W9-BVX-228

DATE DUE

Touching
America's
History

Touching America's History

From the Pequot War through World War II

MEREDITH MASON BROWN

Indiana University Press
Bloomington and Indianapolis

This book is a publication of
Indiana University Press
601 North Morton Street
Bloomington, Indiana 47404–3797 USA
iupress.indiana.edu
Telephone orders 800-842-6796
Fax orders 812-855-7931

∞ The paper used in this publication meets the minimum requirements of the American National Standard for Information Sciences—Permanence of Paper for Printed Library Materials, ANSI Z39.48–1992.

Manufactured in the United States of America

Library of Congress Cataloging-in-Publication Data

Brown, Meredith Mason, [date]-
  Touching America's history : from the Pequot War through World War II / Meredith Mason Brown.
    p. cm.
  Includes bibliographical references and index.
  ISBN 978-0-253-00833-6 (cl : alk. paper) — ISBN 978-0-253-00844-2 (eb) 1. United States—Antiquities. 2. United States—History. 3. Material culture—United States. I. Title.
  E159.5.B76 2013
  973--dc23
                                2012033294

To my family—including several forebears whom,
as I met them working on this book,
I came to know, like, and esteem

CONTENTS

ILLUSTRATIONS AND MAPS

All maps drawn by Mary Lee Eggart

ACKNOWLEDGMENTS

I could not have attempted this survey of more than 300 years of American history without the help of many others, including the authors cited in the bibliography. Jim Boylan, professor emeritus of the University of Massachusetts, brought his deep knowledge of the history of Stonington, Connecticut to his editing of an article I wrote some years ago for the Stonington Historical Society's *Historical Footnotes* that discusses the Pequot war and the torching of the Pequot fort in Mystic. The article was a precursor to the first chapter of this book.

For Kentucky history, I have drawn on the Kentucky Historical Society, the Filson Historical Society (particular thanks to James J. Holmberg, curator of special collections), Liberty Hall Historic Site, and Neal O. Hammon's deep knowledge of early Kentucky and its land laws. Hugh G. Campbell and his colleagues at *The Smithfield Review* helped my attempt to describe the role played by leaders of western Virginia in the opening of Kentucky, from which chapter 2 of this book evolved. Ronald Szudy of Parma, Ohio, whose ancestor fought for the Union in Kentucky during the Civil War alongside my ancestor Colonel John Mason Brown, steered me to several key documents relating to that period. Nelson Dawson, the editor of *The Register of the Kentucky Historical Review*, commented helpfully on my article in that journal on Colonel John Mason Brown during the Civil War, which relates to material discussed in chapter 6 of this book.

DeAnne Blanton, archivist in the Old Military Records section of the National Archives in Washington, D.C., provided invaluable assistance in finding materials relating to the court-martial of Preston Brown for homicide during the Philippine War and to Brown's service and rise through the ranks during the First World War and thereafter. Kenneth H. Williams, who was then the editor of *The Register of the Kentucky Historical Society*, guided me in revising an article I wrote for that journal on that court-martial, which is the subject matter of chapter 8.

My father, John Mason Brown, although he died in 1969, was close to me in thought and in his writing as I sought to describe his uncle General Preston Brown, as well as D-Day as Dad saw it. John F. Thornton kindly reviewed drafts of the book with his expert eye and broad experience in the literary world and encouraged my efforts.

Many libraries shared their broad resources and skills—among them Stonington Free Library, Westerly Public Library (special thanks to Caroline Kreck, reference librarian), and the Library of Congress. Mary Lee Eggart's talents in cartography shine in the maps. I thank ABC PhotoLab, whose skilled employees took the photographs of objects (including earlier photographs) that are not otherwise credited. Thanks also to Bob Sloan and his colleagues at Indiana University Press for their expert guidance.

For all of this, deep thanks. I alone am responsible for errors in the book.

Touching
America's
History

History through Things You Can Touch

As a nation, we're not that old. I count back five generations before me, and the Constitution is being written. Another four or five generations before that, and the Europeans are just starting to settle New England and Virginia and to interact and trade with the Indians: rum and guns for tobacco and furs, smallpox for syphilis.

I do better in history when it becomes concrete and personal to me. Maybe we all do. History is not abstract ideas or theories—mercantilism or imperialism or racism or Marxism. History is the sum of actions of individual human beings. Ideas and theories shape history only to the extent they influence actions by individual human beings. If we can be in touch with those human beings—if they become concrete to us—history comes alive.

This is where relics come into the picture for me. I use *relics* not in the sense of things that work miracles, as the credulous in the medieval Church believed—that doctrine I hold, in the words of the Thirty-Nine Articles of Religion of the Protestant Episcopal Church, as "a fond thing, vainly invented, and grounded upon no warranty of Scripture"—but rather relics in the sense of things left behind, things we can touch, that may not be extraordinary in themselves, but that bring powerfully to mind what was here before, the way a sock or an undershirt can put a bloodhound on the scent of a man on the run.

Henry Ford had the same idea for the Henry Ford Museum. He decided, as one of his biographers put it, that "real history is the stuff you can see and feel." His museum includes George Armstrong Custer's hat, the chair Lincoln sat in when he was shot by John Wilkes Booth, and a test tube holding the last breath of Ford's friend Thomas Alva Edison.[1]

What follows is a reliquary approach to American history—not all American history, not a Grand Unified Theory of American History, but a series of moments in history that have been brought home to me by things I can touch and that together paint an overview of America from 1600 through the Second World War.

Here's my list of relics:

- A stone axe head and a stone adze head
- A compass
- A Kentucky rifle
- A letter from George Washington
- A daguerreotype and the sword of the man who looks sternly out at me from the daguerreotype
- Wood shavings
- Two leather-bound pocket diaries
- A pistol from the 1850s
- A transcript of a 1901 court-martial for homicide
- A citation awarding the Distinguished Service Medal, at the command of General Pershing
- A Western novel called *The Czar of Halfaday Creek*
- A piece of toilet bowl

It may not sound like much of a list. Many of the items are unexceptional in appearance, and many of them could fit in a file drawer, although the rifle and the sword would stick out. But to me, these things I can touch bring to life the killing by and of the Pequots, the opening of the old West, the framing of the Constitution and the election of Washington as America's first president, the forced removal of the Cherokees and the Seminoles from their homeland, the Mexican War, the raid on Harper's Ferry and the hanging of John Brown, the fratricide of the Civil War, the bloodiness of the American fight against the *insurrectos* in the Philippines after the Spanish-American War, the American willingness to die that ended the First World War, and the Allied invasion of Normandy and the collapse of Nazi Germany.

How can this be? It is because of what the relics are:

- The stone tools were likely made by the Pequots or by neighboring tribes who in 1637 joined the English in killing hundreds of Pequots near my home in Connecticut.
- The compass belonged to my forebear Col. William Preston, land speculator, militia officer, and a leader in the opening of Kentucky.
- The rifle was carried by my relative John Floyd, who in July 1776 killed an Indian while helping Daniel Boone rescue Boone's daughter, who had been taken captive by Indians in Kentucky.
- The letter from Washington, written in March 1787, reports that he does not believe he will be able to attend the proposed Constitutional Convention in Philadelphia (fortunately, he changed his mind).
- The daguerreotype and sword are from an ancestor, Richard B. Screven, who fought in Florida in the long Second Seminole War (1835–42) and was brevetted to lieutenant colonel for conspicuous gallantry in the battles of Monterrey and Molino del Rey during the Mexican War.
- The shavings are from the scaffold on which John Brown was hanged.
- The two leather-bound diaries were written by my great-grandfather John Mason Brown when he traveled for thousands of miles in Indian country as the Civil War was breaking out, before he returned to Kentucky to fight for the North.
- The pistol was carried in the Civil War by William Preston's grandson General William Preston, who fought for the South at Shiloh and who held his brother-in-law, General Albert Sidney Johnston, as he bled to death from a wound received in that battle.
- The court-martial was that of my great-uncle Preston Brown, who was convicted of manslaughter for killing a native prisoner in the Philippine War.

- The citation awarded the Distinguished Service Medal, at General Pershing's command, to the same great-uncle, who had become a brigadier general by the end of World War I.
- The Western novel is the actual book General Eisenhower was reading on the day in June 1944 when the Normandy invasion was postponed for a day because of foul weather.
- The piece of toilet bowl was Hitler's—taken from his bomb-shattered bathroom at his home in Berchtesgaden.

Through these things we can touch—disparate though they may seem—we see America born, take shape, and grow. British colonies clustered along the Atlantic coast become a united independent country that grows to the Pacific (see map 0.1). Land is taken from the Indians and from Mexico, and America takes control of the Philippines. The bitter issue of slavery is resolved by bloodshed. America becomes the most powerful country in the world. The tangibles on my list bring to mind that growth and those changes and the central roles played in them by the quest for the new, the hunger for financial betterment, and the recurrent use of military force.

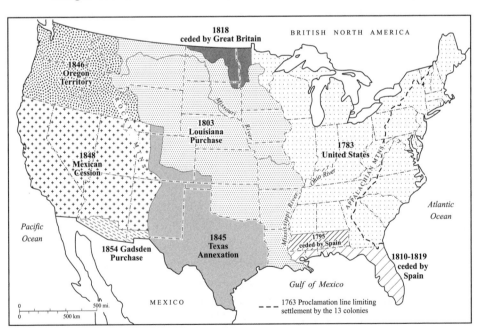

Map 0.1. America's Expansion, 1763–1854

1

Axe Head, Adze Head:
The Pequot War

Most of the relics I inherited or were given to me or to my brother. The only ones I bought were a stone axe head and a stone adze head—both bought in Stonington, Connecticut, where I live—the adze head from a local antique dealer, the axe head at an antique fair in the gym of a local school (see figure 1.1). I was told both were found around Stonington—in Groton, Noank, or Mystic, which is entirely likely. They match nicely with pictures of axe heads and adzes from pre-*Mayflower* New England. Dr. Kevin A. McBride, director of the Mashantucket Pequot Museum and Research Center, who directs all archeological excavations and ethnohistorical research for the Pequot, after hefting the axe head and adze head, told me that if they came from Mystic or Noank, it was likely the Pequot made them, because Pequots had been in that area for hundreds of years before the English arrived in the area—although he also said many tribes made similar objects and had been doing so for thousands of years.[1]

Both of my tool heads were finished by polishing rather than flaking. The adze head is of light gray stone, about seven inches long, a little over two inches wide, less than two inches thick at its thickest. It's flat on the bottom of its length, where it would have been lashed to the top of a wooden handle, and gently curved on the top. A book of Algonquian tools said such an adze would have been used for stripping bark from trees, and Dr. McBride agreed that this was a likely use, as

Fig. 1.1. Stone axe and adze head. *Author's collection.*

was hollowing out dugout canoes. My adze head has a good weight and feel for these uses.

The axe head is of a denser, darker gray (almost black) stone than the adze head. I guessed the stone was basalt; Dr. McBride confirmed this, adding that although basalt was not in our immediate neighborhood there was a vein up near Hartford, and basalt from there was traded into Pequot country. The axe head is six inches long, three inches wide, and two inches thick at its thickest. The back of the head is rounded; the front slopes on both faces to an edge. The stone is girdled at its thickest by a groove the width of your forefinger, for hafting. It weighs a little over two pounds. One side is more finely polished than the other. Some chips have been knocked off the front edge. One good-sized chip is missing from the back of the head, which would have been used like a hammerhead.

The Algonquian tribes who lived near or not far from Stonington before the English came were the Pequot, the Nehantic, and the Narragansett. The Nehantic and, to the east of them, the Narragansett may have been in the Stonington area before the Pequot. There is some support for the idea that perhaps around about the beginning of the seventeenth century, the Pequot and their kinsmen the Mohegan pushed into southeastern Connecticut from the center of Connecticut. Some believe they came from the Hudson River Valley and that they were possibly related to the similar-sounding Mahican. Others doubt this, pointing out that Mohegan or Mahican simply means "People of the River" in Algonquian languages, and that the Mohegan and Mahican languages are not very closely related.[2] Dr. McBride believes the idea of a fairly recent Pequot intrusion into the area is a baseless nineteenth-century hypothesis, which may have been put forward to help justify the white settlers' fights against the Pequot. In any event, the Mohegans and Pequot settled along the Thames and Mystic rivers. In the 1620s, the Pequot defeated other tribes and gained control of trade on the lower Connecticut River. By 1630, they were also receiving wampum as tribute from eastern Long Island.[3] The wampum was important in buying pelts from the Indians of the interior, and the pelts in turn could be used to buy European trade goods.

The Pequot fought their neighbors—the Mohegan, the Nehantic, the Narragansett—who fought them back. And in May 1637, five miles from what is now Stonington, where I am writing this, English settlers from the Hartford area and from Massachusetts, together with Mohegan, Narragansett, and Nehantic, killed close to 500 Pequot early one morning after torching their stockaded village on a hill in what is now Mystic, Connecticut. That killing—and the pursuit and scattering and enslavement of the remnant—ended the Pequot as a threat to the white settlers in Connecticut. Not until the opening of Foxwoods Casino in Ledyard in 1992 did the Pequot again become a regional power.

The English had begun to move into Connecticut in the 1630s, settling around Hartford and New Haven and at Saybrook at the mouth of the Connecticut River, although they traded elsewhere. One of the first results of the contacts between the Indians and the Dutch and English traders was a smallpox epidemic in 1633–1634 that probably killed more than half—one estimate is of an 80 percent mortality—of the Pequot. Before European contact, there may have been 13,000 Pequot; just before the Pequot War, that number was about 3,000, a drop of 77 percent.[4]

Relations between English and Pequot were not always peaceful. In 1633, a trader named John Stone let some Indians come aboard his boat, moored on the Connecticut River. It may be that the trader got drunk. In any event, Stone went to his cabin, fell asleep, and was killed in his bunk, possibly by Western Niantics, a tribe that paid tribute to the Pequot, possibly by Sassacus, a leading Pequot sachem. The Pequot may have killed Stone in reprisal for the Dutch killing in Connecticut of a Pequot sachem named Tatobem, the father of Sassacus.[5]

In 1635, settlers from the Massachusetts Bay Colony, led by John Winthrop, Jr., son of the colony's governor, built Fort Saybrook at the mouth of the Connecticut River, challenging both Pequot trade and Dutch efforts to establish a trading post near Hartford. In 1636, John Oldham, a coastal trader from the Massachusetts Bay Colony, was killed on Block Island, which had been in the Pequot's sphere of influence but had come under the sway of the Narragansetts. His death may have been particularly galling to the English settlers because crop failure caused by a huge hurricane in 1635, followed by bitter cold, had left the growing colonies short of food, and Oldham, through his trading, had been an important supplier.[6] In August 1636, the Massachusetts Bay Colony, in response to the Oldham killing and to the Pequot's failure to deliver Captain Stone's killers and the quantity of wampum the Pequot had promised in a 1634 trade treaty, sent soldiers under Captain John Endicott to punish the Indians on Block Island and to raid the Pequot. Endicott burned some villages on Block Island and sailed up the Pequot River (now called the Thames River), destroyed villages and cornfields on both sides of the river, and sailed back to Massachusetts—not having broken the Pequot power but having riled the Pequot mightily.

In 1636, the Pequot attacked stragglers outside the English fort at Saybrook. Two were tortured to death as their companions, huddled for safety in a strong house, heard their screams. A third was roasted alive.[7] On April 23, 1637, Pequot raided Wethersfield, a little English settlement, just three years old, south of Hartford. The Pequot burned many of the houses in the settlement. Six men, three women, and twenty cows were killed. Two young women were taken captive. As the raiding Pequot went back down the Connecticut River in three large dugouts, they waved English shirts and smocks they had taken from those they had killed at Wethersfield and shouted at the English garrison at Saybrook, saying that Englishmen were all squaws and their God no more than an insect.[8]

That did it. On May 1, 1637, the Connecticut General Court commissioned Captain John Mason to lead a force against the Pequot. Mason had been a soldier much of his adult life: with English troops in Flanders before he came to Massachusetts in 1632 and in Massachusetts as a captain of militia, fighting pirates who preyed on commerce in and out of Boston harbor.[9] The Connecticut settlers sent 42 men from Hartford, 30 from Windsor, and 18 from Wethersfield. Uncas, the sachem of the Mohegans, added another 60 men to the force. After the death of the Pequot sachem Tatobem, Uncas had tried to become sachem of the Pequot, asserting a claim through his wife's family. That did not endear Uncas to Tatobem's son Sassacus, who became the new Pequot sachem and who had driven Uncas and his followers to seek the whites' protection in the Hartford area.

The force under Captain Mason proceeded down the Connecticut River to Saybrook, where they were joined by nineteen men sent from Massachusetts under the leadership of Captain John Underhill. It was not a large force to send against the several hundred warriors of Sassacus in their hill fort overlooking the Thames River.

Mason and Underhill decided to sail east to Rhode Island to seek support from the Narragansetts. As they sailed along the coast, Pequot on the shore in what is now Groton Long Point spotted them and shouted jeers at them. Seeing that the English had sailed by the mouth of the Thames River, the heart of Pequot power, the Pequot may have concluded that the English and their Mohegan allies had decided not to try their strength against the Pequot.

The Narragansetts, under their sachem Canonicus, furnished about two hundred warriors to the force. More troops were said to be coming from Massachusetts, but Mason was worried about the possibility that the Pequot would hear of the force building on their eastern border and that all element of surprise would be lost. Rather than wait for the Massachusetts reinforcements, Mason and Underhill decided to attack the Pequot—not frontally, up the Thames River to the main Pequot fort in what is now Groton, but by coming on them from behind, by land.

They marched west to the Pawcatuck River, crossed at the ford, and followed the Pequot trail to the Northwest, to Taugwonk Hill, and then down the west bank of the Mystic River, from what is now Old Mystic toward what is now Mystic. But let Captain John Mason tell the story of the attack on the Pequot fort on May 26, 1637, in his own way, speaking of himself in the third person:

> And after we had refreshed our Selves with our mean Commons, we Marched about three Miles, and came to a field which had lately been planted with Indian Corn: There we made another Alt, and called our Council, supposing we drew near to the Enemy: and being informed by the Indians that the Enemy had two Forts almost impregnable; but we were not at all Discouraged, but rather Animated, in so much that we were resolved to Assault both their Forts at once. But understanding that one of them was so remote that we could not come up with it before Midnight, though we Marched hard; whereat we were much grieved, chiefly because the greatest and bloodiest Sachem there resided, whose name was Sassacous: We were then constrained, being exceedingly spent in our March with extream Heat and want of necessaries, to accept of the nearest [that is, the fortified village in Mystic, rather than Sassacus's main fortified village in Groton.]. . . .
>
> We continued our March until about one Hour in the Night: and coming to a little Swamp between two Hills, there we pitched our little Camp. . . . The Night proved Comfortable, being clear and Moon Light: We appointed our Guards and placed our Sentinels at some distance; who hearing the Enemy Singing at the Fort, who continued that Strain until Midnight, with great Insulting and Rejoycing, as we were afterwards informed: They seeing our Pinnaces sail by them some Days before, concluded that we were

afraid of them and durst not come near them; the Burthen of their Song tending to that Purpose.

In the Morning, we awaking and seeing it very light, supposing it had been day, and so we might have lost our Opportunity, having purposed to make our assault before Day; rowsed the Men with all expedition, and briefly commended ourselves and our Design to God, thinking immediately to go to the Assault; the Indians shewing us a Path, told us that it led directly to the Fort. We held on our March about two Miles, wondering that we came not to the Fort, and fearing that we might be deluded: But seeing Corn newly planted at the Foot of a great Hill, supposing the Fort was not far off, a Champion Country being round about us; then making a stand, gave the Word for some of the Indians to come up: at length Onkos [Uncas] and one Wequash appeared; We demanded of them, Where was the Fort? They answered On the Top of that Hill: Then we demanded, Where were the Rest of the Indians [i.e., the Mohegans and the Narragansetts]? They answered, Behind, exceedingly afraid: We wished them to tell the rest of their Fellows, That they should by no means Fly, but stand at what distance they pleased, and see whether English Men would now Fight or not. Then Capt. Underhill came up, who Marched in the Rear; and commending ourselves to God, divided our Men: There being two Entrances into the Fort, intending to enter both at once: Captain Mason leading up to that on the North East Side; who approaching within one Rod heard a Dog bark and an Indian crying Owanux! Owanux! which is Englishmen! Englishmen! We called up our Forces with all expedition, gave Fire upon them through the Pallizado; the Indians being in a dead indeed their last Sleep: then we wheeling off fell upon the main Entrance, which was blocked up with Bushes about Breast high, over which the Captain passed, intending to make good the Entrance, encouraging the rest to follow. . . . We had formerly concluded to destroy them by the Sword and save the Plunder.

Whereupon Captain Mason seeing no Indians, entered a wigwam; where he was beset with many Indians, waiting all opportunities to lay Hands on him, but could not prevail. At length

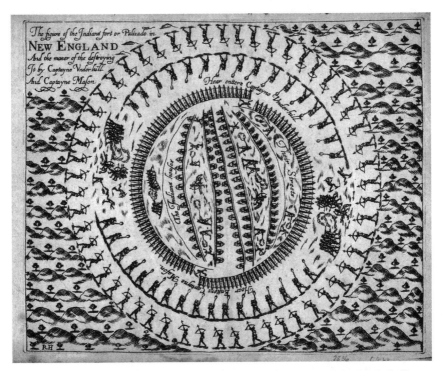

Fig. 1.2. Colonists' attack on the Pequot village, May 1637. From John Underhill, *Newes from America* (1638). *Courtesy of the Mashantucket Pequot Museum and Research Center.*

William Heydon espying the Breach in the Wigwam, supposing some English might be there, entred; but in his Entrance fell over a dead Indian; but speedily recovering himself, the Indians some fled, others crept under their Beds: The Captain going out of the Wigwam saw many Indians in the Lane or Street, he making towards them, they fled, were pursued to the End of the Lane, where they were met by Edward Pattison, Thomas Barber, with some others; where seven of them were Slain, as they said. The Captain facing about, Marched a slow Pace up the Lane he came down, perceiving himself very much out of Breath; and coming to the other End near the Place where he first entred, saw two Soldiers standing close to the Pallizado with their Swords pointed to the Ground: The Captain told them We should never kill them after that manner: The Captain also said, We must Burn them; and immediately stepping into the Wigwam where he had been before, brought out a Firebrand, and putting it into the Matts with which they were covered, set the Wigwams on Fire . . . ; and when it was thoroughly kindled, the Indians ran as Men most dreadfully Amazed.

And indeed such a dreadful Terror did the Almighty let fall upon their Spirits, that they would fly from us and run into the very Flames, where many of them perished. And when the Fort was thoroughly Fired, Command was given that all should fall off and surround the Fort; which was readily attended by all. . . .

The Fire was kindled on the North East Side to windward; which did swiftly over-run the Fort, to the extream amazement of the Enemy, and great Rejoycing of our selves. Some of them climbing to the Top of the Pallizado; others of them running into the very Flames; many of them gathering to windward, lay pelting at us with their Arrows; and we repayed them with our small Shot: Others of the Stoutest issued forth, as we did guess, to the Number of Forty, who perished by the Sword.

Captain Underhill, in his account of the burning of the town, says that he started a fire on the south end with a train of powder, after Mason started a fire on the west side. The two fires met in the center of town, which was completely burned in a half an hour. The fire, according to Underhill, burned through the bowstrings of the Indians, depriving them of their weapons. When the fires were set, the English left the palisaded town and surrounded it to kill the Pequot as they sought to flee from the fire (see figure 1.2):

Great and doleful was the bloody sight to the view of young soldiers that never had been in war, to see so many souls lie gasping on the ground, so thick, in some places, that you could hardly pass along. It may be demanded, Why should you be so furious? (as some have said). Should not Christians have more mercy and compassion? But I would refer you to David's war. When a people is grown to such a height of blood, and sin against God and man, and all confederates in the action, then he hath no respect to persons, but harrows them, and saws them, and puts them to the sword, and the most terriblest death that may be. . . . We had sufficient light from the word of God for our proceedings.[10]

It was not the Indians' way of fighting. Some of Underhill's Narragansett allies "greatly admired the manner of Englishmen's fight, but cried Mach it, mach it; that is, It is naught, it is naught, because it is too furious and slays too many men."[11]

There may have been 500 Indians in the village, perhaps more. Seven were taken captive; seven escaped. The rest were killed. Mason estimated that 600 or 700 Pequot were killed. Two Englishmen were killed and 20 wounded in the fighting. The fighting took less than an hour.

Mason and Underhill and their men made their way from the destroyed village to the Thames River, harassed by warriors coming from Sassacus's fort in Groton, but English guns kept the Indians at a distance and killed many of them. In the harbor were ships with Massachusetts reinforcements, and Mason's force got away safely.

The Pequot scattered. Some went to the Montauks on Long Island—but the sachem there had several of the refugees beheaded and their heads delivered to the English at Saybrook, in response to a request from Lion Gardener, the head of the English settlement there. Sassacus and some immediate followers went northwest to join the Mohawks. A larger group went west along the coast of Connecticut, pursued by ships and troops from Massachusetts under the command of Captain Israel Stoughton, as well as by forty Connecticut Englishmen commanded by John Mason. The Indians were surrounded in a swamp in what is now Fairfield. Some were killed; more were taken captive.

Here is how Captain John Mason ends the story: "The Captives we took were about One Hundred and Eighty; whom we divided, intending to keep them as Servants, but they could not endure that Yoke; few of them continuing any considerable time with their masters. Thus did the Lord scatter his Enemies with his strong Arm!" Mason concluded his history of the Pequot war with further praise to God: "Let the whole Earth be filled with his Glory! Thus the lord was pleased to smite our Enemies in the hinder Parts, and give us their land for an Inheritance."

The Mohawks, seeing which way the wind was blowing, beheaded Sassacus in August 1637 and sent his scalp to the English authorities in

Connecticut. The English forbade the surviving Pequot to return to their villages or to use the name Pequot. In 1650, the Connecticut General Court, in gratitude for what Captain Mason had done, granted him five hundred acres around Lyme and the following year awarded him "The Island commonly called Chippechauge, in Mistick Bay." That island, about four miles from where I write, is still known as Mason's Island.

Less than forty years after the Pequot war, a group of Alquonquian peoples—Wampanoags under Metacomet (known to the colonists as King Philip), Nipmucks, Abenaki, Pocumtucks, Narragansetts—attacked English settlements in Massachusetts and Rhode Island. Springfield and Providence were destroyed. Indian attacks came within ten miles of Boston. The remnant of the Pequot still in Connecticut got back at the Narragansetts by fighting alongside the English against them. When the Narragansett sachem Canonchet was captured, he was taken alive to Stonington, Connecticut. There, according to a militia officer, in order "that all might share in the Glory of destroying so great a Prince, . . . the Pequods shot him, the Mohegans cut off his Head and quartered his Body, and Ninnicrofts Men made the Fire and burned his Quarters, and as a Token of their Love and Fidelity to the English, presented his Head to the Council at Hartford."[12]

The Narragansett were substantially destroyed in what amounted to a larger version of the firing of the Pequot fort at Mystic. On December 19, 1675, English soldiers from the United Colonies, led by an Indian guide, made their way to a palisaded fort in the Great Swamp, near what is now South Kingstown, Rhode Island. Inside were hundreds of wigwams, thousands of Narragansett, and stores of food for the winter. The English set fire to the wigwams and killed the Narragansett as they began to climb over the palisades and through its doors. Survivors were taken captive; many were sold into slavery. Four captains of the English were killed and five mortally wounded—including Captain John Mason, the son of the Captain John Mason who fought the Pequot in 1637.

That was the end of the Narragansetts' fighting strength. King Philip the Wampanoag leader wasn't caught until the following August 12, when he was shot in a swamp near Mount Hope by an Indian named Alderman, fighting with the English captain Benjamin Church. Church called an Indian executioner over to Philip's body. The Indian said over the fallen muddy corpse: "He had been a very great man, and had made many a man afraid of him, but big as he was, he would now chop his arse for him." He proceeded to do just that and then beheaded and quartered the body. Captain Church took Philip's head to Plymouth and received thirty shillings for it, which he deemed to be "scanty reward, and poor encouragement." The decaying head was exhibited on a pole in Plymouth for many years.[13]

And so the Pequot and Narragansetts dwindled, and the white settlers built where the Indians had hunted and grown corn. Where Sassacus had his main fort overlooking the Thames River is now a housing development on Fort Hill Road, as that part of Route 1 in Groton is called. The location of the other fort, the one that Mason burned in 1637, is near the intersection of Clift Street and Pequot Avenue, on the Groton side of the town of Mystic, atop a steep little hill. Recent archaeological surveys, assisted by ground-penetrating radar and magnetometry, have found considerable evidence of the site of the fort, including 67 musket balls, 3 musket rests, and 6 brass projectile points (most likely arrowheads) found in 2010.[14] The ends of three of the points have been bent back, perhaps from hitting metal armor. The name of the town was spelled Missi-tuk or Mistick, a phonetic rendering of an Algonquian name for a wide tidal river, up until the mid-nineteenth century, but "Mystic" must have had a pleasing connotation to the Victorian Americans. The intersection—the putative site of the fort—was marked by a heroic statue of Captain John Mason, helmeted, right hand drawing sword from scabbard, tall swashbuckling boots, erected by the State of Connecticut in 1889. But sensibilities change; the Pequot found the statue a desecration of a sacred place, the place where so many of their ancestors had been killed. One Pequot said that it was like erecting a statue of Hitler at Auschwitz. The statue, therefore, was moved in 1995 to Windsor. The last time I looked, the spot on the hill in Mystic where the statue had been was marked only by a bush and a plaintive hand-lettered sign saying, in essence: "This is a monkey puzzle tree. This is the third time neighbors, with their labor and funds, have put something on this site. We are all sorry that the statue is not here, but planting is better than pavement, and we cannot understand why this site has repeatedly been vandalized. If you have information about the vandalism, please call [a police number]." Someone using black magic marker has crossed out "We are all" and replaced it with "Some of us."

The sword of Captain John Mason can be seen in the Stonington Historical Society's museum in the old stone lighthouse on Stonington Point. It is a long, straight, single-handed sword, with a double-edged blade that measures more than an inch and a half across. The sword is thirty-six inches long from handle end to blade tip. Stamped into the blade toward the hilt are the words "Me fecit Soligen"—Soligen (the famous sword-making town in Germany that now spells itself Solingen) made me. The captain may have wielded the sword when he fought in Flanders, and presumably he brought it with him to the New World. Looking at the size of the sword, you can imagine its weight. Mason must have gotten arm-weary as he hacked his way up and down the lane in the Pequot village that late May morning ("perceiving himself very much out of Breath") before he decided to set fire to the wigwams. Maybe that arm-weariness—as well as fear of the possible arrival of Sassacus's warriors from the fort in Groton—led Mason to torch the village.

The Pequot have found new strength in the past few decades, after dwindling through the nineteenth century. In *Moby-Dick,* Herman Melville described the Pequot as "now extinct as the ancient Medes." In 1850, the historian John W. De Forest reported that only twenty-eight of the Ledyard or Mashantucket Pequot were left: "Nothing is left but a little and miserable remnant, hanging around the seats where their ancestors once reigned supreme, as a few half-withered leaves may sometimes be seen clinging to the upper branches of a blighted and dying tree."[15] Six years later, the state of Connecticut sold off most of what was left of the Mashantucket reservation that had been set up in 1666 north of the headwaters of the Mystic River. The last fluent Pequot speaker, a woman named Fidelia Fielding, died in 1908. In 1973, only two elderly half-sisters were left on the reservation. One of them, Elizabeth George, who had been fighting to preserve the tribe and its history, died that year.

In 1976, the tribe brought suit against property owners in Ledyard to recover former reservation land that the State of Connecticut had sold in 1856, in violation of federal law. In 1979, the tribe, relying in large part on historical and genealogical information that had been gathered by Elizabeth George, applied for federal recognition. In 1983, the Mashantucket Pequot Indian Land Claims Settlement Act was signed into law. The act recognized the tribe, and, in settlement of its land claims, set up a $900,000 trust fund, $600,000 being designated for land acquisition and $300,000 for economic development.

In 1986, the tribe opened a high-stakes bingo operation, and in 1992, backed by Malaysian Chinese, opened Foxwoods Resort Casino in Ledyard. Within a decade, Foxwoods became the largest resort casino in the world. The casino and other tribal enterprises have about eleven thousand employees. Under a 1993 agreement with the State of Connecticut that permitted the tribe to operate slot machines, 25 percent of the slot machine revenues is paid to the state. In February 2009, the casino had 7,998 slot machines, and the casino won $58 million that month from its slots. Not surprisingly, tribal membership has increased in recent years—from 150 in 1987 to about 800 in 2009.[16]

Twelve miles away, the Pequot's traditional rivals, the Mohegan, opened a competing casino in the late 1990s, the Mohegan Sun, backed by a South African casino operator. In February 2009, the Mohegan Sun had 6,787 slot machines, winning $62.8 million for the month—even more than the winnings at the Pequot casino. The Mohegan casino, like the Mashantucket casino, is estimated to gross more than $1 billion a year. The two casinos each gross more than any other casino in the United States, even though, thanks to the recession and to increased competition from other casinos, revenues dropped starting in 2007, and the Pequot have had trouble meeting the interest and principal on the roughly $2 billion in debt they had incurred. Nevertheless, by May 2010, the two tribes together had paid more than $3 billion to the state of Connecticut out of slot machine revenues—which means that the two tribes themselves received over $9 billion as their share of the take from the slots. Neither tribe makes public how much it makes from other forms of gambling. The Pequot publicly celebrated reaching the $3 billion milestone. Their neighbors the Mohegan did not attend but sent flowers.[17]

On Route 2, which runs between Pawcatuck and Norwich and which used to be a lightly traveled road past cornfields, traffic jams mark the front of the Foxwoods casino entrance at all hours of the day and night. I used to climb Lantern Hill, near Pequot land in Ledyard, each fall to look at the changing colors of the leaves. I still do—it's one of the highest hills in the neighborhood, and the views are big—but my eye now gets distracted by the sunlight bouncing off the roofs of tour buses and cars in the casino's acres of parking lots.

The tribe in 1998 opened a 308,000–square foot museum and research center at a cost of $193 million. In the museum, the word Pequot is translated as "People of the shallow waters." Earlier histories, written by whites, had said that Pequot is a contraction of the Algonquian Indian word *pasquatanog*, meaning "destroyer." Inside the museum is a rebuilt Pequot village of the 1550s, with wigwams, a running stream, and fifty artificial trees bearing a total of five million green polyester leaves. A highlight of a visit to the museum is a bloody and compelling thirty-minute film of the destruction of the fort in Mystic in 1637. Near the auditorium, in glass cases of Indian tools, are axe heads and adze heads very like the ones that sit beside me on my desk. By 1637, Dr. McBride told me, the Pequot were mostly using metal-headed weapons, but in a recent archaeological survey of the Mystic fort McBride's team had found chips of stone weapons, as well as pieces of metal weapons.

2

A Compass, a Rifle, and the Opening of the West

The crushing of Pequot power in the 1630s and the taking of Pequot land by settlers of European descent were mirrored over the next 250 years throughout what became the United States of America, as the white population shot up and pushed westward and as Indians from east of the Mississippi were driven farther and farther west. Nowhere were the changes more abrupt than in what is now western Virginia and Kentucky, an area which was transformed between 1755 and 1785. To me, that transformation is called to mind by a small compass, mounted in a square wooden box about two and a half inches on each side (see figure 2.1a), and by a heavy rifle, a muzzle-loading flintlock about five feet long (see figure 2.2). The rifle weighs nine pounds, has an octagonal barrel forty-six inches long, and has ornamental brass on its fourteen-inch stock.

The compass belonged to my ancestor Colonel William Preston. Written on the bottom of the compass are the words "Genl—This compass was used by the first Preston in surveying the land granted to the Prestons in Montgomery County Virginia" (see figure 2.1b).[1] Thanks to a host of official positions and a driving personality, Preston, from the 1770s until his death in 1783, was the most powerful figure in western Virginia and in the westward expansion of its settlers into what became Kentucky. One of the positions that underlay his power and his accumulation of land was that of the surveyor in a succession of western counties of Virginia. My cousin, the portrait painter William F. Draper, another descendant

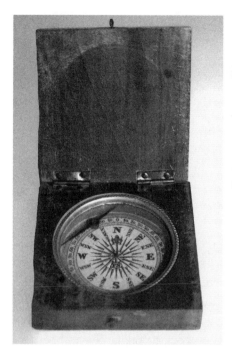

Fig. 2.1a and b. Hand compass of William
Preston (1729–1783). *Author's collection.*

of William Preston, gave me the compass in the 1990s, not many years
before his death. The rifle was carried by Preston's talented younger friend
and protégé John Floyd, also a relative of mine, who led in the surveying
and opening of Kentucky and in the fights with Indians there, before he
was killed by Indians in the same year William Preston died. When I was
a child, the rifle hung on the wall of my father's study in Manhattan. The
rifle had come down to Dad in the Floyd and Preston families.[2] It now
hangs in my brother's house.

William Preston's compass calls to my mind the settlers' ceaseless drive
to locate, survey, and claim new lands in the West. John Floyd's rifle evokes
the settlers' bloody fights with the Indians that ended with the Indians,
their numbers reduced by warfare and by European diseases, being driven
farther west, out of the lands claimed by the whites. Preston was exposed
to the risk of Indian attack—but Floyd, whom Preston sent west into
Kentucky, was far more exposed (ultimately fatally) to that risk.

William Preston was born in 1729 near Londonderry, a descendant
of Presbyterian settlers encouraged to settle in northern Ireland by the
British. He came to America as a child in 1738, as part of the forefront

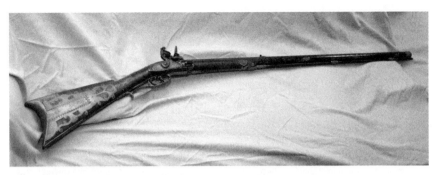

Fig. 2.2. Rifle owned by John Floyd (ca. 1751–1783). *Courtesy of Preston Brown. Photograph by Omar J. Mitchell.*

of the opening up of trans-Allegheny Virginia to British settlement. Preston himself was of modest birth, his father, John Preston, being a ship's carpenter—but John Preston prospered as a result of having eloped with Elizabeth Patton, the sister of a highly successful merchant-shipper named James Patton, who traded extensively with Virginia (bringing indentured servants to Virginia and furs and tobacco back to England—and perhaps smuggling in much of the tobacco to avoid customs duty).[3]

In 1737, Patton became a partner with William Beverley, owner of a manor on the Rappahannock River, to develop a grant by the Virginia Council of 30,000 acres of land on the Calfpasture River, west of the Blue Ridge Mountains, in what became Augusta County. Patton, who had a quarter share of the grant, offered John Preston 4,000 acres if he and his family would settle on the grant. Preston agreed, and the Preston and Patton families sailed to Virginia in 1738 and settled in Augusta County.[4] Not satisfied with his Augusta County acreage, Patton in 1742 and 1743 sent out exploring parties farther south and west in Virginia, to the New River and two rivers to the west, the Holston and the Clinch.[5] In 1745, the Virginia Council granted Patton and his associates (one of whom was John Preston) 100,000 acres (more than 150 square miles) in western Virginia, where Patton's agents had explored, on the condition that they settle one family on each 1,000 acres. Part of this "Great Grant" (as Patton called it) was on or close to the New River, near what is now Blacksburg, Virginia.[6] Five hundred acres of that land was sold to a settler named George Draper. The little settlement that grew up around his land became known as Draper's Meadows.[7] Looking for the ability to acquire land even farther west, in 1752 Patton was one of the commissioners who negotiated with the Iroquois, Delaware, Shawnee, and Wyandot the Treaty of Logstown, in which Virginia asserted claims to lands south of the Ohio River.[8] He took with him to Logstown, as his secretary, his nephew William Preston, then 22 years old, who had begun to keep Patton's official correspondence, as well as accounts of his land investments, and who that year became a licensed surveyor.[9]

By 1755, Patton owned 17,007 acres in his own name and was a colonel in the militia, a leading negotiator with the Indians, the lieutenant of Augusta County, president of the Augusta Court, county coroner, county escheator, and county customs collector, as well as burgess from Augusta County in the Virginia Assembly.[10] He was the dominant political figure in Augusta County and a central figure in the British colonists' expansion to the west.

That expansion conflicted not only with Indian claims, but also with French efforts to expand into the Ohio Valley, to gain control of the fur trade, and to forestall the possibility that British western settlement would sever trade between French Canada and French Louisiana. A clash between the British settlers and the French and Indians became inevitable. To strengthen their own claims to the Ohio Valley and its fur trade, the French stirred up western Indians to attack Ohio Valley Indians who had begun to trade with British traders instead of French traders. In 1752, Ottawa, Ojibwa, and Potawatomi, at French urging, attacked the Miami village of Pickawillany in what is now western Ohio; killed one English trader and ate his heart; and killed, dismembered, and ate the village chief, who had broken away from alliance with the French and was trading with the British. Not surprisingly, the Miamis in the village decided to resume trading with the French. The French also began talking to the Indians about building a fort on the Allegheny River. By 1753, the French were building a series of forts west of the Alleghenies. Alarmed by the increased French military presence in the Ohio Valley, the Iroquois and other tribes that traded with the British asked Pennsylvania and Virginia to protect them and to build a fort where the Allegheny and Monongahela Rivers join to form the Ohio River—the strategic location that was to become the site of Pittsburgh. When the British colonies dragged their feet, the Ohio Company, formed by British investors and settlers to develop a land grant west of the Alleghenies, began on its own to build a fortified trading post there. Not until early 1754 did Virginia send a few dozen militiamen to help to build the fort.

In 1753, George Washington, only 22 years old but already a colonel in the Virginia militia, was sent by Virginia's Governor Dinwiddie to the French forts in western Pennsylvania to assert Britain's claims to the Ohio Valley and to request the French to leave. The French made their views clear. As Washington noted in his journal, the French army officers, after they had "dosed themselves pretty plentifully with wine," which "gave a License to their Tongues to reveal their Sentiments more freely," told him "it was their absolute Design to take possession of the Ohio, & by G_____ they would do it."[11] In April 1754, the French seized the Ohio Company's fledgling fort and renamed it Fort Duquesne, after the governor general of New France. In July, the French forced George Washington to surrender Fort Necessity, the small fort he had built just east of Fort Duquesne.

In the French-British struggle for control of the Ohio Valley, most of the Ohio Valley Indians decided to join forces with the French. The number of Indians in the Ohio Valley had dropped drastically—estimates range from 25 to 90 percent—from the ravages of European diseases such as smallpox and measles in the century following exposure to the new viruses, but the Indians still were a formidable force.[12] The Indians saw both the French and the British as threats to their own rights to the Ohio Valley but viewed the British as the greater threat. There were far more British than French in North America—around 1.6 million British but only perhaps 75,000 French.[13] As one Delaware explained it, the Indians needed French aid to defeat the British who coveted their land, because the British were "such a numerous People," but "we can drive away the French when we please."[14] Moreover, many of the British were settlers and farmers, more likely to stake permanent claims to land than were the French trappers and traders.

With French aid, Indians in June and early July 1755 began to attack and kill British colonists in Virginia's westernmost settlements, including those that were part of the Great Grant on the Holston and New Rivers. At the same time, Britain was mounting a massive effort to retake Fort Duquesne and drive the French from the Ohio Valley. In February 1755, the British sent two regiments of regulars to America under Major General Edward Braddock, with the mission of capturing a series of French forts, starting with Fort Duquesne and going on to Frontenac in Canada. Braddock scoffed at a warning from Benjamin Franklin about the risks of ambushes by Indians, declined the offer by a Delaware chief to provide scouts, and refused to promise the Delaware that the British would assure them sufficient hunting grounds. In May 1755, Braddock's regiments, supported by Virginia militia, set off from Frederick, Maryland, toward Fort Duquesne at a ponderously slow pace (as George Washington, part of the Virginia militia, wrote, "halting to level every Mole Hill, & to erect Bridges over every brook"), beginning to have their ranks reduced by Indian killings of stragglers and outliers.[15]

On July 9, 1755, several hundred French and Indians—many more Indians than French—encountered, in a clearing not far from Fort Duquesne, Braddock's advance party, which had just crossed the Monongahela. The French and Indians spread out in the woods around the clearing, flanking Braddock's troops, and started firing from behind the trees. The American militia made for the nearest trees, for frontier-style fighting—firing individually, behind the shelter of tree trunks. The British regulars stayed put for a while in the clearing, under withering cross fire. The American militiamen were shot both by the British regulars firing from the clearing and by the French and Indians firing from the woods. Braddock's forces were cut to pieces. Of the 1,300 British and American men with Braddock, more than 900 were killed or wounded. The French and Indians reported 23 killed and 16 wounded. Braddock himself was fatally wounded.[16]

The day before Braddock's defeat, Virginia's governor Dinwiddie had ordered James Patton to form a company of rangers to protect Virginia's western settlements. Patton gave William Preston a commission as a captain in the company, and Preston recruited as many men as he could—perhaps about twenty. Recruiting was not easy, since settlers were fleeing the western settlements following the killings by Indians in June and early July.[17] Patton and Preston then rode west toward the New River, to Draper's Meadows, slightly ahead of the new company of rangers. They probably were attempting to encourage the western settlers to stay and to assure them that help was on the way, although they may also have ridden ahead seeking to collect a debt from a purchaser of land in the Great Tract.[18] Their separation from the rangers proved fatal for Patton. More than a dozen Shawnee warriors were waiting near Draper's Meadows. Within days of Braddock's defeat, the Shawnees killed and scalped Colonel Patton and killed or captured several of the Draper's Meadows settlers.[19]

It is likely that the killing of Patton was targeted. Patton was well-known to the Indians. In light of his leadership in exploring and developing western land, killing him was a good way for the Shawnees to endeavor to stop the British settlers' westward push into the Ohio Valley. Moreover, Patton may have alienated the Indians by the inept manner in which he had spoken during the preliminaries to the Logstown treaty meeting; the Indians there interpreted his request for a council as a threat and were "greatly affronted."[20] It is also possible that the French had put a bounty on Patton's scalp, as they did on the scalps of some other frontier leaders.[21]

In the Draper's Meadows attack, the Shawnees just missed killing William Preston, then 24 years old. Early that day, Patton had sent Preston to a neighbor to seek help in harvesting. When Preston returned, he found the bodies of Patton and other settlers. According to one family tradition, near Patton's body were two Indians he had killed with his broadsword before he was shot to death. Two other accounts by relatives give less heroic versions of Patton's slaying. Floyd's daughter said that Patton was seated at the cabin door shaving when the Indians fell upon him, and another relative reported that "the Indians approaching unobserved shot him while he was writing in his office."[22]

Settlers and rangers (probably including Preston) sought to catch up with the Shawnees and to rescue their Draper's Meadows captives but returned empty-handed after a 200-mile pursuit.[23] In February 1756, Preston, as a militia captain, commanded a company of rangers as part of an expedition that marched in bitter weather from settlements in southwestern Virginia, intending to attack the Shawnees in their own villages north of the Ohio River. The Virginians, with a number of Cherokee allies, made it as far as the mouth of the Big Sandy River on the Ohio (in what is now the northeast corner of Kentucky). Captain Preston recorded on March 5, a day on which the increasingly famished expedition crossed and recrossed Sandy Creek twenty-four times: "This day my . . . horse expired and I was left on foot with a hungry belly, which increased my woe. Nothing but hunger and fatigue appears to us."[24] Soon many of the men refused to go further, and on March 13, the day Preston's journal abruptly ends, he recorded that "hunger and want was so much increased that any man in the Camp would have ventured his life for a supper." The men, after being reduced to eating hide harness, were so debilitated by cold and hunger that they turned back without striking a blow. Of the 100 horses they brought, only four or five came back, the rest having been eaten.[25]

To defend its western frontier from the French and Indians, Virginia built a string of forts, which George Washington inspected in the fall of 1756. On part of the inspection, Washington was, as he wrote Governor Dinwiddie, "attended by Captain Preston, who was kind enough to conduct me along." Washington was not impressed by the frontier militiamen. He described those at Fort William (built by and named after William Preston) as "irregulars with whom order, regularity, circumspection, and vigilance are matters of derision and contempt" and reported that in the frontier counties, the militia "were in want of order, regulations, and obedience"; "every petty person must assume command, direct, and advise; otherwise he takes huff, thinks his wisdom and merit affronted, and so marches off in high contempt of every social Law. . . . Of the many forts I passed, I saw but few that had the captain present: most of them absent on their own business, and had given leave to many of the men to do the same," with the result that the settlers had fled and "a rich and once thick-settled country is now quite deserted and abandoned from the Maryland to the Carolina line." In Washington's words, "the ruinous state of the frontiers, and the vast extent of land we have lost since this time twelve-month, must appear incredible to those who are not eye-witnesses of the desolation."[26]

The tide of French and Indian victories finally turned, thanks to a combination of diplomacy and military force. In October 1758, Pennsylvania, in the treaty of Easton, to induce Indians to stop backing the French, relinquished to the Six Nations Pennsylvania's claims to land west of the Alleghenies. The following month, the French, no longer having Indian support, yielded Fort Duquesne to a superior approaching British force. In 1759, the British took Quebec from the French, a victory that led the French, in the 1763 Treaty of Paris, to turn over to the British all of Canada, as well as America east of the Mississippi.

During the French and Indian War, Preston grew in his surveying and other official positions, which in turn helped him to increase his landholdings. Soon after the failure of the Sandy Creek expedition, he began to fill offices similar to those in the array Patton had held. In the Augusta County militia, Preston became a major in 1758 and lieutenant colonel in 1759, in which year he also became the county's sheriff, coroner, and escheator. In 1761, when the town of Staunton, Virginia, was incorporated, Preston was named as a trustee. In 1766, he was elected to the Virginia Assembly as one of the two burgesses from Augusta County. When Botetourt County was formed in 1769, he became colonel of its militia, as well as surveyor, coroner, and escheator. In 1772, when Fincastle was formed as Virginia's western-most county, including most of what is now Kentucky, Preston became the county's surveyor, lieutenant, and sheriff. Montgomery County was split off from Fincastle County in 1776, and Preston became its surveyor in 1780.[27] As a result of holding all these positions, as leading Ohio Valley historians have noted, "practically all public business passed through his hands."[28]

Preston kept adding to his landholdings in western Virginia and what is now Kentucky. By 1773, in addition to other holdings, he had assem-bled, starting with land bought in 1759, 2,175 acres in a tract he called Greenfield, north of Roanoke, near what is now Daleville, Virginia, on what was called the Great Road leading southwest through the Valley of Virginia to northeast Tennessee. In 1773 and 1774, he bought four tracts of land at Draper's Meadows, aggregating 980 acres in Montgomery County that Patton had owned. On this land, Preston set up a plantation he called Smithfield, in honor of his wife, whose maiden name was Susannah Smith. The site is a few miles west of the Appalachian Ridge, where waters start to run not to the Atlantic but, ultimately, to the Mississippi. Being beyond where the waters run to the Atlantic, the Smithfield region was beyond the line of permitted settlements established by the British government in the Royal Proclamation of 1763, which sought to limit western settlements in Indian lands to reduce the risk of military expenditures of the sort that had badly strained Britain's finances during the Seven Years' War. But settlers had started to arrive in this region before there was a Proclamation of 1763—and settlers in the region, including men like William Preston, never paid much attention to that proclamation anyway. Smithfield was strategically located on a natural route parallel to the Clinch and Holston Rivers that leads to the southwest, between mountain ridges, into north-east Tennessee and through the Cumberland Gap up into Kentucky (see map 2.1). The plantation was far enough west to be exposed to possible Indian attack. Preston's brother-in-law Rev. John Brown, in May 1774,

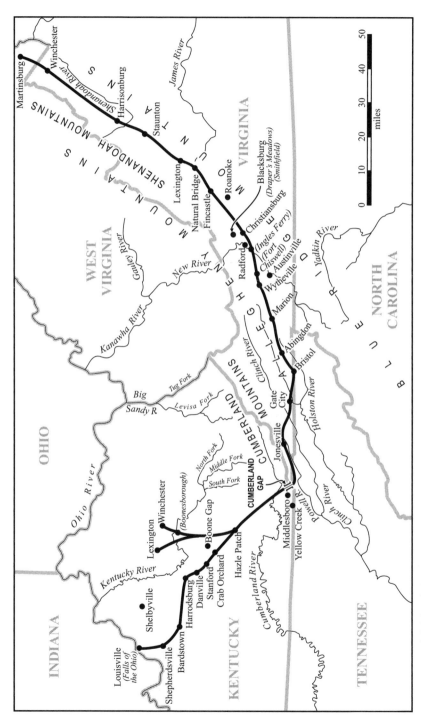

Map 2.1. Smithfield and the Opening of Kentucky

wrote Preston, "I can asure you that I am no ways satisfied with your situation; you lay too much in the way of the Indians."[29] But Preston remained at Smithfield. The location made it easier for him to coordinate exploration and surveying in Kentucky and to send support to the settlers in Kentucky. Moreover, if Preston had pulled back east, many other western settlers would likely have followed his example.

By the time Preston died in 1783, he owned 17,251 acres—nineteen tracts in Virginia and three tracts aggregating three thousand acres in what is now Kentucky, including valuable lands that were to become a large part of Louisville, as well as a choice tract Floyd had surveyed for him near Lexington.[30] He had become substantially rich—in part by trading in slaves and indentured servants, in part from distilling whiskey but most of all by his dealings in land.[31]

Being a county surveyor contributed to Preston's success as a land dealer—as it also contributed to George Washington's large landholdings and to the fortunes of many other investors in western lands. Preston never lost sight of the importance of surveying. When he died, the personal property in his estate included not only "42 Negroes valued at $4,431.65" and "273 volumes of books valued at $194.60," but also "surveyor's instruments."[32] I like to think that among those instruments—along with metal chains of standardized length to measure distances to identifiable markers and circumferentors or theodolites to give angles (see figures 2.3a and 2.3b)—was the handheld compass that was passed down to me, which would have been useful for rough approximations of bearings.[33]

Why was being a surveyor so important to men like Washington, Preston, and Floyd? Above all, because the surveyors of the unsettled frontier were in an ideal position to spot what land tracts were most promising—and then to file claims to those tracts for themselves. At the age of 17, George Washington, after a summer surveying Lord Fairfax's vast land claims in Virginia, noted: "The greatest Estates we have in this Colony were made . . . by taking up & purchasing at very low rates the rich back Lands which were thought nothing of in those days, but are now the most valuable lands we possess." He acted on this insight. At age 20, he bought 1,459 acres in the Virginian Piedmont.[34] He also acquired significant land ownership by inheritance and by marriage (Martha Dandridge Custis owned 18,000 acres when Washington married her)—but much

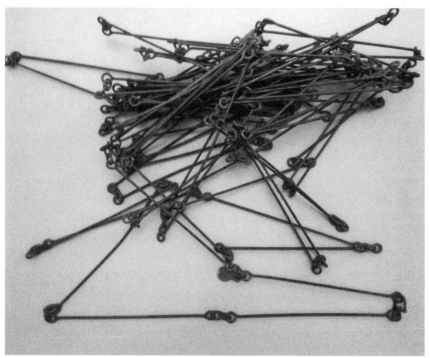

Fig. 2.3. Other eighteenth-century surveying instruments: (a) a circumferentor, or surveyor's compass, to measure angles; and (b) surveyor's chains, to measure distances. *Courtesy of Smithfield Plantation. Photograph by David McKissack.*

of his acreage came from land to the west of the established settlements, claimed based on explorations and surveys made by him (as a young man) or by others, including John Floyd, on his behalf.[35] As George Washington wrote in 1771, "What Inducements have Men to explore uninhabited Wilds but the prospect of getting good Lands?"[36] Eventually, Washington came to own over 52,000 acres, across six different states.[37]

Surveying was also important because without a survey by an official surveyor, land would not be allocated and registered. In addition, surveying was highly profitable. George Washington, surveying Fairfax claims as a young man of 17, earned a doubloon a day, sometimes six pistoles—say $15–$22.50 a day, or about $100 a week—close to what he earned 40 years later as president of the United States. Charles Mason and Jeremiah Dixon in 1763 were paid £3,500 by the Calverts of Maryland and the Penns of Pennsylvania to survey the boundary between Maryland and Pennsylvania—the Mason-Dixon Line.[38] That was a princely sum—but without an accurate survey, the proprietors of Maryland and Pennsylvania could not convey clear title to land on either side of the boundary and therefore could not realize the value of their land ownership.

Although Preston knew how to survey, by the 1770s, when thousands of acres were being surveyed for British colonists, he was not surveying frontier land himself but was having it done for him, in large part by his young protégé John Floyd and by Floyd's assistants. Floyd was a young widower, not yet 20, when he was recommended to Preston in 1770 as well-qualified to be a deputy surveyor. To test out Floyd's skills and diligence, Preston had him teach the Preston children and other children at Greenfield. Preston liked what he saw. Floyd was smart, wrote well and in a clear hand, and had surveying skills. He was also a commanding figure—trim, over six feet tall, with piercing black eyes and straight black hair, perhaps from his mother's mother, whose father was said to have been a Catawba chief.[39] Preston soon used Floyd as his private secretary and assistant surveyor, in addition to his teaching responsibilities. When Fincastle County (including most of what is now Kentucky) was organized in 1772, Preston caused Floyd to be appointed as a deputy surveyor and deputy sheriff of the county.

In April 1774, Preston, as county surveyor of Fincastle County, sent out a group of surveyors under Floyd to make surveys along the Kanawha River in what is now West Virginia and in Kentucky.[40] Early in that trip, Floyd's party, carrying out a promise Preston had made to George Washington, surveyed 2,000 acres for Washington on the Kanawha River, under land warrants that had been issued to Washington for his services as an officer in the French and Indian War.[41] Washington had decided to claim lands west of the mountains despite the bar in the 1763 proclamation, because, as Washington had put it in 1767 to another land speculator, "I can never look upon that proclamation in any other light (but this I say between ourselves) than as a temporary expedient to quiet the Minds of the Indians" that "must fall in a few years. . . . any Person therefore who neglects the present opportunity of hunting out good Lands & in some Measure Marking & distinguishing them for their own (in order to keep others from settling them) will never regain it."[42]

Floyd's party, after surveying the Washington claim, continued further west to the Falls of the Ohio.[43] Near the Falls, at what was to become Louisville, they laid out thirty tracts for such leading Virginians as William Preston, William Christian (colonel in the militia of Fincastle County and brother-in-law of Patrick Henry), William Byrd (militia colonel and member of one of Virginia's first families), and Martha Washington's nephew Alexander Spottswood Dandridge.[44] Floyd also laid out two 1,000 acre tracts for himself near Beargrass Creek, not far from the falls.[45] In a period of ten days, Floyd and his men surveyed more than 40,000 acres in and near the future Louisville.[46]

Despite hearing rumors that war was likely between the Shawnees and the whites, the Fincastle surveyors continued laying out tracts. In June and July 1774, they moved east to the bluegrass region of central Kentucky, surveying land around what would become Frankfort and Lexington.[47] These surveys included one tract of 1,000 acres for Floyd and one of the same size for Preston, both near what was to become Lexington, and tracts aggregating 7,000 acres for Patrick Henry.[48] The land entranced the surveyors. One entered in his journal for July 1: "All the land that we passed over today is like a Paradise it is so good & beautiful."[49]

It was becomingly increasingly dangerous for whites to be in Kentucky, particularly after the brutal killing by whites at Yellow Creek of the relatives of the Mingo chief Logan and the ensuing Mingo raids on white settlers. In early June 1774, Preston received reports that "an Indian War is commenced, and the out Inhabitants are all Forting [or] fleeing in."[50] On

June 10, Lord John Dunmore, the last British governor of Virginia, began mobilizing British troops and American militia to defend the settlements. He planned to invade the Shawnee lands north of the Ohio River and to "destroy their Towns & magazines and distress them in every other way that is possible."[51] It may not be coincidental that Dunmore was personally interested in British title to lands in Kentucky, having invested in a large tract of land there.[52] In early July, after Shawnees killed two settlers near Harrodsburg, the first settlement by British settlers in Kentucky, its residents abandoned the station and returned to the Clinch River settlements.[53]

The imminence of what came to be known as Lord Dunmore's War put the Fincastle surveyors at great risk of their lives. Not knowing whether the surveyors were already aware of that risk, Preston, on June 20, 1774, authorized Captain Russell, the commander of a settlement on the Clinch River, to engage two "faithful woodmen" to find the Virginia surveyors in Kentucky and warn them. Russell chose Daniel Boone and his friend the German-American frontiersman Michael Stoner, telling Preston that Boone and Stoner were "two of the best Hands I could think of" and that "by the assiduity of these Men, if it is not too late, I hope the Gentlemen [the surveyors] will be apprised of the eminent Danger they are Daily in." In a later letter, Russell wrote Preston that if the surveyors were still alive, "it is indisputable but that Boone must find them."[54] Boone and Stoner traveled all the way to the Falls of the Ohio in search of Floyd and the other Fincastle surveyors, only to find that Floyd and his group had already set out back to the relative safety of the settlements on the Clinch—so Boone and Stoner themselves returned to a station on the Clinch in August 1774, having covered 800 miles in 62 days.[55]

By that time, war had broken out in earnest. In late July, Shawnees killed two of the Fincastle surveyors as they were paddling a dugout across the Kentucky River. In response to Indian attacks on the Clinch settlements, with Floyd's strong encouragement, Preston appointed Boone a captain in the Virginia militia and placed him in charge of three stations on the Clinch River.[56] In October 1774, many hundreds of Shawnees and allied Indians crossed the Ohio River to attack more than a thousand members of the Virginia militia who were massing at Point Pleasant, where the Kanawha runs into the Ohio, to raid the Shawnee villages in Ohio. Floyd, as a captain in the Fincastle County militia, rode north to join the fight, but the Fincastle militia was not able to reach Point Pleasant until midnight on the day of the battle. After the Virginian militia pursued the Shawnees north of the Ohio River to their towns on the Scioto River, the Shawnees, in the Treaty of Camp Charlotte, agreed to yield their hunting rights in Kentucky in exchange for Lord Dunmore's promise to keep the colonists south of the Ohio River.[57]

Although Lord Dunmore's War was over, the bloody struggles between settlers and Indians in Kentucky were only beginning. Floyd was in the midst of those struggles. In April 1775, on Preston's instructions, Floyd went back to Kentucky and helped to found St. Asaph's Station, later known as Logan's Station, on Dick's River, about 25 miles southeast of Harrodsburg. There Floyd surveyed more land for Preston and others, but the question of who had the right to award title to land in Kentucky became less and less clear. While Floyd was assisting in the founding of St. Asaph's Station, Daniel Boone and a party of axemen blazed the way to a site on the Kentucky River northeast of St. Asaph's to set up a stockaded settlement soon called Boonesborough, built for Richard Henderson and his Transylvania Company, which had bought from the Cherokees all their rights in a vast area including most of Kentucky and much of northern Tennessee, with the objective of establishing their own proprietary colony (Transylvania) and selling land to settlers.[58]

The white settlers in Kentucky were sorely confused by conflicting claims of right to award land. Floyd wrote Preston in May 1776 that there was "the D-l to pay here about land," and if Virginia did not straighten out the land situation, "there'll be bloodshed soon."[59] At the same time, the Shawnees and other Indians of the Ohio Valley saw the increase in surveying and the influx of settlers as a threat to their lands. Floyd, on his way back to Kentucky to build the St. Asaph's station, wrote Preston that "when I consider that the settlements of the land will ruin the hunting ground of [several Indian] nations, I a little dread the consequence."[60] The risk to Floyd and other white settlers in Kentucky and elsewhere west of the Alleghenies soared after fighting broke out in April 1775 between Americans and British troops, because the British encouraged Indian attacks on the American frontiersmen to further three objectives: to strengthen their position in the Ohio Valley; to hold on to Canada, which in 1775 was being attacked by American troops; and to divert American military forces from the coastal colonies, the main theater of operations during the Revolutionary War. For all these reasons, Henry Hamilton, the lieutenant governor of Canada who commanded the British garrison at Detroit, sought (and in June 1777 obtained) authorization from London to employ Indians "in making a Diversion and exciting an alarm upon the frontiers of Virginia and Pennsylvania." The British began to supply the Indians with large amounts of war goods—guns, tomahawks, ammunition, scalping knives, and war paint.[61]

In April 1776, a delegation of Shawnee, Ottawa, Mohawk, and other northern Indians, their faces blackened for war, visited the towns of the western Cherokee who were against accommodation with the settlers, to urge joint action against the Americans who were taking Indian land. The leading Shawnee delegate produced a war belt of wampum some nine feet long, described the American encroachments, and said it is "better to die like men than to diminish away by inches." The Cherokee chief accepted the belt, and the warriors joined in singing the war song. The warriors of the different tribes represented by the singers far outnumbered the number of men then in Kentucky—probably fewer than 200—who were capable of bearing and firing a rifle.[62]

In July 1776, the Indian threat to the western settlers was translated into action in a way that directly involved Floyd and his rifle. On Sunday, July 14, Indians near Boonesborough seized Boone's 13-year-old daughter Jemima, along with two other girls from Boonesborough, the daughters of Colonel Richard Callaway: Fanny Callaway, aged 14, and her 16-year-old sister Betsy, who was engaged to marry Colonel Henderson's nephew Samuel Henderson.

That Sunday afternoon had been a quiet one at Boonesborough. The men and the few women at the settlement were wearing their Sunday best. Most of the men wore pantaloons rather than their usual weekday breechclouts and leggings. Boone was resting in bed. Samuel Henderson was halfway through his weekly shave. Jemima Boone, who had hurt her foot stepping on a broken cane stalk, wanted to cool the injured foot in the water of the Kentucky River; she was tired of being confined in the squalid little station because of the risk of Indian attack.[63] She and the Callaway girls decided to take a canoe out into the river. Boone had warned Jemima to keep the canoe close to Boonesborough's cabins, but the current took the girls downriver and toward the north bank. A war party of two Cherokees and three Shawnees was waiting for them. When the canoe got close to the bank, one Indian dove in and grabbed the buffalo-hide tug at the boat's bow. The Indians pulled the canoe to shore. The girls screamed until an Indian grabbed Betsy Callaway by the hair and made a scalping gesture to make plain what would happen if they did not shut up. The Indians then dragged the girls into the woods.[64]

Boonesborough settlers heard the girls' cries across the river. A Callaway boy ran up to Floyd and his friend Nathan Reid, screaming: "The savages have the girls!" Boone jumped up from his bed, pulled on his pants, and ran barefoot to the riverbank. Samuel Henderson ran there, too, his face half-shaved and half-covered with shaving soap. So did Floyd and Reid. The Kentucky River behind Boonesborough was not wide. Floyd and the other settlers who had run to the riverbank could see on the far side the capsized canoe. John Gass, aged 12, stripped, swam the river, and brought back the canoe. In it, Floyd, Reid, Boone, Samuel Henderson, and others crossed to the north shore of the river. Once there, the settlers split to search for and follow the Indians' trail in what little daylight was left before making camp for the night. Boone sent young Gass back to the fort in the dark for ammunition, food, moccasins, and breechclouts. Boone was barefoot, and, as Reid put it, pantaloons "impeded our movements." Frontiersmen like Boone found they could move more quickly in the woods dressed like Indians in breechclouts and leggings than in European pants.[65]

The girls had been dressed up for Sunday. After cutting off their dresses at the knees so the girls could move more quickly, the Indians led the girls off at a fast pace north toward the Ohio River and the Shawnee towns across it. By the afternoon of the second day, the Indians and their captives were 25 miles from Boonesborough. The girls kept breaking branches and dropping bits of cloth as signs for the settlers to follow.[66]

For three days the settlers pursued, led by Boone. On the second day, Boone became concerned that they were not gaining on the Indians, because the captors' trail was hard to follow through the heavy cane. There was also the risk that if the settlers followed in the Indians' footsteps, the Indians would hear them coming and have time to tomahawk the girls before the settlers could get to the Indians. As Floyd later wrote Preston, the settlers' goal was "to get the prisoners without giving the Indians time to murder them after they discovered us."[67] The tracks told Boone that the Indians intended to cross the Licking River at the Blue Licks. Boone decided not to follow the tracks but to head directly to where he thought the Indians were likely to cross. As Reid remembered it, "paying no further attention to the trail, [Boone] now took a strait course through the woods, with increased speed, followed by the men in perfect silence."[68] Later in the day, the settlers once again came on the tracks of the Indians. At mid-morning on the third day, Boone, Floyd, and the others struck the Indians' trail again.[69] Boone started jogging, and the other men followed. The pace was dauntingly fast. Some of the men were quite young—Floyd was around 25, Henderson was 30, Reid 23—but Boone, the pacesetter, was 41. They came on the carcass of a recently killed buffalo calf, blood still trickling down from its back; part of its hump had been cut off. Boone was sure the Indians would stop to cook the buffalo meat at the first water they reached.[70] Near the Licking River, the Indians made a fire to cook the piece of buffalo hump. Jemima heard a sound in the woods, looked up, and saw her father, a hundred yards away, "creeping upon his breast like a snake."[71] She kept still. Fanny Callaway, who was looking at an Indian standing by the campfire, saw blood spurt from the Indian's chest before she heard the gun that shot him.[72]

"That's Daddy!" Jemima cried out.[73]

Floyd fired at the same time as Boone and was certain he had shot his target through the body.[74] The settlers' rifles were single-shot muzzle-loaders. Deadly accuracy was essential, because at least a minute was generally needed to reload such a rifle. Floyd, Boone, and the others raised the war whoop and charged the camp. The Indians fled, as Floyd wrote Preston, "almost naked, some without their mockisons, and not one of them with so much as a knife or tomahawk."[75] Betsy Callaway ran towards the rescuers, disheveled, her dress cut short, her dark hair loose. One of the rescuers, thinking she was an Indian, raised his just-fired rifle to club her. Boone yelled out "For God's sake, don't kill her when we've traveled so far to save her!"[76] Boone's yell stopped the man just before he brained her. The girls' clothes were torn to shreds. Their legs were bleeding. Boone covered them with blankets. "Thank Almighty Providence," Boone said, "for we have the girls safe. Let's all sit down by them now and have a hearty cry." Jemima remembered "there was not a dry eye in the company."[77]

The capture of the girls showed the extent of the Indian threat to the white settlers in Kentucky. It was not a good sign that Shawnees and Cherokees, traditional enemies, had worked together in the capture and in the trip toward the Shawnee towns north of the Ohio River. That alliance presaged more Indian attacks of greater size. As Floyd put it in his letter to Preston, the situation of the settlers in Kentucky was "truly alarming." Some of the settlements in Kentucky were being abandoned, with the settlers going back east. Floyd said he wanted "as much to return as any person can do, but if I leave the country now there is scarcely one single man hereabouts, but what will follow the example," so he had concluded "to sell my life as dear as I can . . . rather than to make an ignominious escape."

For two years, however, Floyd's career was to diverge from the imperiled settlements in Kentucky. In December 1776, Virginia drove a stake into the heart of the Transylvania Company's pretensions by carving out of Fincastle County a new county, Kentucky County, which included most of the land the company had claimed.[78] Floyd, who had been appointed as the Transylvania Company's principal surveyor, went east to Williamsburg to look for an attractive position, since the Transylvania Company no longer had any land-granting power. In December 1776, he wrote Preston that others had been appointed the surveyors of all the new counties in western Virginia and that he had become a partner in a "vessel fitted out for privateering."[79] Floyd and the ship went after British commerce in the Caribbean, but the privateer was soon captured by a British man of war. Sent to prison in England, Floyd escaped, made his way to France, borrowed money from Benjamin Franklin in Paris, and sailed back to Virginia. He brought with him a scarlet cloak he had bought in Paris with the hope of wearing it when he married William Preston's ward Jane Buchanan. Not until 1778 did Floyd make it back to Virginia and to Smithfield—just in time to prevent Jane Buchanan from being married to another suitor and to marry her himself. By November 1779, Floyd and his family were back in Kentucky, building a cabin on Bear Grass Creek near what was to become Louisville, where the settlers were sick (of scurvy, one suspects) from eating only meat and where Indian attacks were a constant hazard.[80]

In 1780, Floyd, who by then was one of the original trustees of Louisville as well as the head of the militia for Jefferson County, wrote Preston how quickly the settlers were coming down the Ohio River to the Louisville area.[81] The fighting with the Indians continued, despite the surge of settlers. "Hardly one week pass[es]," Floyd wrote Preston, "without someone being scalped between [Floyd's home on Bear Grass Creek] and the Falls and I have almost got too cowardly to travel about the woods without company." In September 1781, Floyd came close to death when he led 26 men into an ambush by a much larger force of Indians. Floyd was wounded and most of his men were killed.[82]

The fighting between Indians and whites in the Ohio Valley continued long after the British army under General Cornwallis in October 1781 surrendered to the Americans at Yorktown, basically ending the fighting between the British and the Americans, although the treaty of Paris formally ending the Revolutionary War was not signed until September 3, 1783. Indeed, the fighting with Indians in Ohio did not end until August 1794, when General Anthony Wayne defeated an Indian confederation at the Battle of Fallen Timbers, near what is now Toledo, Ohio, more than a dozen years after the Yorktown surrender.

On August 19, 1782, at the Battle of Blue Licks—near where Floyd and Boone in 1776 had rescued Jemima Boone and the Callaway girls— hundreds of Indians, led by British officers, in less than 15 minutes killed more than a third of Kentucky's militia in the worst defeat ever sustained by Kentuckians at Indian hands. Also in August 1782, Indians fatally wounded Floyd's brother-in-law William Buchanan, who died a lingering death several days later. In November 1782, Floyd, as part of the retaliatory expedition commanded by George Rogers Clark after the Battle of the Blue Licks, led battalions from Jefferson and Fayette Counties in destroying Shawnee villages, driving the Shawnees further away from the Ohio River and reducing the Indian threat to Kentucky.

After returning to Kentucky in 1779, Floyd had become a substantial landowner, one of the original trustees of Louisville, and in 1780 the county lieutenant (the head of the militia) for Jefferson County (Louisville's county). Floyd continued as a surveyor of lands around Louisville. Surveying was a risky occupation. As a white captive of the Shawnees recorded, Indians felt "the deepest hatred" for surveyors and considered them "the agents who take their lands from them, because they are invariably the forerunners of settlement by the whites."[83]

In late March 1783, Floyd wrote his final letter to Preston. Much of it had to do with land and surveying. "We have endeavored to stick to survey-ing," Floyd wrote, "but have been so often interrupted by the savages that we have made but little progress." After reporting that Indians had killed his brother-in-law Buchanan, Floyd added: "I have long expected some-thing like this to be my own lot, & if the war is continued much longer I can hardly escape, tho' I am now determined to be more cautious than I have been heretofore, yet every man in this country must be more or less exposed to danger." He ended his letter by saying that he did not expect to have the pleasure of seeing Preston again "till the War is ended, if ever I should survive that time. But let me see you or not, or let me enjoy all the Blessing of peace or be involved in every calamity of war & distress, I shall ever remain your very affectionate Friend & Servt."[84] Within days of send-ing the letter, Floyd's forebodings came to pass. On April 8, 1783, while wearing his scarlet cloak and riding with his friend Captain Alexander Breckinridge, he was fatally wounded by Indians on his way to a salt lick not far from Louisville. He died of his wounds two days later. He was not yet 33 years old. Perhaps he was shot simply because the scarlet cloak made him so visible a target—but it is hard not to believe that the Indians knew who he was and killed him because of his prominence in the settle-ment of Kentucky, just as Indians had killed James Patton almost thirty years earlier. Floyd's widow eventually married (and outlived) Alexander Breckinridge. When she died in 1812, at her request Floyd's scarlet cloak was placed in her coffin.[85]

During the Revolutionary War, Preston did not himself fight Indians, although from his fortified stronghouse at Smithfield he was centrally involved (through men like Floyd and Boone) in the settlement and defense of Kentucky and, directly, in the provisioning of militia sent into Kentucky or against the Cherokees. He also was a leader in guarding western Virginia and its vitally important lead mines and gunpowder works against possi-ble attacks by Tory sympathizers, who were rife in Montgomery County. In addition, he sought to keep Loyalists from taking up arms against the Continental troops and supporters of the Revolutionary cause. In 1780 he acted as chief justice in the trials of 55 Loyalists accused of treason.[86]

In late 1776, when the ungainly expanse of Fincastle County was split into several counties, Preston, who had been the lieutenant and

commander in chief of the militia of Fincastle County, became the lieutenant of Montgomery County and head of its militia.[87] He stayed at
Smithfield, close to settlements being attacked by Indians, even though
many of his neighboring settlers fled eastward, and he sent his wife and
children to the greater safety of Greenfield.[88] In 1780, after implementing
Thomas Jefferson's directions to "take the most immediate measures for
protecting the Lead Mines" against possible attack from Tories or Indians,
Preston helped plan the campaign that led to the defeat of a Tory force
at King's Mountain, on the border between North and South Carolina.[89]
Early in 1781, Preston led a force of 350 riflemen from Montgomery County
from the Virginia lead mines south into North Carolina to join the
American fight against Banastre Tarleton's rangers. In March 1781, while
fighting alongside his men against British troops, Preston was thrown from
his horse at the skirmish at Weitzel's Mill, several days before the decisive
Battle of Guilford Court House that led the British to relinquish control
of North Carolina. By then, Preston was in his fifties. He had been in bad
health and, in his daughter's words, was not only tall (5'11") but "large,
inclined to corpulency." Fortunately, a fellow officer helped Preston to
remount and ride away. Within days, before the Battle of Guilford Court
House, Preston's militia melted away—illustrating George Washington's
views as to the unreliability of militias. In a letter to Jefferson, Preston
attributed the disappearance of his men to their being "greatly straitened
for provisions" and having been "overpowered by numbers" in two actions,
in the second of which they were "broken and dispersed with the loss of
their blankets." Preston said he and a fellow officer went home "accompanied by only two or three young men." He wrote Jefferson: "It gave me
great pain that our militia returned so soon, but I will venture to say, they
did duty on the Enemy's Lines, as long as any other that went from behind
the mountains, & much longer than some."[90]

When Floyd heard of Preston's fall from his horse, he wrote Preston to
express his desire to stand in Preston's place "if you have any more of that
sort of business to do." Floyd went on to tell Preston that 47 from Louisville's
county had been killed or captured by Indians since the start of 1781 and
to note that "no surveying can possibly be done till better times." Those
themes—Indian attacks and their effect on surveying—dominated Floyd's
letters to Preston until Floyd's fatal wounding by Indians in April 1783.[91]

William Preston survived Floyd by only two months, dying in June 1783. He was 52 years old. He was overweight and dropsical (in March 1783 he had told his daughter his "legs & feet swell every evening like posts"). The news of Floyd's death stunned him; his daughter said "he was never seen to smile afterwards." On June 28, an exceedingly hot day, Preston reviewed a muster of the Montgomery County militia not far from Smithfield. He complained of pain in his head, could not mount his horse, lost the ability to speak, and died that night.[92]

From the time Preston and Floyd met in 1770, their lives had been closely intertwined. That intertwining continued after their deaths. Preston's daughter Letitia married Floyd's son, another John Floyd, who was governor of Virginia (from 1830 to 1834), as was his son John Buchanan Floyd (governor from 1849 to 1852), who was to become secretary of war under President Buchanan.[93]

America had changed enormously in the lifetimes of Preston and Floyd, who helped to bring about some of those changes. What had been disparate British colonies had become an independent nation, thanks in part to the efforts of men like Preston against the British and their Tory sympathizers. Settlement had expanded westward in western Virginia and into Kentucky, thanks to a large extent to the surveying of the wilderness by Preston and Floyd and others like them and to the driving of Indians out of Kentucky by militiamen like Floyd, with planning and supplies provided by men like Preston. The increase in western settlement was overwhelming. In 1774, when Preston sent Floyd and the Fincastle surveyors into Kentucky, there may have been 200 settlers there from the American colonies. By 1783, when Floyd and Preston died, the population of Kentucky was at least 30,000 and perhaps over 45,000.[94] Kentucky was well on its way to having the 60,000 minimum population needed to be able for it to separate from Virginia and become a state, which it did in 1792. Locating and claiming land and fighting to defend it and to expel rival claimants underlay much of the transformative change in the western frontier. The compass and the rifle—tools of the surveyor and of the fighter—are fitting emblems of these changes.

3

Y^r Most Ob^t Servt, G. Washington: The Constitutional Convention

History records things that happened. Many of those events would have been far different if they had taken place as initially appeared likely. The differences in outcome can shed light on major forces (and weaknesses) at work at the time of the event. An example: what would have happened to the young United States if George Washington had not attended the Constitutional Convention in 1787 and if he had not agreed to become our first president?

On the wall of my study is a letter from George Washington, dated March 15, 1787, to a man named James Mercer. I inherited the letter from my father, who inherited it from his uncle, Major General Preston Brown. Much of the letter is a dry discussion of a legal matter. Mercer was a lawyer, and Washington was writing to him about how best to pay off and settle a bond Washington had given to pay for a large parcel of land in Virginia. But the end of the letter is extraordinary and calls to mind just how uncertain matters were in America before the Constitution was written and ratified and Washington became the first president of the United States: the fragility of the Confederation, the need for a constitution, and the doubt as to whether Washington would attend the Constitutional Convention. In the next to last paragraph of the letter, Washington wrote:

> However desirous I am, and always shall be, to comply with any
> commands of my Country, I do not conceive how I can, with

Fig. 3.1 "Washington at the Constitutional Convention" (1856). Painting by Junius Brutus Stearns, *Wikimedia*.

consistent conduct, attend the proposed convention to be holden in Philadelphia in May next. For besides the declaration which I made in a very solemn manner when I was about to retire, of bidding adieu to all public employment; I had just before the appointment of delegates to this Convention, written and dispatched circular letters to the several State Societies of the Cincinnati [former officers in the Continental Army] informing them of my intention not to attend the General Meeting [of the Cincinnati] which was to be held about the same time and at the same City, and assigned reasons which apply as forcibly in the one case as in the other. Under these circumstances, to attend the Convention might be considered disrespectful to a worthy set of men for whose attachment and support on many trying occasions, I shall ever feel the highest gratitude and affection.[1]

Bear in mind where matters stood with Washington and with the young United States in March 1787, when Washington wrote Mercer. During the long Revolutionary War with Great Britain, Washington had been the commander in chief of the Continental Army from May 1775 until the war's end in 1783. In early December 1783, Washington bade farewell to his officers at Fraunces Tavern in New York City. Three weeks later, before the Congress sitting at Annapolis, he resigned his commission as commander in chief, saying "I retire from the great theater of Action." Washington rode from Annapolis to his home at Mt. Vernon on the Potomac, resolved to tend to his plantation and build up his extensive landholdings and his fortune. He was 51 at the time—not at all a young man in that era. For more than three years, although his correspondence reflected interests that included natural history, art, and the building of a Potomac canal that would link the East Coast to the Ohio River and the Mississippi (and greatly increase the value of his western land holdings), Washington carried out his resolution to be a country squire, building up his estate at Mount Vernon and supervising its many businesses. Those businesses came to include raising wheat, corn, and other crops; milling; weaving; blacksmithing; and catching and selling the hundreds of thousands of herring and other fish that in those days ran seasonally in the Potomac. For example, on the day before his letter to James Mercer expressing doubt about whether he could attend the constitutional convention, Washington wrote a letter consigning for sale "45 Barrls. of Herrings" and telling the consignee "It is hardly necessary to add that, the sooner these fish are disposed of the higher the Sale of them probably will be."[2]

Washington also stayed in touch with his former officers, attempting to be loyal both to the men who had fought with him so long and to the central government of the new United States. That effort had not always been easy. Congress was chronically short of funds and had delayed paying salaries or meeting officers' requests for pensions. In March 1783, an anonymous manifesto was circulated to officers gathered at Newburgh, New York, proposing to confront Congress with an ultimatum: if the officers' back pay and pension requests were not met, the army would disband if the war continued; if the war ended, the army would not dissolve. Washington managed to quash the implied threats of treason and tyranny after an eloquent speech to the officers in which he pulled out all the stops, including saying, when he donned spectacles to read his remarks: "Gentlemen, you must pardon me. I have grown gray in your service, and now find myself growing blind." Two months later, Major General Henry Knox, the chief artillery officer of the Continental Army, started the formation of the Society of the Cincinnati to band together the Continental Army officers into a permanent union, with membership to be inherited by the eldest son. The Society was named after the Roman Cincinnatus, who, in the fifth century BC, had left his farm when asked by the Roman senate to lead in Rome's defense against attack by rival tribes. Many saw the Society as a step toward military control of the United States and viewed the Society's primogeniture as an attempt at hereditary nobility. Washington became the Society's first president general in December 1783 and remained in that position until his death in 1799, although he rarely attended its general meetings, and he sought (unsuccessfully) to have the Society eliminate its hereditary aspect. Given the controversy stirred up by what some saw as the Society's aristocratic leanings, Washington's aide David Humphreys, after consulting with several officers, advised Washington in September 1786 that the unanimous sentiment was that "it would not be of any good consequence, or even advisable for you to attend the next General Meeting" of the Cincinnati.[3]

Out of military office, Washington kept in touch with national political developments. One matter that had concerned him for years was the weakness of the power of the federal government under the Articles of Confederation, written in 1777 by a committee of the Continental Congress and not finally ratified until 1781. In order to gain support of the former colonies, many of which feared the development of a strong central government that would dominate the states, the Articles (as indicated by their name) created a loose confederation with little central power. Each state, regardless of the size of its population, cast one vote. There was no executive branch. Congress had no power to impose taxes—so it could not pay its war debts to soldiers or suppliers or fund the raising of an army. Nor did Congress have any power to regulate commerce. Indeed, under the Articles, states were imposing tariffs on goods from other states. Many saw the need to strengthen the Articles, but changing them was not easy, because any amendment had to be approved by the legislatures of every state.[4]

Washington had seen during eight years as commander in chief how weak and disorganized the central government had been. He had witnessed the turmoil of promotion and demotion of senior officers by Congress, as well as the chronic lack of funding that led to the mutinous murmurings by unpaid officers at the time of the Newburgh Address in March 1783. As early as 1780, Washington wrote a Virginia delegate in the Congress: "unless Congress speaks in a more decisive tone; unless they are vested with powers by the several States competent to the great purposes of War, or assume them as a matter of right . . . our Cause is lost." Two weeks after his speech in Newburgh, Washington wrote Hamilton "No Man in the United States is, or can be more deeply impressed with the necessity of reform in our present Confederation than myself." In June 1783, writing a circular to the states in support of an impost to fund payment of obligations to soldiers, Washington said it was a time of "political probation" for the states that would determine whether the United States "will be respectable and prosperous, or contemptible and miserable as a Nation." To him, it was "indispensable to the happiness of the individual States, that there should be lodged somewhere, a Supreme Power to regulate and govern the general concerns of the Confederated Republic, without which the Union cannot be of long duration." In December 1783, at a dinner in his honor given by Congress in Annapolis the night before he resigned his commission, Washington offered as the final toast of the evening: "Competent powers to Congress for general purposes." But the Confederation bumbled on, without a stronger central government. As Washington wrote in 1784, the "foederal Government is a name without substance," because the states were not "bound by its edicts." In a 1785 letter, he said that if America is not "a united people under one head," "we are thirteen independent sovereignties, eternally counteracting each other." Washington was not, however, anxious to play a large part in framing a stronger charter. When John Jay in 1786 wrote Washington about the possibility of "a general convention for revising the articles of Confederation" and his belief that Washington would not be "an unconcerned Spectator," Washington doubted that the time was ripe and wrote that as to his own role, "having happily assisted in bringing the ship into port & having been fairly discharged; it is not my business to embark again upon a sea of troubles." In February 1787, Congress called the summoning of a Constitutional Convention, to be held in May of that year in the centrally located city of Philadelphia. That was the convention at which the Constitution of the United States was drafted—the convention that, as he wrote Mercer, Washington did not see how he could attend.[5]

Washington ultimately decided to go to the Constitutional Convention, making that decision less than two weeks after his letter to Mercer explaining why he couldn't attend. What led him to change his mind? Washington was never one to bare his soul to others or in his diary, but several factors were presumably at work. The soundings by his aide David Humphreys indicated that members of the Cincinnati would have no objection to Washington's attendance at the convention. As Madison reported to Washington, it had become more and more likely that the delegates to the convention would favor a complete reworking of the nation's charter, not just some tinkering with the existing Articles. Washington may well have been concerned that his reputation, which had soared with the victory over Britain and the grace with which he resigned his commission, would be damaged if he took part in a constitutional convention that failed. As the prospects for a successful convention grew, so did the chance that Washington's reputation would suffer if he did not participate in the convention—particularly if the convention's efforts bore no fruit. Many whom Washington deeply respected—among them Hamilton, Madison, Jay, and Knox—urged him to go to the convention, appealing both to his patriotism and to his desire to protect and build his reputation. Early in March, Washington had expressed to Knox a concern "whether my non-attendance in this convention will not be considered as a dereliction to republicanism." On March 19, Knox wrote Washington that he took it for granted that Washington would be elected president of the convention and that if the convention framed a vigorous federal government, "it would be a circumstance highly honorable to your fame . . . and doubly entitle you to the glorious republican epithet "The Father of Your Country." In addition, Washington must have known that the convention was likely to lead to the creation of a chief executive for the country. Being the nation's first chief executive would not be a bad way for Washington to cap his career. He was ambitious, but he was also driven by a sense of duty to do the best he could for his country. Washington could well have thought that no one was as well qualified as he was to hold the country and its factions together, treading the untrod path of the presidency under a brand-new constitution. For whatever assessment of these or other factors, on March 28, Washington wrote Virginia's governor Edmund Randolph that he would go to the convention and that he planned to go to Philadelphia a week early to address the Cincinnati, so his attendance at the convention would not appear to demonstrate "a disrespectful inattention to the Society."[6]

At their first session, the delegates to the Constitutional Convention unanimously chose Washington to be the convention's president. The tasks before the delegates were not easy. Issues, notably the tensions between large states and small ones, came close to wrecking the outcome— to the point that on July 10, 1787, Washington told Hamilton "I *almost* despair of seeing a favorable issue to . . . the convention and do therefore repent having had any agency in the business." What the convention ultimately achieved, however, is both familiar and remarkable. Instead of a few amendments to the Articles of Confederation, the convention wrote a constitution that built on, but was far different from, the Articles. The Constitution prescribed not just a legislature, but three branches of government—a legislature, a judiciary, and an executive branch, with the executive power vested in the president of the United States of America, who was to be the commander in chief of the army and navy of the United States. The legislature was to have two chambers, the House of Representatives and the Senate. Representatives were to serve two-year terms, and the number of representatives from a state was to be proportionate to its population. Senators were to be elected for six-year terms, and there were to be two senators from each state, regardless of the size of its population. Congress had broad powers, including to impose and collect taxes, pay debts, provide for the common defense, borrow money, regulate commerce with other nations and among the states, and declare war. The Constitution could be amended by amendments proposed by two-thirds of both houses and ratified by three-fourths of the states. This was a compact that gave the national government the tools it needed—the "competent powers for general purposes" Washington had proposed in his 1783 toast. In his diary for September 17, 1787, the day on which the Constitution was approved by twelve states, Washington recorded that after the members "adjourned to the City Tavern, dined together, and took a cordial leave of each other," he "returned to my lodgings . . . and retired to meditate on the momentous wk. which had been executed." He was to write Lafayette a few months later that the system of government formed by the Constitution "approached nearer to perfection than any government hitherto instituted among men."[7]

Washington had played a large part in the convention—not by speaking, which he did rarely, but by presiding, keeping order, and supporting the effort to create a strong national charter. His presence alone was persuasive, given the delegates' and the nation's respect for Washington, a man of imposing stature, their commander in chief for more than eight years of warfare, a man who since 1775 had been referred to as His Excellency (see figure 3.1). After the signing, Washington also took a large role in the effort to have the Constitution ratified—not least by encouraging Hamilton and Madison to use their "good pens" in soliciting support for ratification in what became *The Federalist* essays. Supporters of ratification repeatedly invoked Washington's name, arguing, for example, that the Constitution must be a good document, or Washington would not have supported it. By the early summer of 1788, eleven states had ratified the Constitution.

Not surprisingly, Washington was elected the first president (by the unanimous vote of all electors), taking office in April 1789. He was re-elected (again by unanimous electoral vote) in 1792 for a second four-year term, starting in March 1793. During Washington's first term as president, he visited every state in the union and appointed Hamilton as secretary of the treasury and Jefferson as secretary of state; Congress passed the Bill of Rights, set up the federal court system, and, with Washington's backing, passed (over vehement opposition by Jefferson and his adherents) a Hamilton-fathered bill creating the Bank of the United States. In his second term, Washington issued a proclamation of America's neutrality in the war between France and Great Britain, led the successful quashing of the effort by western frontiersmen to refuse to pay tax on whiskey, appointed Anthony Wayne to command the army that defeated the Indians at the Battle of Fallen Timbers, and appointed Thomas Pinckney to negotiate what turned out to be a favorable treaty with Spain, opening up to the United States navigation on the Mississippi River and access to New Orleans. In brief, Washington's achievements as president were remarkable.[8]

What would have happened if Washington had not gone to the Constitutional Convention and had not agreed to stand for election to the presidency? Adoption and ratification of the Constitution would have been far harder. Gouverneur Morris, delegate from Pennsylvania to the convention and chairman of the Committee on Style that did the final drafting of the Constitution, wrote Washington a few weeks after the convention adjourned: "I have observed that your name [attached] to the new constitution has been of infinite service. Indeed, I am convinced that, if you had not attended the convention and the same paper had been handed out to the world, it would have met with a colder reception. . . . As it is should the idea prevail that you would not accept of the presidency, it would prove fatal in many parts."[9]

If Washington had not served as America's first president, who would have done so, and with what consequences? John Adams, Alexander Hamilton, Thomas Jefferson, and James Madison were all able men. Madison, an astute politician and a gifted writer, wrote many of the *Federalist Papers* and most of the Constitution, and he was to write much of the Bill of Rights. But he was young (only 37 in 1788) and physically unimpressive (sickly, inaudible, and 5'4"; John Adams in his journal referred to him as "His Littleness"), and he had joined Jefferson in deep distrust of Hamilton's projects for fiscal reform. Jefferson, a man of immensely ranging knowledge and interests, wrote most of the Declaration of Independence. He had, however, been a doubter of the wisdom of a strong constitution, fearing that the president—like a pope or a Roman emperor—would have too much power. Although he came to accept the Constitution, he was vehemently opposed to the Bank of the United States and other policies favored by Hamilton to bring fiscal stability to the new republic, and he and Madison soon began organizing what became the Democratic-Republican Party, opposed to the Federalists such as Adams and Hamilton. Adams, who was Washington's vice president before becoming president himself, was a patriot and a smart man—but he talked too much, took umbrage readily, and, being of at most medium height and quite plump, lacked Washington's physical presence. When Adams suggested in the Senate that the president should be referred to as "His Elective Majesty" or perhaps "His Mightiness," someone suggested that Adams should be known as "His Rotundity." Hamilton was brilliant, brave, strong on finance, and the author of more *Federalist* papers than anyone. He was also eligible for the office of president under the Constitution, despite having been born on a Caribbean island, because he was unquestionably a U.S. citizen when the Constitution was adopted. He was, however, loathed by many as a manipulator and schemer (Jefferson believed Hamilton planned, after Washington's departure, to seize power and to establish his banker friends as a new American aristocracy), and the animosity between Adams and Hamilton was deep and personal, although both were Federalists. They did not speak kindly of each other. Hamilton said Adams displayed "the unfortunate foibles of a vanity without bounds and a jealousy capable of discoloring every object." Adams believed that Hamilton's financial system would release the "gangrene of avarice" into the American atmosphere. He described Hamilton—who had been born out of wedlock on the island of Nevis, and who was prone to extramarital indiscretion—as a "Creole bastard" and a man who had "a superabundance of secretions which he could not find whores enough to draw off."[10]

Americans can only be grateful that Washington changed his mind, went to the Constitutional Convention, and agreed to be the first president of the United States.

4

Daguerreotype and Sword: Seminole and Mexican Wars

etween the end of the Revolution and the beginning of the Civil
War, the United States, by diplomacy, land purchases, and military
force, more than tripled its size, from 888,811 square miles to 3,022,387
square miles. At the same time, white Americans drove Indians further
and further west and settled what had been Indian land. Both of these
transforming changes come to my mind when I look at a daguerreotype
and a saber that were both given to me when I was a child by my uncle
Richard Screven Meredith (see figures 4.1 and 4.2). The daguerreotype is
of a handsome, dark-haired man in a dark uniform adorned with epaulets
and bright buttons. The man's arms are crossed. The sternness of his gaze
may result—at least in part—from the immobility required to avoid blur-
ring the daguerreotype. The sword is in a steel scabbard hanging from
a white buff leather belt, closed by a brass belt buckle marked US. The
curved steel blade is thirty-six inches long. The leather hilt is wrapped in
braided brass wire, which makes for a firm grip. The image is of, and the
sword belonged to, my maternal ancestor Richard Bedon Screven (1808–
1851), who served as an officer in America's small regular army from 1829
until his death. Screven fought the Seminoles in Florida, participated in
their forced removal to what is now Oklahoma, and went on to fight in
the Mexican War, gaining brevet promotions first to major and then to
lieutenant colonel for gallant and meritorious conduct in the battles of
Monterrey and Molino del Rey. That war and subsequent treaties with

Fig. 4.1. Daguerreotype of Colonel Richard B. Screven (1808–1853). *Author's collection.*

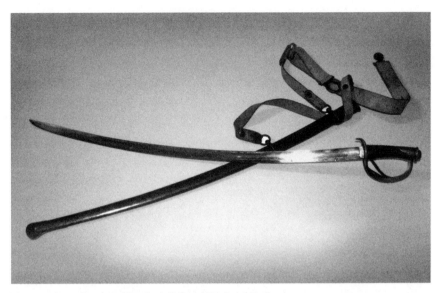

Fig. 4.2. Sword and scabbard of Colonel Richard B. Screven. *Author's collection*

Mexico increased the size of the United States by 558,657 square miles (see maps 0.1 and 4.2).

Even as a teenager, Screven foresaw a life in the army. His family were members of the South Carolina establishment, descendants of Landgrave Thomas Smith, who became governor of South Carolina in 1693. In January 1823, before Screven had turned 15, his father wrote John C. Calhoun, former congressman from South Carolina, who at the time was secretary of war in the cabinet of President James Monroe: "My Son Richd B Screven a youth of nearly 15 and whom I had the pleasure of shewing you in the Town of Beaufort in the year 1819 is very anxious to obtain a military education at West Point, and I request an appointment for him there. Richd has obtained a tolerable education thus far in the grammar schools of our State, and I think from his anxiety would persevere and probably become a soldier. He is the grand-nephew of Genl James Screven who fell in the revolutionary war in the State of Georgia."[1]

Secretary Calhoun evidently pulled the appropriate levers. In January 1825, Screven's father wrote to Calhoun accepting his son's appointment to West Point and asked to be excused "for adding/what a parents solicitude extends/that I trust his . . . industry will render him a fit subject on whom the funds and patronage of his country may fitly be bestowed." The young man, who had spent the previous two years attending a school in Norwich, Vermont, imposingly named "The American Literary, Scientific, and Military Academy," showed up at West Point on July 1, 1825—aged 17 years, 3 months. The cadets then were much fewer in number and younger than they are today. Screven's graduating class numbered only 46 (as contrasted with the current graduating classes, each of which numbers about 1,000). Of Screven's graduating class, 27 (well over half the class) had been 17 or younger when admitted to West Point. One had been only 14—not much older than the twelve-year-old who was admitted as a cadet soon after West Point was founded in 1802.

Only two things stand out about Screven's performance at West Point: he played a prominent part in a riot in December 1826 (the behavior of cadets at the time was as immature as their age), and he graduated last in his class. More than 50 years later, Albert E. Church, who graduated at the top of his West Point class one year ahead of Screven, and who had a distinguished career teaching mathematics at the academy for fifty years, described that riot in a farewell address of reminiscences about West Point between 1824 and 1831: "On Christmas eve 1826, occurred one of the most violent outbreaks ever known at the Academy. A large number of the cadets got on a spree, and became excessively riotous, setting all officers at defiance and even, with a drawn sword, chasing one to his room—throwing missiles through the halls, breaking windows and the railings of the stairs, &c. The scene, as described to me two days afterwards, was fit for Bedlam." Professor Church noted that "a large number of cadets was dismissed." The riot became known as the Eggnog Mutiny, because cadets, to celebrate Christmas, had sneaked off to a nearby tavern, bought a gallon or two of spirits, made eggnog, and overindulged grossly. According to one student of the mutiny, "Cadet Richard B. Screven was particularly wild, shouting, breaking tables and brandishing a musket." Seventy cadets were arrested. After hearings from January to March 1827, nineteen were sentenced to be expelled. Screven, found guilty of disorderly but not mutinous conduct, was sentenced to be dismissed, but the court recommended the sentence be remitted because of his excellent character and "frank admission of his errors." Screven managed to stay at the Academy. In this respect he resembled the future Confederate President Jefferson Davis, a class ahead of Screven, who in 1825 was court-martialed and sentenced to be dismissed from West Point for an unauthorized visit to the same off-campus tavern that supplied the liquor for the 1826 eggnog and whose sentence was remitted for his previous good conduct.[2]

Screven graduated from West Point in June 1829. One of his classmates was Robert E. Lee, who was second in the class. Screven ranked 46th in a class of 46. He shared the distinction of being last in his West Point class (a position that later came to be known as "goat") with, among others, George E. Pickett, of Pickett's Charge at Gettysburg (class of 1846), and George Armstrong Custer, of Custer's Last Stand (class of 1861). On graduation, Screven became a member of a regular army that was still diminutive— only 6,332 officers and men. He started as a second lieutenant with the Second Infantry; was transferred to the Fourth Infantry in August 1831; became a captain in the Eighth Infantry in 1838; and remained a captain until his death in 1851, although promoted by brevet first to major and then to lieutenant colonel during the Mexican War. The brevet system of promotion, borrowed by the U.S. Army from the British, was at once inexpensive and confusing. A brevet rank was an honorary higher rank awarded to an officer for meritorious conduct—but without any increase in the officer's pay and without any practical effect in the ranking of the officer's own regiment (although it might be recognized as a real rank when the officer was assigned to provisional formations made up of several regiments, or to detachments composed of various arms of the service, or in courts-martial, or "on other occasions").[3]

The first hard fighting Screven saw was in the Second Seminole War (1835–1842). The Seminoles were a powerful group of affiliated Indian bands in Florida who fought to remain there. The Americans battled the Seminoles off and on, in three separate wars, between 1816 (although some say the First Seminole War started in 1814) and 1858. The Seminole Wars were the largest wars fought by the U.S. Army between the War of 1812 and the Mexican War. By 1839, the fighting with the Seminoles had gone on so long that soldiers made up a song about its duration:

> Ever since the creation,
> By the best calculation,
> The Florida war has been raging;
> And 'tis our expectation

That the last conflagration
Will find us the same contest waging.[4]

Most of the Seminole bands had originally been part of the Creek confederation, living to the north and west of Florida and speaking Muskogean languages. The bands came into Florida at least as early as the mid-eighteenth century, after disease and Creek warriors (some brought in by the British to fight Indian allies of the Spanish, who controlled Florida at the time) had killed off many of the earlier Indian inhabitants of Florida. The immigrating Indians were drawn to Florida by the available land, the quantity of deer and other game, and the abundance of food for horses and cattle. The last large movement of Indians into Florida was in 1814, in the wake of the bloody defeat Andrew Jackson's Tennessee militia inflicted on the Red Stick group of Upper Creek at the battle of Horseshoe Bend. Many of the surviving Upper Creek moved to Florida rather than live on the small portion of land left to the Creek under the post-battle treaty. One who made the move was a boy later known as Osceola, who became the best known Indian leader in the Second Seminole War (see figure 4.3 for Catlin's portrait of the adult Osceola). The differing bands of Indians had different names—among them Alachua, Mikasuki, Eufaula, and Tallahassee—but collectively came to be referred to as Seminoles, meaning "wild ones," because of their desire to live apart from the Creek confederation.[5]

Starting not long after the War of 1812, the Americans—above all those in the southern states—sought to acquire Florida for its land, to create a new pro-slavery state to offset the anti-slavery states being formed in the northern territories, and to eliminate Florida's role as a haven for runaway slaves from Georgia and other southern states. This quest led to repeated conflicts with the Seminoles and, in the Second Seminole War, to a massive commitment of American funds and military forces. In 1816, when Florida was still Spanish territory, American troops and sailors, on orders of Andrew Jackson, then a major general and the commander of the U.S. Army's southern district, destroyed a fort in the Florida panhandle controlled by renegade slaves. After more border fighting in 1817, Andrew Jackson, in 1818, with 1,500 American troops and 2,000 Creek warriors but with little express authorization from President Monroe, went down the Apalachicola River into Florida, destroyed the Mikasuki towns, and seized control of most of northern Florida from the Spanish, who, in 1819, in the Adams-Onís treaty, agreed to cede Florida to the United States. Jackson's 1818 campaign ended the First Seminole War but not the continued American pressure on the Seminoles.[6]

In 1823, several Seminole chiefs agreed, in the treaty of Moultrie Creek, to give up Seminole claims to all of Florida in exchange for a reservation of slightly more than 4 million acres in central Florida and American undertakings of future supplies worth less than a penny per acre for the Florida land the chiefs were giving up.[7] Worse was yet to come for the Seminoles. Andrew Jackson, elected president of the United States in 1828, pushed for removal of all the remaining eastern Indians to reservations west of the Mississippi. In 1830, Congress passed the Indian Removal Act, empowering the president to exchange lands west of the Mississippi for lands claimed and occupied by any Indian tribe or nation east of the river and to aid the Indians to remove to and settle in the western lands. In 1832, a number of Seminole chiefs whose tribes had been on the point of starvation attempting to subsist in their Florida reservation signed the treaty of Payne's Landing, agreeing, if seven of their chiefs were satisfied with proposed western lands, to move west of the Mississippi within three years to lands to be shared with the Creeks and to give up their claims to the four million acres in Florida for considerations worth about $80,000—or two cents an acre. Seven Seminole chiefs were taken west of the Mississippi and purportedly signed a treaty approving the proposing western lands (although the chiefs later denied that they gave their approval). Many of the Seminole chiefs, led by Osceola, refused to leave Florida.

In the spring of 1835, Wiley Thompson, the American agent to the Seminoles, had Osceola put in chains until he acknowledged the treaty of Payne's Landing. To Osceola, the manacling was a degradation that called for revenge. In November 1835, Osceola shot dead a Seminole chief, Charley Emathla, who was preparing to migrate out of Florida. On December 28, 1835, Osceola and his followers killed and scalped agent Thompson outside of Fort King in north-central Florida. That same day, a column of 108 American soldiers, commanded by Major Francis Dade, was on its way north from Fort Brooke to relieve Fort King. Seminoles who had word of the column's approach lay in wait and cut the column to pieces. Only two wounded whites survived to make it back to Fort Brooke. One of the two died of his wounds within months. On December 31, 1835, at the Battle of the Withlacoochee, about fifty miles west of Fort King, Seminoles led by Osceola repulsed an attack by perhaps 250 U.S. regulars and 500 Florida volunteers, commanded by General Duncan Clinch. The Second Seminole War had broken out bloodily (see map 4.1).[8]

The population of the United States in 1835 was just under fifteen million. The number of Seminoles in Florida at the time has been estimated at about four thousand. Why, then, did it take America eight years of fighting to deport or kill most of the Seminoles? For one thing, the American army was small in 1835, when the Second Seminole War began—in actual strength, about four thousand, and those four thousand manned more than fifty posts scattered across the United States. Although at least one thousand regulars were kept in Florida during most of the war, that resembled in number the estimated thousand warriors with which the Seminoles started the war. The Americans could also draw on state militias—but many in these militias were ill-trained, ill-armed, and would enlist for no more than three months of service. The American firearms were hardly better than those borne by the Seminoles. The U.S. Army, unlike the Seminoles, had artillery—but cannons were not easily moved in Florida's trackless hinterland. For shoulder arms, most of the Americans carried flintlock muskets. Many of the Seminoles had rifles, although powder came to be in increasingly short supply as the war continued. The Seminoles could find their way around the marshy interior of Florida far better than the U.S. Army could. The American soldiers, in the words of one of their generals in Florida, had "as little knowledge of the interior of Florida as of the interior of China." The terrain—rivers, lakes, swamps, sawgrass—was a constant challenge to the Americans, as were heat, malaria, and yellow fever. Disease killed far more U.S. troops than the Seminoles did. The warfare was guerrilla warfare—something not then taught at West Point. In a typical clash, Seminoles would kill or wound as many whites as they could and then melt away into the landscape, rather than engaging in a pitched battle to the death. Finally, the Seminoles were fighting for land they viewed as theirs. As a Mikasuki head chief had said in 1826, resisting white pressure for removal to the west, "Here our navel strings were first cut, and the blood from them sunk into the earth and made the country dear to us."[9]

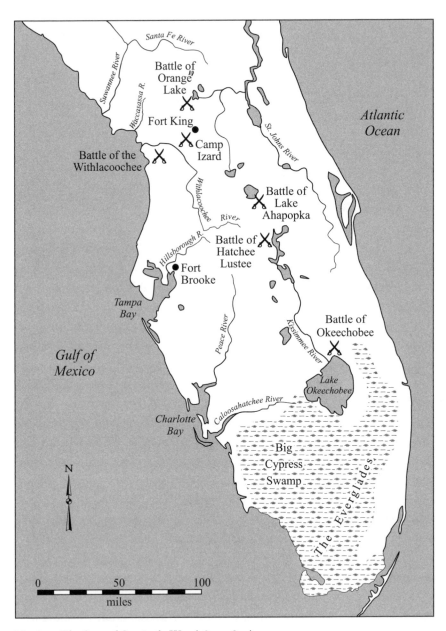

Map 4.1. The Second Seminole War (1835–1842)

The United States was still not comfortable with the idea of having a large army of regulars—partly because of the expense, partly because of a concern that dated back to the Revolution about the threat a large stand-ing army posed to a republican form of government. During the War of 1812, the U.S. Army ballooned from 6,686 in 1812 to 38,186 in 1814 but shrank again after the war to a mere 5,773 in 1821. The Second Seminole War brought a renewed increase in the size of the active army, to 12,449 in 1837. It also brought an increased deployment of regulars and militia into Florida. Richard Screven was part of that deployment. From 1831, when he was transferred to the 4th Infantry, to early 1836, he had been stationed in Louisiana and Mississippi. By February 1836, he was in Florida, serving as part of the columns under Brevet Major General Edmund Pendleton Gaines. On February 26, 1836, the Seminoles stopped an attempt by Gaines's troops to cross the Withlacoochee River. The Americans built and manned a makeshift log breastwork they called Camp Izard, after an American lieutenant who had been fatally wounded by the Seminoles as he sought to lead men across the river. A relief column did not arrive until March 6, after five of Gaines's men had been killed and 46 wounded. Screven was also part of another engagement near Camp Izard, in late March 1836, when three wings of troops commanded by General Winfield Scott attempted without success to engage and crush the Seminoles in the Cove of the Withlacoochee.[10]

The war with the Seminoles by this time looked less and less like a pushover for the American troops. The size of the American army and the appropriations for the war began to soar. In May 1836, Congress autho-rized enlistment of 10,000 emergency troops. By 1837, the regular army had grown to 12,449—nearly twice the number of troops there had been when Screven graduated from West Point in 1829. General Scott also rounded up about 4,000 militia from states neighboring Florida. It was hard to keep troops in service, however. Militia left as soon as their short terms of service expired. Morale slumped. The incidence of disease was high. Pay was miserable: a private made only $6 per month. One Tennessee volunteer, in his diary, described the soldier's life: "A life of dirt and toil, privation and vexation, and the poorest pay in the world." The pay wasn't much better for officers: in 1841, a second lieutenant in the infantry made $25 per month; a captain, $40; a major, $50. Even if one multiplies these numbers by 20 to get a sense of the worth of these amounts in 2010, the pay was abysmal. Not surprisingly, many enlisted men deserted, and many officers (103 in 1836 alone) resigned.[11]

Although with frequent reverses, the U.S. troops were increasing the pressure on the Seminoles. In March 1837, several Indian chiefs agreed to migrate west of the Mississippi. One of the Indian chiefs turned himself and two hundred of his followers in at an American fort to be shipped to the west from Tampa. Screven's record shows he was engaged "on Indian duty" from April 20 to August 7, 1837. Presumably he was rounding up and escorting Seminoles to detention camps. On June 2, however, the thrust toward transporting Seminoles to the west suffered a major setback when Osceola and another militant chief known to the whites as Sam Jones, at the head of two hundred warriors, visited the principal detention camp at night and led away as many as seven hundred Seminoles who had been scheduled for shipment west. Later on in the year, however, American troops captured several Seminole leaders and their followers and, in October 1837, on instructions from General Thomas S. Jesup, took Osceola captive near St. Augustine, even though he had come to the American camp under a flag of truce to negotiate a peace. At Osceola's direction, his family and several of his warriors and Negroes also surrendered to the Americans.[12]

Starting in October 1837, Jesup launched a campaign intended to trap many Seminoles remaining at liberty between several converging columns, including one commanded by Colonel Zachary Taylor, by birth a well-born Virginian, kin both to James Madison and to Robert E. Lee, but nicknamed "Old Rough and Ready" for his dislike of ostentation and his willingness to fight. By December, Jesup commanded more than 4,600 regular troops and over four thousand volunteers. In mid-December, Jesup permitted Taylor to take his column south from central Florida toward Lake Okeechobee in search of Seminoles. Taylor had over a thousand troops, including 180 volunteers from Missouri and more than seven hundred regulars, including Screven's regiment, the Fourth Infantry. As Taylor's men marched south, over a hundred Indians surrendered to them. North of Lake Okeechobee, however, in excess of four hundred warriors, commanded by the war chiefs Sam Jones, Alligator, and Coacoochee, awaited Taylor's advance in a swamp hammock. They had cut down a corridor through the tall sawgrass for a field of fire and notched trees to steady their guns. Soon after noon

Fig. 4.3. "Osceola, the Black Drink, a Warrior of Great Distinction" (1838). Portrait by George Catlin. *Smithsonian American Art Museum. Gift of Mrs. Joseph Harrison, Jr.*

on Christmas Day, the two forces met. Taylor ordered a frontal attack by the Missouri volunteers, followed by the Fourth and Sixth Infantry, with the First Infantry held in reserve. It was the biggest pitched battle in any of the Seminole wars. The fighting lasted until three o'clock, when the Indians retreated after the First Infantry attacked the Seminoles' right flank. Although outnumbered two to one, the Indians inflicted many more casualties than they suffered. Twenty-six of Taylor's men were killed and 112 wounded; 11 Seminoles were killed and 14 wounded. But Taylor, who reported that he had taken 180 Indians as prisoners, was promoted to brigadier general as a result of the Battle of Okeechobee.[13]

Most of the Seminoles' ability to fight had been broken by this time, although fighting continued. On January 31, 1838, Osceola died of quinsy and malaria in captivity at Fort Moultrie in Charleston. The American doctor who had been treating him cut off Osceola's head, embalmed it, and took it to his home in St. Augustine. There, if one of his young children was disobedient, the doctor would hang Osceola's head on the child's bedstead for the night. The head passed down through a series of doctors but eventually went missing. The rest of Osceola was buried at Fort Moultrie. In May 1838, Jesup turned over command in Florida to Taylor. In the nearly eighteen months of Jesup's command, some one hundred Indians had been killed and 2,900 captured. Taylor continued pressure on the Seminoles, in part by dividing all of North Florida into twenty-mile squares, each with a garrison. He also had hundreds of miles of wagon roads and thousands of feet of causeways and bridges built, to enable quicker troop movements throughout Florida, and arranged to ship west of the Mississippi all Seminoles in his custody.[14]

Many in the northern states had come to hate the war in Florida, although many in the South supported it. By May 1838, the direct cost of the war had climbed to $9,400,000, or about $180 million in 2010 dollars. Despite the expenditure already incurred, Congress, in July 1838, in addition to increasing the authorized size of existing regiments, created a new regiment, the Eighth Infantry. On July 8, Screven was commissioned a captain in that regiment, which was soon sent to be part of the armed force of 7,000 commanded by General Winfield Scott that rounded up some 13,000 Cherokees into camps in Tennessee before taking them out to Oklahoma in the fall and winter of 1838 on what the Cherokee called the Trail of Tears—a trek on which an estimated 4,000 Cherokees (over 30% of those on the trail) died. Faced with the mounting costs from the Florida war, Washington began looking for ways to stop the fighting. In May 1839, Major General Alexander Macomb, commanding general of the United States Army, after a parley with Seminole leaders, who agreed to withdraw into southern Florida, proclaimed that the war was at an end—but the fighting did not stop. In May 1840, Taylor was succeeded in the Florida command by Brevet Brigadier General Walker Keith Armistead, who sought to force more Indians to surrender by systematically destroying the Seminoles' crops, continued scouting and fighting, and large payments to Indian chiefs who brought their followers in to be shipped to the west. The three-pronged policy worked. By the time Armistead left Florida in May 1841, he had shipped 450 Indians and Negroes westward and had 236 more awaiting shipment from the Tampa area. Captain Screven presumably took part in the round-up and shipment, as he was stationed at Fort Brooke, near Tampa, at least part of the time between 1840 and 1842.[15]

Armistead's successor as commander in Florida was Colonel William Jenkins Worth, who had commanded Screven's regiment, the Eighth Infantry, since it was organized in July 1838. Worth, who had been badly wounded during the War of 1812, was handsome, brave, a splendid horseman, and unbearably vain. His forces managed to capture the ablest remaining intransigent Indian war chief, Coacoochee, who in turn convinced most of his followers to join him in being shipped west in October 1841. More war chiefs came in with their followers, and others were captured. In February 1842, Worth was able to report that he had just shipped 230 Seminoles, including 68 warriors. He estimated that about 300 Indians were left in all of Florida. His troops also destroyed settlements belonging to recalcitrant Seminoles. On December 10, 1841, for example, Captain Screven and his men destroyed the "town" belonging to Sam Jones and his followers. A fellow soldier in the Eighth Infantry, Collinson R. Gates, recorded in his journal, "there were about twenty huts there; mosquitoes and fleas very thick." Screven's action against the Sam Jones camp was part of a two months' campaign near the Big Cypress Swamp in central Florida. Excerpts from Gates's journal tell us what those two months were like: December 14: Screven returns from a day in the swamp and reports "two raccoons and a large rattlesnake were killed today; a ground-rattlesnake was killed whilst making my bivouac." December 30: columns went out, although many were sick; Screven, ill, "was unable to proceed after a short distance, so returned." February 7, 1842: "Thus ended the Big Cypress campaign, like all others: drove the Indians out, broke them up, taught them we could go where they could; men and officers worn down; two months in water; plunder on our backs; hard times; trust they are soon to end. . . . Indians asking for peace in all quarters. The only reward we ask is the ending of the Florida war."[16]

On April 19, 1842, Worth directed a force of some 400 regulars, including the Eighth Infantry, to attack a band of about 40 warriors led by the fierce Mikasuki chief Halleck Tustenuggee near Lake Ahapopka in central Florida. The troops fought their way through mud and vegetation that stank so much that some of the soldiers vomited. Halleck and most of his warriors escaped, but they had no food and were lured to Ft. King by the promise of a feast with much liquor. At Worth's direction, all were captured: 43 warriors, 37 women, and 34 children. On May 10, 1842, John C. Spencer, the secretary of war, notified General Winfield Scott that the administration wanted hostilities to end as soon as possible. On July 14, Halleck and his band were shipped out of Florida. "I have been hunted like a wolf," Halleck declared, "and now I am sent away like a dog." In early August, Worth and most of the remaining chiefs worked out an agreement under which Seminoles not willing to be shipped west could settle within a reservation in south Florida—and on August 14, Colonel Worth (soon brevetted to brigadier general) declared the war was over. The declaration was a precedent for the suggestion made in October 1966 by Senator George Aiken of Vermont on how the United States should end the prolonged and bloody Vietnam War: declare that we have won, and leave.[17]

Most of the regulars left Florida soon after Worth's declaration. After April 1843, the Eighth Infantry was the only regular unit in the territory. It continued to round up Indians who refused to be confined to the reservation. On December 30, 1843, the regiment's four companies, on drill at Ft. Brooke under Captain Screven, on a preconcerted signal, surrounded and captured the recalcitrant chief Octiarche and his followers, who were promptly shipped to New Orleans. The long war broke the power of the Seminole in Florida. By the end of 1843, more than 3,800 had been shipped west. An unknown number had been killed. In November 1843, Worth reported that of the 300 Indians remaining in Florida, only 95 were warriors. The result had come at a high cost in money and in men. The war was estimated to have cost from $30 million to $40 million—around $570 million to $760 million in 2010 dollars. Of the roughly 10,000 regular soldiers who served in the war, 1,466 (about 14% of the total) died, including 328 who were killed in action. Most of the other deaths were from disease. Despite the cost, the war yielded benefits to America. Florida was opened for settlement, and its population grew from 34,730 in 1830 to 87,445 in 1859. In

1845, it became a state. The war also was a rigorous training ground for many (among them Zachary Taylor and Winfield Scott) who were to lead American forces in the Mexican War that followed soon after the Seminole War, as well as for others (including Sherman, Thomas, Bragg, Johnston, Pemberton, and Meade) who were to lead armies in the Civil War.[18]

The drive to expand America that underlay the fighting in Florida continued in a way that left the U.S. Army little time for rest after Worth's declaration that the Seminole war was over. Much of the pressure to expand was directed against Mexico. In 1836, Texas had won its independence from Mexico, after Sam Houston's army at San Jacinto had beaten Mexican troops commanded by General Antonio López de Santa Anna. In 1844, James K. Polk of Tennessee, a slaveholder and a protégé of old Andrew Jackson, was elected president on a platform calling for annexation of Texas. Although not in the platform, Polk also hoped, if elected, to acquire California and enough of northern Mexico to be able to link the eastern United States to the Pacific coast by rail. In 1845, Texas was admitted as a state. The southern border of Texas was unclear: was it the Nueces River, as Mexico contended, or the Rio Grande, south and west of the Nueces, as the Texans argued? Polk made clear to the Texan leaders that the United States would defend Texas against Mexico and would "not be satisfied with the less than the whole territory claimed by Texas—namely to the Rio Grande." American troops—among them, Captain Screven— were sent to protect Texas from Mexican attack.[19]

Colonel (Brevet Brigadier General) Zachary Taylor commanded the U.S. soldiers who were stationed initially at Corpus Christi on the mouth of the Nueces. This was not a small force of scouts but close to 4,000 regulars: five infantry regiments (including Screven's Eighth Infantry), one regiment of dragoons, and 16 companies of artillery. The total number of American troops under Taylor was nearly half of all the regulars in the U.S. Army in 1845 (8,509). The latter number was to shoot up to 47,319 by 1848, the year of the treaty that ended the Mexican War. It soon became clear that President Polk was looking to provoke a fight between a large and prosperous America, with more than 17 million people in 1840, and a much poorer Mexico, with a population of about 7 million. On February 4, 1846, Taylor received orders from Washington to take his men to the Rio Grande. There, across from Matamoros, Taylor's troops built Fort Texas (now Brownsville), as if to thumb their noses at the Mexican forces gathering on the south side of the river. One of Taylor's officers, Colonel Ethan Allen Hitchcock, wrote in his diary: "We have no particle of right to be here. . . . It looks as if the government sent a small force on purpose to bring on a war, so as to have a pretext of taking California and as much of this country as it chooses."[20]

The Mexican commander, Pedro de Ampudia, requested Taylor to withdraw his forces north of the Nueces. Taylor, after replying that his orders did not permit retreat from the Rio Grande, ordered the U.S. Navy to blockade the mouth of the Rio Grande, cutting off supplies to the Mexicans at Matamoros. Some 1,600 Mexican cavalrymen crossed the Rio Grande and, on April 25, attacked and killed or captured most of a U.S. scouting party under Captain Seth Thornton. On the afternoon of May 8, about two thousand of Taylor's men encountered some 3,300 Mexican troops awaiting them in a double line across the Matamoros road at Palo Alto, about ten miles northeast of Fort Texas. This was the first battle for Ulysses Grant (West Point, class of 1843), who was then 24 years old and a second lieutenant. In his memoirs, he recalled the decisive role played by the American artillery, which included eighteen-pounders with a long range and howitzers that threw exploding shells, while the Mexican guns fired only solid shot. When the Mexican cannon opened up before the Americans were within range, their cannon balls struck the ground before reaching the American line "and ricocheted through the tall grass so slowly that the men would see them and open ranks and let them pass." Taylor's infantry "was armed with flint-lock muskets, and paper cartridges charged with powder, buck-shot and ball. At the distance of a few hundred yards, a man might fire at you all day long without your finding out about it." The American guns told heavily on the Mexicans. The Americans kept closing with the Mexicans, who were able to do some execution at the shorter range. Grant was to remember a cannon ball that passed through the ranks close to him: "It took off the head of an enlisted man, and the under jaw of Captain Page of my regiment, while the splinters from the musket of the killed soldier, and his brains and bones, knocked down two or three others." The wound led to Page's death more than two months later. The U.S. troops continued to move forward, with the Fifth and Eighth Infantry charging the Mexican batteries, until the Mexicans broke and ran. Nine Americans were killed and 47 wounded—but the Mexicans pulled out from their position during the night.[21]

The Mexican army withdrew about five miles to the south and west on the Matamoros road, to Resaca de la Palma, where they formed a defensive line fortified by dead trees and brush and protected by artillery. Taylor, though outnumbered, nevertheless ordered his troops to advance. Lieutenant Grant led his company up through thick chaparral. As he remembered it, "At last I got pretty close up without knowing it. The balls commenced to whistle very thick overhead, cutting the limbs of the chaparral right and left. We could not see the enemy, so I ordered my men to lie down, an order that did not have to be enforced." But the Americans kept advancing, and the Mexicans abandoned their position, enabling Taylor and his troops to get back to Fort Texas, which they renamed Fort Brown in honor of Major Jacob Brown, who had been killed at the fort by a Mexican shell a few days earlier. The city of Brownsville later grew up around the fort. On May 18, Taylor crossed the Rio Grande and occupied Matamoros.[22]

On April 26, Taylor had written to inform Washington of the Mexican ambush of Captain Thornton's scouting party. Not until Saturday, May 9, did Taylor's dispatch reach Polk, who on Monday, May 11, delivered to Congress a message stating that Mexico "has invaded our territory and shed American blood upon the American soil" and recommending that Congress recognize the existence of the war, empower the president to call a large body of volunteers, and make liberal provision for sustaining the American military. Polk's recommendation was overwhelmingly adopted by the House and the Senate, and the House soon authorized the president to call up and accept up to 50,000 volunteers. Polk accepted Scott's proposal to start by calling up 20,000 volunteers.[23]

"The Mexican war was a political war," as Grant correctly noted in his memoirs. Polk was a Democrat. Each of the thirteen men he appointed as a general of volunteers during the war was a loyal and long-time Democrat. Scott, however, a major general who was the general-in-chief and the most experienced American army officer, was from a rival political party, the Whigs—as were Taylor and many other army officers. "General Scott was also known to have political aspirations, and nothing so popularizes a candidate for high civil positions as military victories"—again in the words of Grant, who became president on the strength of his Civil War record.

Because Polk wanted to win the war, he had to use Whigs like Scott and Taylor, because they were outstandingly able military leaders—but he sought to juggle the roles of Scott and Taylor so that neither became too prominent. He also attempted, unsuccessfully, to make Senator Thomas Hart Benton, a staunch Democrat with scanty military experience, a major general with command in the field or perhaps general in chief, in place of Scott. On May 21, Scott wrote to William Marcy, the secretary of war, that he did not "desire to be put into the most perilous of all positions—*a fire upon my rear, from Washington, and a fire in front, from the Mexicans.*" When Congress authorized only one new major general position, Polk appointed Taylor to the post.[24]

Taylor, his forces increased by numerous but unruly volunteers, pushed further into Mexico, going west along the Rio Grande, then turning south and west to Monterrey, which his men reached in mid-September 1846. The fortress-like town, its stone houses overlooked by fort-topped craggy hills and a dark citadel the Americans called the Black Fort, was defended by some 10,000 Mexican troops under General Ampudia. Taylor commanded about 6,500 troops. On September 21, a division led by Colonel (Brevet Brigadier General) William J. Worth, under whom Screven had served in Florida, defeated a Mexican cavalry unit, cut off the road west and south of Monterrey, and stormed the larger of the town's protective hills. A captain in Screven's regiment was killed when a nine-pounder ball went through his breast, taking his heart and lungs with it. On the same day, Taylor lost one out of ten men engaged in seizing a fortified position to the east of town. On September 22, Worth's men took the other hill that protected Monterrey. On September 23, Americans attacking from the east and, under Worth, the west sides of Monterrey pushed toward the center of town in house-to-house fighting, smashing in common walls with picks and crowbars, then tossing lit shells into the next house.

When the 4th infantry was almost out of ammunition, Grant volunteered to ride back to headquarters to ask for more. The ride exposed him to Mexican fire every time he crossed one of the town's straight streets. He made the trip unscratched, riding on the side of his horse away from the Mexican soldiers "with only one foot holding to the cantle of the saddle, and an arm over the neck of the horse" and galloping through the perilous street crossings "at such a flying rate that generally [he] was past and under cover of the next block of houses before the enemy fired." Before morning the next day, Ampudia opened negotiations for the surrender of Monterrey and an armistice of several weeks. On September 25, the surrender was signed, the Mexicans marched out of the Black Fort, and American troops marched in while their band played "Yankee Doodle." On October 3, Grant wrote to his fiancée about the beauty of Monterrey and how nearly incredible the American capture of the city was—and added: "But our victory was not gained without loss. 500, or near abouts, brave officers and men fell in the attack. Many of them were only wounded and will recover, but many is the leg or arm that will be buryed in this country while the owners will live to relate over and over again the scenes they witnessed during the siege of Monteray." For "gallant and meritorious conduct in the Battle of Monterey," Screven received a brevet promotion to major, as of September 23, 1846, signed by Polk and Secretary of War Marcy.[25]

The American public viewed Taylor as a hero for the taking of Monterrey, and Whig papers began to talk of him as a presidential candidate. Not coincidentally, Polk sought to downplay Taylor's role in the war, even at the risk of giving greater visibility to another Whig, Winfield Scott. In November 1846, Polk gave Scott command of operations in Mexico and endorsed Scott's plan of a large landing at Vera Cruz on the Gulf of Mexico and a campaign inland to take Mexico City (see map 4.2). The plan involved taking from Taylor most of the regular troops that had been in his command in northern Mexico and shifting those forces to Scott's proposed army. Among the thousands moved were Colonel Worth and Captain (now Brevet Major) Screven.[26]

In the meantime, Mexico had rallied its own forces under the resilient, colorful, and devious General Antonio López de Santa Anna. Santa Anna had fallen into disgrace in Mexico after his defeat by Sam Houston at San Jacinto in 1836 and his signing of a peace treaty acknowledging the independence of the Republic of Texas. By 1841, he had once again become president of Mexico, after his public esteem rose when he led a Mexican attempt in 1838 to repel a French occupation of Vera Cruz to collect Mexican debts to France and, in the process, was wounded in the left leg. The leg was amputated and buried, at Santa Anna's orders, with full military honors. In 1844, Santa Anna had been forced from the presidency and into exile in Cuba. In 1846, a Spanish colonel who purported

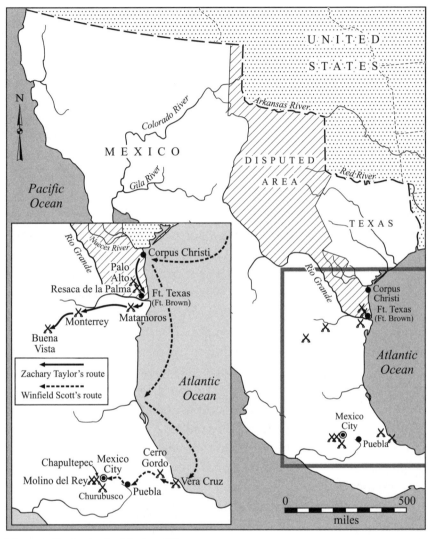

Map 4.2. Battles in the Mexican War

to be close to Santa Anna proposed to Polk that Santa Anna, if permitted to get back to Mexico, would once again become Mexico's president and would be willing to sell to the United States, for $30 million, Texas north of the Rio Grande, all of what is now New Mexico, and all of what is now northern California. Pursuant to instructions from Polk, the U.S. Navy permitted Santa Anna to pass through the U.S. blockade and reenter Mexico. Hailed as a hero, he resumed control of the Mexican government, proclaiming that his goal was "to devote myself, until death, to the defence of the liberty and independence of the Republic." Rather than negotiating for the sale of Mexican territory to the United States, he assembled at San Luis Potosí in central Mexico, northwest of Mexico City, an army of some 20,000—far more than the forces of Scott or of Taylor—to defeat the American invaders of Mexico. Santa Anna's plan was to crush Taylor's reduced forces in the north and then to turn south and east to defeat Scott's troops at Vera Cruz.[27]

Things did not go in accordance with Santa Anna's plan. He led his 20,000 men some 200 miles to the north, losing perhaps 5,000 on the long hard march, to attack Taylor's troops, who were outnumbered at least three to one. On February 22, 1847, at Buena Vista, the Americans, aided by superior artillery and by the stubbornness and skill of Colonel Jefferson Davis and his First Mississippi Rifles, defeated Santa Anna at a cost of 673 killed or wounded and about 1,500 desertions. One of those killed was Henry Clay's son, Lieutenant Colonel Henry Clay, Jr., who was stabbed to death by Mexican lancers. Buena Vista was Taylor's last battle in Mexico—but it had the crucial effects of safeguarding the territory America had gained in northern Mexico and in weakening Santa Anna's ability to defeat Scott's forces in their drive to Mexico City.[28]

On March 9, in what John S. D. Eisenhower described as "the largest amphibious invasion yet attempted in history," Scott's forces—close to 12,000 troops—landed on a beach about three miles from Vera Cruz. The ever-bold William Worth was the first man on the beach, leading a brigade that included Screven and the Eighth Infantry. Scott began a heavy and growing bombardment of Vera Cruz and its fifteen thousand inhabitants, aided by huge thirty-two pounders from the navy ships. The battered town surrendered on March 27.[29]

Santa Anna, realizing that Scott's army was likely to proceed along the National Highway from Vera Cruz to Mexico City, by mid-April had placed some twelve thousand troops on a broad hill, Cerro Gordo (meaning Fat Hill), which commanded the highway. The position looked impregnable—until two young American engineers and future Confederate generals, Pierre G. T. Beauregard and Robert E. Lee, discovered a path to a hill behind Cerro Gordo. The Americans hacked a trail to widen the path and managed to haul a twenty-four pounder up the hill. On April 18, after the Americans shelled Cerro Gordo from behind, other U.S. troops stormed the center. Santa Anna and most of his men scattered. The Americans captured Santa Anna's personal carriage, his wooden leg (American soldiers promptly turned the song "The Girl I Left Behind Me" into "The Leg I Left Behind Me"), and three thousand Mexican troops. The captured men were soon released on parole, because Scott lacked the means to feed them. The wooden leg, picked up by troops from Illinois, was shipped back to America and displayed as a trophy in the Illinois state capitol.[30]

Scott's forces shrank after Cerro Gordo, not from deaths in battle, but because many of the volunteer soldiers, having served the year for which they had enlisted, left to go home, and because close to two thousand men were sick or wounded. But Scott kept driving on toward Mexico City, through Jalapa, Perote, and Puebla, although he now had fewer than six thousand men who were able to fight. To strengthen his attacking force, he brought west to Puebla all of the troops that had garrisoned towns along the highway from Vera Cruz—in effect, severing his supply route from the Gulf of Mexico. By August, thanks to reinforcements, Scott's troops numbered about 14,000, although more than 3,000 of these were sick or convalescing. In June, Santa Anna indicated to Nicholas Trist, a civilian from the Department of State authorized to negotiate a peace treaty with Mexico, that he was willing to negotiate a peace that would be favorable to the United States if he were paid a million dollars. Santa Anna pocketed a $10,000 advance from the Americans but continued to build up his forces until by August he had close to thirty thousand troops.[31]

The Americans drove toward Mexico City from the south. On August 20, at Churubusco, Worth's division, including the Eighth Infantry in which Screven served, stormed a strongly held Mexican position by means of a bayonet charge which, Worth reported, filled his mind with wonder. In the day's fighting, about four thousand Mexican troops were killed or wounded, and three thousand more were taken prisoner. After an attempt at a truce failed on September 7 (according to Santa Anna, because of his unwillingness "to sign a treaty which would lessen considerably not only the territory of the republic, but that dignity and integrity which all nations defend to the last extremity"), Scott ordered Worth to take a Mexican position at Molino del Rey ("mill of the king"), a mass of stone buildings around an old flour mill. Santa Anna had installed five brigades, supported by artillery, in the Molino and placed four thousand cavalry nearby to destroy Worth's rear and flank. The battle, on September 8, lasted only two hours—but it was bloody. One hundred sixteen Americans were killed and 671 wounded—twice the casualties suffered by Taylor at Monterrey, even though the American force at Molino del Rey was half the size of Taylor's at Monterrey. Mexican losses were estimated at two thousand killed or wounded, two thousand deserters, and seven hundred captured. After the war, Screven was brevetted to lieutenant colonel effective September 8, 1847, for gallant and meritorious conduct in the battle of Molino del Rey.[32]

On September 13, the Americans attacked the castle of Chapultepec, a half mile to the east of Molino del Rey. The initial attack was led by a brigade under Brigadier General (and future U.S. president) Franklin Pierce. Worth's troops were part of the assault. In Screven's Eighth Infantry, Lieutenant James Longstreet was shot carrying the regiment's colors at the foot of the castle wall. George Pickett took the colors from the wounded Longstreet and carried them up the wall and into the castle. By 9:30 AM, the Americans were in the castle killing its defenders. Six young cadets from Mexico's Military College, which had been based in the castle, died rather than surrender. One jumped to his death from the castle wall, holding the Mexican flag. By the end of the day, Worth had pushed on into Mexico City itself. Santa Anna evacuated the city. By noon on September 14, Scott rode in triumph through the city's central square.[33]

What followed was the occupation of Mexico City, some gambling and carousing by the occupying troops (according to one Mexican observer, orgies, from nine in the evening until two or three in the morning, "which had never before been seen in Mexico"), unseemly public squabbling among the American generals (including Worth) over who should get the credit for the victories—and Trist's negotiation of the peace treaty, the terms of which reflected not only the achievements of Scott and Taylor but also the taking by the American military in 1846 and 1847 of New Mexico, Arizona, and California. On February 2, 1848, Trist and his Mexican counterparts signed the treaty of Guadalupe Hidalgo, under which the southern boundary of Texas was fixed at the Rio Grande and the United States acquired what is now New Mexico, Arizona, and California—529,017 square miles, increasing the country's size by more than 20 percent (see map 0.1). The United States also agreed to assume Mexico's debts to U.S.

citizens and to pay $15 million to Mexico—or about 5.5 cents for each of the acres acquired in the treaty. The U.S. Senate ratified the treaty in March 1848. In December 1848, in his final annual message to Congress, Polk was able to say: "The Mississippi, so recently the frontier of our country, is now only its center." In 1854, the United States, in the Gadsden Purchase, bought from Mexico (once again under the presidency of the resilient Santa Anna) another 29,640 square miles in what is now southern Arizona and New Mexico, for $10 million—about 53 cents per acre.[34]

The Mexican War's large additions to the size of the United States came at a high price. The out of pocket cost of the war exceeded $100 million—roughly equivalent to $2.3 billion in 2010 dollars. American dead numbered 13,780—about 1,500 in battle or from wounds and more than 12,000 from disease (in particular, diarrhea, dysentery, and yellow fever) or accidents. In Screven's Eighth Infantry, however, over 36 percent of the deaths were battle related—the highest percentage of such deaths in any of the regular infantry, artillery, or dragoon regiments that fought in the war. The total number of deaths was 11 percent of the number of Americans who served—the highest mortality rate of any U.S. war, other than the Second Seminole War. The war also provided a bloody training ground for soldiers and sailors who were to fight in the Civil War that broke out little more than 13 years after the U.S. Congress ratified the treaty that ended the Mexican War. Practical lessons learned in the war included the key roles of artillery, engineering, reconnaissance, intelligence, and field fortification. Officers who fought in the Mexican War included many who served as generals for the North (among them Ulysses Grant, Philip Kearny, George B. McClellan, George G. Meade, Winfield Scott, and George H. Thomas) or for the South (for example, P. G. T. Beauregard, Braxton Bragg, Albert Sidney Johnston, Joseph E. Johnston, Robert E. Lee, James Longstreet, and George Pickett). Grant was to say in his memoirs that his experience in the Mexican War "was of great advantage to me afterwards"—not only for "the many practical lessons it taught" but because "the war brought nearly all the officers of the regular army together so as to make them personally acquainted." In the war of the rebellion—as Grant called the Civil War—he found of immense service what he had "learned of the characters of those to whom I was afterwards opposed." Much of the Union army and most of the press clothed Lee with "almost superhuman abilities," but

Grant said, "I had known him personally, and knew that he was mortal; and it was just as well I felt this."[35]

The Mexican War created national political leaders as well as military ones. Despite the efforts of Polk, a Democrat, to prevent the war from giving rise to a Whig president, in 1848, Zachary Taylor, the hero of Monterrey and Buena Vista, was elected president on the Whig ticket. Franklin Pierce, a Northern Democrat with Southern sympathies, was elected president in 1852 (running against Winfield Scott, the Whig candidate), in part because of Pierce's service as a brigadier general of volunteers in the Mexican War. Jefferson Davis's distinguished service in Mexico helped his selection in 1861 as president of the Confederate States of America. The war also increased the polarization of America on the issue of slavery. Many in the North (among them James Russell Lowell and Henry David Thoreau) believed that Polk's primary goal in promoting the war with Mexico was, in the words Grant used to describe the occupation and annexation of Texas, "a conspiracy to acquire territory out of which slave states might be formed for the American Union." The reverse side of the coin was the South's increasing view that, because much of the North opposed the spread of slavery, secession from the Union might be the only way for the Southern states to preserve their "peculiar institution."[36]

The Civil War came after the deaths of many Mexican War veterans from ailments that could well have been the lingering effects of diseases contracted in Mexico. Brevet Major General William J. Worth, Screven's commanding officer in Florida and in Mexico, died in Texas in 1849 of cholera. One of the Texas frontier posts he had established was named Fort Worth in his honor. Screven himself was never in good health after the Mexican War. He was assigned to recruiting service in 1848, placed on sick leave in 1850, and died in New Orleans on May 15, 1851, aged 43, leaving a wife and four children. His widow, applying for a pension, stated "that her husband, the said Richard B. Screven, returned ill from Mexico, and continued to suffer intensely from disease resulting from fatigue and exposure, while in the discharge of his duties in Mexico—prostrating him in body and mind." The widow Screven was allowed a pension of $20 per month, which was increased in 1860 to $25 per month (retroactive to the date of Screven's death) and cut off completely in 1861 because she lived in Louisiana, a seceding state.[37]

5

Shavings from a Scaffold:
The Hanging of John Brown

My father John Mason Brown was a drama critic, writer, and lecturer who spoke all over America from the 1930s into the 1960s. In the 1950s, after he gave a lecture in Charles Town (known before 1912 as Charlestown), West Virginia, a woman came up to him and asked if he were related to the abolitionist John Brown, who had been hanged there. Dad said he didn't have that distinction. He noted that there were quite a few people named John Brown. The woman said it didn't matter; she nevertheless wanted him to have some shavings from the scaffold on which John Brown was hanged, which had come down in her family from the son of one of the carpenters who built the scaffold in 1859.

Dad gave me the shavings when I was a bookish bespectacled boy of about 12. The shavings are in a little cardboard box, surrounded by a note on which my father's secretary had neatly typed:

SHAVINGS FROM THE SCAFFOLD ON WHICH
JOHN BROWN WAS HANGED—CHARLESTOWN, VA.,
(NOW WEST VIRGINIA,) DECEMBER 2, 1859.

THESE ARE APPLE WOOD SHAVINGS, AND WERE
GOTTEN FROM A MAN NAMED CHARLES PHILLIPS,
WHOSE FATHER WAS ONE OF THE CARPENTERS
WHO BUILT JOHN BROWN'S SCAFFOLD.

Fig. 5.1. Shavings from the scaffold on which John Brown was hanged. *Author's collection.*

The curled shavings (see figure 5.1) look as if they'd be good in starting a fire. That's apt, considering the impact on the United States of John Brown's raid on Harpers Ferry and of his hanging.

John Brown, from young manhood on, was a driven, God-fearing man. Captains Mason and Underhill, as Puritans, looked to the Old Testament for justification of their killing of the Pequots in 1637—but John Brown outdid them. He had large portions of the Old Testament by heart and frequently summoned words from those portions to his lips or his pen to demonstrate the righteousness of his cause. He did not stay part of an organized church throughout his adult life. He was expelled from a Congregational church in Ohio, ostensibly because he didn't tell the church he had moved. Brown believed the real reason was that he had escorted Negroes in the town to sit in his family pew.[1] He never belonged to another church after that, but he held his own family services regularly and preached sermons influenced by the elder Jonathan Edwards and heavily laced with strict Calvinist doctrines of predestination and punishment for sin. As he preached in one sermon: "Is not the reflection that full & complete justice will at last be done enough to make the very Heavens & Earth tremble?"[2]

John Brown did not have an easy life. His mother died when he was eight. He studied for the ministry but had to abandon his studies because of an eye inflammation and a lack of funds. He had recurring bone-aching fevers most of his adult life. His first wife died insane in 1832 soon after the birth and death of their fifth child, a boy. Another son had died at age four less than two years earlier. He married again and had more children—he had a total of twenty by his two wives. In 1843, four of his children died. Three other children died young, in 1846, 1852, and 1859. And Brown bore up, although, as he put it, "smarting under the rod of our Heavenly Father."[3] After a daughter died in 1846, he wrote his second wife:

> I feel assured that notwithstanding that God has chastised us often and sore, yet He has not entirely withdrawn Himself from us nor forsaken us utterly. The sudden and dreadful manner in which He has seen fit to call our dear little Kitty to take her leave of us, is, I need not tell you, much in my mind. But before Him I will bow my head in submission and hold my peace. . . . I have sailed over a somewhat stormy sea for nearly half a century, and have experienced enough to teach me thoroughly that I may most reasonably buckle up and be prepared for the tempest. Mary, let us try to maintain a cheerful self-command while we are tossing up and down, and let our mottoe still be action, action,—as we have but one life to live.[4]

John Brown had recurrent financial reverses, as well. He speculated in land, and suffered under the repeated money contractions of the 1830s and 1840s. In 1842, he was declared bankrupt. The court took all he had, except for some farm animals and equipment, eleven Bibles and Testaments, a book called *Church Member's Guide,* and another book called *Beauties of the Bible.*[5]

One constant in his life was a hatred for slavery, which he said dated back to an experience in the War of 1812 when, in his early teens, he stayed for a short time "with a very gentlemanly landlord" who had a slave boy about John Brown's age. The landlord "made a great pet" of John Brown, but before John Brown's eyes beat the slave with an iron shovel or whatever came first to his hand. John Brown later wrote that seeing this beating made him "a most *determined Abolitionist* and led [him] to declare, *or Swear, Eternal war* with Slavery."[6] In November 1837, when Brown was 37, the abolitionist newspaper editor Elijah Lovejoy was murdered in Alton, Illinois, by a pro-slavery mob from across the Mississippi River in Missouri. Brown went to a prayer meeting held in the Congregational Church in Hudson, Ohio, to commemorate Lovejoy. Toward the end of the meeting, stirred up by the speeches, Brown stood up, raised his right hand, and vowed before God, in the presence of these witnesses, that he would consecrate his life to the destruction of slavery.[7]

He started in a small way. He helped runaway slaves on their way to Canada, but this was at a time when he still had other interests—trying to extricate himself from his financial entanglements and, by selling wool directly in England, to assist wool growers in their fight against what he believed were unfair buying practices on the part of Northeastern wool buyers. Nevertheless, at least as early as 1847, he began to think big thoughts about undermining slavery throughout the South. About that time, he began quoting as a favorite text Hebrews 9:22: "almost all things are by the law purged with blood; and without shedding of blood is no remission."

In November 1847, Brown invited the prominent black abolitionist Frederick Douglass to his house in Springfield, Mass. Douglass had escaped from slavery in Maryland, lectured in the North and in England, raised funds to buy his freedom, and started his own abolitionist newspaper, *The North Star*, which carried as its slogan "Right is of no Sex—Truth is of no Color—God is the Father of us all, and we are all Brethren." Douglass had heard of Brown from leaders in the free black community. Brown told Douglass that slavery was a state of war and that slaves had a right to gain their freedom "any way they could." He produced a map of the United States and ran his finger down the spine of the Alleghenies. Brown said that God had placed the mountains there "for emancipation of the Negro race; they are full of natural forts, where one man for defense will be equal to a hundred for attack; they are full also of good hiding-places, where large numbers of brave men could be concealed, and baffle and elude pursuit for a long time." Small squads of armed men could go out and induce the slaves to come and join them in the mountains. The object would be "to destroy the money value of slavery property . . . by rendering such property insecure." Douglass was skeptical (wouldn't Southerners with bloodhounds hunt you out of the mountains; wouldn't they surround you and cut off your provisions?) but impressed by Brown's fervor. Even if the worst came, Brown told Douglass, "he could but be killed, and he had no better use for his life than to lay it down in the cause of the slave."[8]

Brown spent the early 1850s in continuing (and financially disastrous) attempts to sell U.S. wool directly to English buyers, lawsuits arising out of his tangled finances, and attempts to help a community of black farmers in North Elba, New York, in the Adirondacks, struggle with poor land and long cold winters. The Kansas-Nebraska Act of 1854, which threatened to spread the reach of slavery by providing that the citizens of territories not yet states (including Kansas and Nebraska) would be the ones to decide whether the territories were to be free or to permit slavery, gave the 54-year-old frail and frequently fever-ridden John Brown an opportunity for action.

Settlers from North and South poured into Kansas, as much to influence the vote on the slavery question as to stake claims in the newly opened territory. In October 1854, five of John Brown's sons emigrated from Ohio to Kansas, with eleven head of cattle, three horses, a plough, and a box of fruit trees and grapevines. Earlier that year, border crossers from Missouri had swung the vote to elect a pro-slavery legislature. A Free Soil convention repudiated that election and refused to honor the legislature's enactments. Something very like war was brewing, and John Brown's sons asked him to send arms and ammunition. John Brown raised funds at an abolitionist convention and came out himself to Kansas in October 1855, concealing a load of arms—revolvers, rifles, dirks, and broadswords—in a covered wagon under some conspicuously displayed surveying instruments.

In December, Brown and his sons went to Lawrence, Kansas, heavily armed, when that town was rumored to be the target of a pro-slavery attack. Peace was made before fighting broke out, but rumors of murders and atrocities on both sides persisted. Brown longed to take action. On May 21, 1856, he heard that pro-slavery forces were about to attack Lawrence. Brown and his sons rode off to its defense, but federal troops restored order in the town. On May 22, in the U.S. Senate in Washington, Congressman Preston Brooks of South Carolina clubbed the abolition-ist Senator Charles Sumner of Massachusetts senseless, striking his head repeatedly with a weighted cane as he sat at his seat. When Brown and his sons heard the news, they went crazy, as one of the sons remembered it.[9] Brown decided to kill some of the pro-slavery activists who had settled near his family not far from the Pottawatomie Creek. The Browns sharp-ened their broadswords. "I hope you will act with caution," a Free Soiler volunteer said to Brown. "Caution, caution, sir," Brown replied. "I am eternally tired of hearing the word caution. It is nothing but the word of cowardice."[10]

Brown and his followers set out to kill the leaders of the pro-slavery faction on Pottawatomie Creek. They went from cabin to cabin in the night, dragging the menfolk out into the darkness and hacking them to death with their broadswords. In all, on the nights of May 23–24 and May 24–25, they killed five pro-slavery men before washing the blood off their swords in the Pottawatomie. Some years later, Brown told a friend that he himself hadn't killed the five men, "but I do not pretend to say that they were not killed by my order; and in the doing so I believe I was doing God's service." The friend's wife asked Brown if he thought God used him as an instrument to kill men. Brown said: "I think He has used me as an instru-ment to kill men; and if I live, I think he will use me as an instrument to kill a good many more."[11]

The result of the Pottawatomie killings was chaos and guerilla war in southeastern Kansas. The Brown family cabins were burned to the ground. At Black Jack, Kansas, on June 2, 1856, Brown and his men captured a captain of Missouri militia and 24 followers after a skirmish in which four Missourians were killed. Brown wrote his wife Mary: "May God still gird our loins & hold our right hands, & to him may we give the glory."[12] A column of 50 U.S. cavalrymen forced Brown to surrender his prisoners but did not take Brown himself captive.

Brown, after going into hiding in the bush, organized a Free Soil company that, among other things, liberated pro-slavery settlers' cattle. Missourians poured into the state to support pro-slavery settlers in Kansas. One Missourian shot Brown's son Frederick to death. The Missourians set fire to the Free Soilers's cabins in the town of Osawatomie. Brown, seeing the fire and smoke, told his son Jason: "I have only a short time to live—only one death to die, and I will die fighting for this cause. There will be no more peace in this land until slavery is done for."[13]

A new governor came to Kansas and managed to disband militia on both sides. Brown, ill with dysentery and fever, left Kansas for Ohio and the East to lecture and raise funds for the abolitionist cause. He began building an arsenal—rifles, pistols, even an order of a thousand pikes—and planning to overthrow slavery. His plan was to raid the Federal armory and arsenal at Harpers Ferry (which at that time was part of Virginia; like Charlestown, Harpers Ferry become part of West Virginia when that pro-Union state was carved out of Virginia during the Civil War), carry off arms, and move into the mountains, where he expected to be joined by runaway slaves from Virginia and Maryland. At the same time, he hoped that supporters in New England would call a Northern Convention to "overthrow the Pro-Slavery Administration." Brown prepared to execute his plan. He studied census data for the counties in the South with the highest percentage of slaves, and he read military history. He started training his followers in Tabor, Iowa, for guerrilla warfare. Kansas, at the time, was peaceful. Where were they to fight, the recruits wanted to know? "Our ultimate destination," he told them, "is Virginia."

Later on, unfolding pieces of his plan gradually, as Jesus had unfolded his mission to his disciples, Brown told some of his recruits that "God had created him to be the deliverer of the slaves the same as Moses had delivered the children of Israel."[14] Perhaps because he saw himself as Moses, Brown, whose stern face had hitherto been clean-shaven, grew a long white beard. In seeking support from the New England abolitionist Frederick Sanborn, he used a different Biblical conception of himself, with a different view of the outcome of his efforts: "I expect nothing but to endure hardness; but I expect to effect a mighty conquest, even though it be like the last victory of Samson."[15] In May 1858, when Brown was in Chatham, Ontario, framing a Provisional Constitution for the United States and seeking support among Canada's fugitive blacks, he looked to the New Testament for example. To a Canadian black who pointed out how hopeless Brown's plan was and that the blacks could not spare men of his stamp, Brown said: "Did not my Master Jesus Christ come down from Heaven and sacrifice himself upon the altar for the salvation of the race, and should I, a worm, not worthy to crawl under His feet, refuse to sacrifice myself?"[16] But he also thought in warlike terms, which may explain his willingness to kill supporters of slavery. The preamble to his Provisional Constitution described slavery as "none other than a most barbarous, unprovoked, and unjustifiable War of one portion of [America's] citizens upon another portion."[17]

By this time, ahead of Abraham Lincoln and most political leaders, Brown had become convinced that, as he told one Kansas Free Stater, "Peaceful emancipation is impossible. The thing has gone beyond that point." In January 1859, he told another Kansas Free Stater, "we have reached a point where nothing but war can settle the question." After attending an anti-slavery convention in Boston, he burst out: "Talk! talk! talk! That will never free the slaves! What is needed is action—action!"[18]

Rumors about Brown's plans began to spread, some of them quite concrete. Three Quakers in Iowa in August 1859, who later claimed their goal was "to protect Brown from the consequence of his own rashness," sent an anonymous letter to John Buchanan Floyd, the secretary of war, that "*old John Brown, late of Kansas*," was planning to effect "the liberation of the slaves at the South by a general insurrection" and that the group planned to enter Virginia at Harpers Ferry. The anonymous writer said Brown "will arm the negroes and strike the blow in a few weeks; so that whatever is done must be done at once." Floyd (the grandson of Colonel William Preston and of the surveyor John Floyd) filed the letter away, finding the alleged scheme incredible and believing, as he later testified to a Senate committee, that "a scheme of such wickedness and outrage could not be entertained by any citizens of the United States." At about the same time, Secretary Floyd began transferring weapons—nearly 115,000 rifles and muskets—from arsenals in the North to ones in South Carolina, North Carolina, Alabama, Georgia, and Louisiana—as U. S. Grant put it in his memoirs, spreading the arms "throughout the South so as to be on hand when treason wanted them."[19]

After a series of delays and worries about premature disclosure of his plans, Brown began to move his few close followers near to Harpers Ferry. He thought the location was perfect: a federal arsenal in a slave state (Virginia), less than 30 miles from Pennsylvania, and nestled in a gap in the Blue Ridge Mountains through which he and his men (and, he hoped, hundreds of runaway slaves) could flee for safety. In the summer of 1858, Brown sent ahead one of his followers, John E. Cook, to scout. Cook checked out the government armory and managed to impregnate a local girl, whom he had to marry in April 1859. Brown himself came to Harpers Ferry in July 1859 and, under the name of "Isaac Smith," rented a farmhouse a few miles from Harpers Ferry on the Maryland side of the Potomac, as his men gathered, hid, and trained from a manual of arms.

On August 19, Brown met for the last time with Frederick Douglass in Chambersburg, Pa., not far from Harpers Ferry. He tried to induce Douglass and a friend of Douglass's, an ex-slave named Shields Green, to join him. "Come with me, Douglass," Brown said. "When I strike, the bees will begin to swarm, and I shall want you to help hive them." But Douglass thought the idea of an attack on the federal property in Harpers Ferry was doomed to failure and would rouse the whole country against them. Douglass asked Shields Green what he had decided to do. Green said: "I b'lieve I'll go wid de old man."[20]

Brown's own followers—the small band in the farmhouse—were not happy with Brown's plans. They had thought Brown planned just to run slaves off into the mountains. Few of Brown's followers had known that the first step was to be a raid on the federal armory. At one point, John Brown resigned as commander in chief. His followers re-elected him and sent him a formal letter, of less than ringing support (although written by Brown's son Owen): "Dear Sir—We have all agreed to sustain your decisions, until you have *proved incompetent,* & many of us will adhere to your decisions so long as you will."[21]

Through the late summer and early autumn, the men waited, often hiding in a garret to avoid the curiosity of visiting neighbors, often near the breaking point from confinement, boredom, and the possibility of being lynched if discovered. Brown hoped for a flood of recruits. Only one came during the entire month of September. Finally, on October 15, three more straggled in, increasing Brown's force to twenty-one recruits—sixteen whites, five Negroes—and himself. He decided to strike the next day, Sunday, October 16. Brown started that day, as he started every day, with a worship service. He read a text from the Bible about slavery and then, as a black recruit who survived the raid remembered it, "offered up a fervent prayer to God to assist in the liberation of the bondmen in that slaveholding land."[22] The group held a council of war. Final orders were given. At 8 PM, Brown said: "Men, get on your arms; we will proceed to the Ferry." They set off into the cold, drizzly, moonless night, Brown leading in a one-horse farm wagon laden with pikes and tools, the men marching behind. One of the men later told Brown's daughter Annie that the men in the procession "all felt like they were marching to their own funeral."[23]

The raid itself lasted not much more than a day and a night. The raiders cut the telegraph wires on Sunday night. Before dawn on Monday, Brown's men had captured the armory and the arsenal and both bridges into town and seized hostages from the countryside, including Colonel Lewis W. Washington, great-grandnephew of George Washington. One of the raiders shot a baggage master who refused to halt on command. The man, a freed Negro, died in great pain, the first to die in the raid. A train to Washington, passing through the town in the night, was halted by Brown's men but allowed to pass—spreading word of the insurrection throughout northern Virginia and, thanks to the telegraph, Washington.

Militia from the neighboring communities recaptured both bridges on Monday morning, trapping Brown in Harpers Ferry. One of the black recruits was shot dead by a sniper. Someone sliced off the dead man's ears as souvenirs. Others beat his body with sticks. A pack of hogs came to root on the body.[24] Brown, from the engine house of the armory, tried to negotiate under a flag of truce. The first recruit he sent out was dragged off at gunpoint. He sent out two more—one his son Watson—under a white flag. Both were shot. Brown's son Watson crawled back into the firehouse and doubled up in agony at his father's feet.

More raiders were killed in the afternoon. One of Brown's recruits, a Quaker, saw a man coming near the engine house to see what was happening. Thinking the man was trying to shoot him, the Quaker fired and killed the man. The man, who had not been armed, was the mayor of Harpers Ferry. The townspeople, already outraged, many of them filled with strong liquor, redoubled their fire on the armory, wounding Brown's son Oliver. One of Brown's prisoners remembered Oliver, in his pain, begging his father again and again to shoot him. "If you must die," Brown said, "die like a man." Later he called to Oliver. There was no answer. "I guess he is dead," Brown said.[25]

When dawn broke on Tuesday morning, Brown saw that he was now besieged, not by ill-organized militia, but by a company of U.S. Marines. The company was commanded by Brevet Colonel Robert E. Lee, assisted by Lieutenant J. E. B. Stuart. Lee sent Stuart to the firehouse under a flag of truce, with a note demanding that the raiders surrender unconditionally to be turned over to the proper authorities. As Brown looked at the note, Stuart, who had been in Kansas, recognized him. "Why, aren't you old Osawatomie Brown of Kansas, whom I once had there as my prisoner?"

"Yes," Brown said, "but you didn't keep me."[26]

Brown said he would surrender only on terms that allowed him and his men to escape. Stuart said the only terms possible were those in Lee's note. "I prefer to die here," Brown said.

Stuart stepped back and waved his cap, signaling his company to attack. A storming party of Marines with sledgehammers and a heavy ladder charged the engine house and battered at the oak doors as the raiders fired back. The Marines tore down a door and poured in the breach. The prisoner Colonel Washington pointed out Brown to Lieutenant Israel Green, who led the storming party. Green hit Brown with his sword before Brown could fire, then tried to run him through, lifting him completely from the ground. The light dress sword hit Brown's belt buckle and bent double. Brown fell forward and Green beat him repeatedly on the head with his sword hilt, knocking him unconscious.[27]

It was 8 AM on Tuesday morning, thirty-six hours after Brown had started from the farmhouse to Harpers Ferry. There had been no slave uprising. No slaves had come to join Brown, except ones that the raiders had forcibly liberated—and those refused to join in the fighting. Ten of the small raiding party—including two of Brown's sons—had been killed or mortally wounded. Three residents of Harpers Ferry, a slaveholder, and a Marine had been killed.[28] The raid had been a complete failure. But, wounded and facing the certainty of death by hanging or lynching, Brown lived, and, by his answers to his questioners, by his testimony, by his letters, by his fierce example, kept on fighting.

On Tuesday afternoon, as he lay a captive on the floor of the paymaster's office of the armory, Brown, his head bandaged, was questioned first by Henry Wise, the governor of Virginia, who, impressed by Brown's composure and candor, told a reporter: "He is the gamest man I ever saw."[29] Brown was then questioned by Senator James Mason of Virginia and others for more than three hours. Several reporters were there, and the interview was published throughout the country.

> Mason: "How do you justify your acts?"
>
> Brown: "I think, my friend, you are guilty of a great wrong against God and humanity—I say it without wishing to be offensive— and it would be perfectly right for any one to interfere with you so far as to free those you wilfully and wickedly hold in the bondage."
>
> A bystander: "Upon what principle do you justify your acts?"
>
> Brown: "Upon the Golden Rule. I pity the poor in bondage that have none to help them: that is why I am here; not to gratify any personal animosity, revenge, or vindictive spirit. It is my sympathy with the oppressed and the wronged, that are as good as you and as precious in the sight of God."

Toward the end of the long interview, a reporter said: "I do not wish to annoy you; but if you have anything further you would like to say, I will report it."

> Brown: "I have nothing to say, only that I claim to be carrying out a measure that I believe perfectly justifiable, and not to act the part of an incendiary or ruffian, but to aid those suffering great wrong. I wish to say, furthermore, that you had better—all you people of the South—prepare yourself for a settlement of this question, that must come up sooner than you are prepared for it. The sooner you are prepared, the better. You may dispose of me very easily—I am nearly disposed of now; but the question is still to be settled—this negro question I mean; the end of that is not yet."[30]

The authorities moved as quickly as they could, partly to forestall a lynching that could do even more harm to the Southern cause. One week after his capture, Brown underwent a preliminary examination before the magistrates' court in Charlestown, Virginia. The special prosecutor told the court to observe "the judicial decencies," but "in the double quick time."[31] The trial itself, begun on October 27, was completed by November 4.

Brown's trial, and the evidence uncovered before it, polarized the nation more than the raid itself had done. Brown had not destroyed his correspondence with his Northern supporters but kept it all in a carpet bag in the farmhouse he and his men had stayed in before the raid. J. E. B. Stuart and a detachment of Marines found the bag and the letters on the afternoon of the day on which Brown was captured. Newspapers throughout the nation published the names and the maps on which Brown had marked locations of armories throughout the South. Troops sent by Lee also found in Maryland an immense quantity of weapons, including hundreds of carbines and revolvers, a swivel gun, knives, and close to a thousand pikes—in Lee's words, "all the necessaries for a campaign."[32] Throughout the South, many became convinced that prominent men in the North (several of whom fled to Canada or England when their names were published) were in on a plot to destroy slavery by force and that secession was the only way for Southerners to defend their property and their rights. As the Richmond *Enquirer* put it, the Harpers Ferry invasion "has advanced the cause of disunion more than any other event since the formation of the Government; it has rallied to that standard men who formerly looked upon it with horror; it has revived with tenfold strength the desires of a Southern Confederacy."[33] The raid intensified the perennial Southern fear of bloody slavery insurrections like the slave uprising that had killed so many whites in Haiti. Throughout the South, militia were formed and trained.

In the North, abolitionists set about making Brown a martyr even before Brown was executed. Wendell Phillips called Harpers Ferry "the Lexington of today." Emerson called Brown "the new saint awaiting his martyrdom, and who, if he shall suffer, will make the gallows glorious like the cross." Henry Ward Beecher, preaching on October 30, thundered: "Let Virginia make him a martyr! Now, he has only blundered. His soul was noble; his work miserable. But a cord and a gibbet would redeem all that, and round up Brown's failure with heroic success." Brown saw a newspaper report of Beecher's sermon while he was in the jail. "Good," he wrote above the passage about making him a martyr.[34] From his jail cell, Brown poured out inspiring letters to his acquaintances. "Tell your Father," he wrote one young friend, "that I am quite cheerful, that I do not feel myself in the least degraded by my imprisonment, my chains, or the *near prospect* of the Gallows. *Man* cannot *imprison, or chain, or hang,* the *soul.* I go joyfully in behalf of Millions that have no rights that this 'great & glorious', 'this Christian Republic', is bound to respect."[35]

The trial was another platform for Brown. His assigned defense counsel, seeking to save him from the gallows, argued that Brown was insane. Brown rejected the defense. After the jury on October 31 convicted him, the judge on November 2 asked Brown if there was any reason why he should not be sentenced. Brown's speech was published in newspapers across the country:

> "I see a book kissed, which I suppose to be the Bible, or at least the New Testament, which teaches me that 'all things whatsoever I would that men should do to me, I should do to them.' It teaches me further to 'remember them that are in bonds, as bound with them.' I endeavored to act up to that instruction. I say that I am yet too young to understand that God is any respecter of persons. I believe that to have interfered as I have done in the behalf of His despised poor, is no wrong, but right. Now, if it is deemed necessary that I should forfeit my life for the furtherance of the ends of justice, and mingle my blood with the blood of millions in this slave country whose rights are disregarded by wicked, cruel and unjust enactments, I say let it be done."[36]

On November 2, the judge sentenced Brown to hang on December 2. The month's delay between sentencing and execution gave Brown more time to be heard. Some of his supporters in the North thought of a rescue attempt. Let them hang me, Brown said; "I am worth inconceivably more to *hang* than for any other purpose." As he wrote his wife, he believed "that for me at this time to seal my testimony for God and Humanity with my blood will do vastly more toward advancing the cause I have earnestly endeavored to promote, than all I have done in my life before."[37] And he wrote with similar strength and composure to friends and family and supporters from around the country. On November 30, he wrote a final letter to his family. "Do not feel ashamed on my account," he wrote, "nor for one moment despair of the cause; or grow *weary* of *well doing*. I bless God; I never felt stronger confidence in the certain & near approach of a *bright Morning; & a glorious day*."[38]

On his way to the scaffold on December 2, 1859, he handed to an attendant a last message: "I John Brown am now quite *certain* that the crimes of this *guilty, land: will* never be purged *away;* but with Blood. I had *as I now think: vainly* flattered myself that without *very much* bloodshed; it might be done."[39]

Brown sat on his own coffin on the wagon as he rode out to the scaffold. Fifteen hundred cavalry and militia were at the site, because the authorities feared a last-minute rescue attempt. Others there included John Wilkes Booth, who assassinated Lincoln in 1865, and Edmund Ruffin, a leading Virginia secessionist, who wrote in his diary for the day his hope that Brown's raid would "stir the sluggish blood of the South" to take up arms and form an independent country.[40] On the scaffold, the sheriff put a white hood over Brown's head. It took ten minutes for the soldiers to get into their assigned positions. Brown stood as motionless as a statue. Below the platform, the sheriff cut the rope. The platform fell. Brown's body struggled for a time, until it dangled straight down, swayed by the wind, while the onlookers were still (see figure 5.2). Breaking the silence, Colonel J. T. L. Preston (one of the founders and first faculty members of the Virginia Military Institute and, like Secretary of War Floyd, a grandson of Colonel William Preston), called out: "So perish all such enemies of Virginia! All such enemies of the Union! All such foes of the human race!"[41]

John Brown's body was taken to his family home in North Elba, New York, and buried on December 8, 1859. The abolitionist Wendell Phillips said in his eulogy of Brown: "Marvellous old man! . . . He has abolished slavery in Virginia. You may say this is too much. . . . True, the slave is still there. So, when the tempest uproots a pine on your hills, it looks green for months—a year or two. Still, it is timber, not a tree. John Brown has loosened the roots of the slave system; it only breathes,—it does not live, hereafter."[42] On the day Brown was buried, Jefferson Davis (the future president of the Confederate States of America) told the Senate: "To secure our rights and protect our honor we will dissever the ties that bind us together, even if it rushes us into a sea of blood."[43] On December 20,

Fig. 5.2. Execution of John Brown. Engraving in *Frank Leslie's Illustrated Newspaper*, December 10, 1859. *Library of Congress.*

1860, just over a year after the hanging, South Carolina seceded from the Union. In the following two months, Mississippi, Florida, Alabama, Georgia, and Louisiana followed suit. On April 12, 1861, less than 18 months after Brown's hanging, Confederate artillery began to fire on the federal troops in Fort Sumter in Charleston harbor, starting the purging by blood Brown foresaw and helped to bring about by his acts, his words, and his hanging.

6

Diaries from Indian Country, Civil War Back Home

The months after the hanging of John Brown saw the polarization of America into Northern and Southern camps, largely over the issue of slavery. Nowhere was that polarization more acute than in the Border States. Kentucky was the most deeply divided of these, because slaves made up almost 20 percent of its population in 1860 (much more than Maryland and Missouri's less than 13 percent each, western Virginia's less than 4 percent, and Delaware's 1 percent).[1] Between the time of John Brown's execution and the start of the Civil War, settlers and prospectors continued to pour into the West, causing friction and fighting with Indians west of the Mississippi, as well as the continued destruction of buffalo and other game and of the Plains Indian way of life. All of these developments are made real for me by two small leather-bound pocket diaries, each 5½ inches by 3¼ inches by ¾ inch, kept by my great-grandfather John Mason Brown (no kin to John Brown of Harpers Ferry), a Kentuckian, during two long trips (the first covering some eight thousand miles, the second five thousand miles), mostly in Indian country, in 1861 and 1862, before he came back to Kentucky and joined the Union army, becoming a colonel and a leader in the successful fight against Confederate raids into Kentucky led by Colonel John Hunt Morgan. Brown was a young man when he wrote these diaries. He had just turned twenty-four when he left St. Louis in May 1861, bound for Montana and beyond. His curiosity was as limitless as his energy. By writing what he saw—the Indians, the

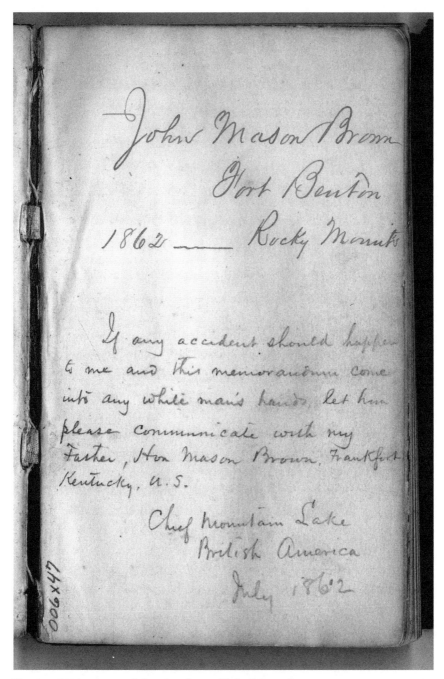

Fig. 6.1. Opening page of the 1862 diary of John Mason Brown. *Collection of Filson Historical Society. Gift of the author.*

reservations, the annuities, the violence, the killing of the game, the quest for gold, the Civil War news that slowly reached the Rockies, the deeply split loyalties of Kentuckians—he opens to us a world that was radically changing as he lived in it. More of that world—including the fighting of Kentuckians against Kentuckians—is revealed in regimental histories and in wartime correspondence by Brown and his fellow officers.[2]

John Mason Brown was born in Frankfort, Kentucky's state capital, on April 26, 1837, in Liberty Hall, an imposing brick house built in about 1800 for his grandfather, John Brown, a leading lawyer, a U.S. congressman, and, when Kentucky became a state, one of its first two senators. John Brown's oldest son, Mason, who inherited Liberty Hall when the senator died in August 1837, had been a circuit judge in Kentucky, had served as its secretary of state, and, like his father, was a substantial landowner and slave owner.[3] According to the 1860 census, Mason Brown then owned fifty-one slaves— thirty-one in Franklin County (site not only of Brown's home Liberty Hall in Frankfort but also of Brown's farm about two miles away) and twenty in Owen County, where he had another farm in a rich farming area with the unfortunate name of Brown's Bottom. Kentucky was far from a classless society in John Mason Brown's time. The Browns, although not among the largest landowners and slave owners in the state, were one of a small number of families, many connected by marriage or kinship, who had much of the best land and wielded much of the political influence in the state.

When Mason Brown's son John Mason Brown was nine, his right leg was badly crushed in an accident when he was playing with other boys in a grist mill. It took the boy more than a year to recover substantial use of the injured leg—during which time, studying at home under his father's super-vision, Brown became what he remained throughout his life, an omnivo-rous reader and an eager and excellent student. In 1854, he entered Yale, his father's alma mater, as a junior. His class of 1856 numbered only ninety-seven (considered a large class at the time) but included many who were to excel. Among Brown's close friends in the class were Timothy Dwight, later president of Yale; David Brewer and Henry Brown, later justices of the U.S. Supreme Court; and Chauncey Depew, later president of the New York Central Railroad and senator from New York. After teaching school and working on a geological survey, Brown studied law. Admitted to the bar in 1859, he moved to St. Louis, where his half-brother Benjamin

Gratz Brown, an emancipationist and a future senator from and governor of Missouri, was a leading lawyer. In St. Louis, John Mason Brown practiced law and made friends with senior officials of Pierre Chouteau, Jr. & Company (often referred to as American Fur Company), which for years had been a large fur trader on the Missouri River and which was trading farther and farther up that river, using steamboats designed for the river's shallow waters. In 1859, *Chippewa*, one of the company's steamboats, had gone farther upriver than any steamboat had gone, reaching close to Fort Benton in what is now Montana.[4] In addition, Brown had befriended the Jesuit priest Father Pierre-Jean De Smet, who, with his colleagues, had established missions among many of the Indian tribes of the Plains and the Rocky Mountains, including the Pottawatomie, the Pend d'Oreilles, and the Blackfeet. De Smet had a strong influence on Brown, a Presbyterian who was more than 35 years younger than De Smet.[5]

Why did Brown in 1861 and 1862 decide to travel into the heart of Indian country, thousands of miles northwest from St. Louis? According to Brown's son Preston, his father was inspired by De Smet's accounts of the Indians and "a natural love of adventure"—and, in the case of the 1862 trip, by the hope of finding gold. According to Brown's relative Preston Davie, the family story was that Brown "in his early manhood had grown so tall and had become so thin that his family feared he might be going into what was then termed a 'decline,' and to improve his health he had been sent out West where the vigorous life soon restored his constitution."[6] Could it also have been that Brown was not in a hurry to take part in the Civil War, particularly as many of his relatives from Kentucky were pro-Confederate and were likely to fight for the Confederacy? But Brown's first trip began on May 1, 1861, soon after secessionists fired on Fort Sumter and before the major battles of the Civil War had begun, at a time when Kentucky's legislature had proclaimed its neutrality and its pro-slavery governor sought to keep Kentucky out of the fight and opposed providing troops in response to President Lincoln's call for volunteers. By the time Brown's second trip started, on May 13, 1862, the Civil War was raging in earnest. That was long after the Union defeat at First Bull Run (July 1861) and more than a month after the bloody two-day battle of Shiloh (April 6–7, 1862). However, by May 1862, Unionists controlled Kentucky's legislature, and Union troops had driven most Confederate soldiers out of

Kentucky, so there then appeared to be no Confederate threat to the state.[7] It may be that Brown, in his early 20s, was bored by practicing law and was anxious to see the Wild West before the game was killed off and all of the Indians were confined to reservations.

Brown's first diary entry gives us a foretaste of what he hoped to find in his trip through Indian country: "May 1st, 1861 Wednesday—Left St. Louis in Am. Fur Company's Steamer 'Spread Eagle' at 12¾ o'clock. Passage to Fort Benton paid at Pierre Chouteau Jr. & Co.'s $100. Carry with me a Hawken rifle, 7 canisters powder and other ammunition, a few articles of clothing and a small assortment of beads, vermilion, &c. for presents. Find the boat very roomy and pleasant. . . . Weight this day 160½ pounds." From these few sentences we conclude that Brown was trim verging on skinny, able to afford a long and fairly expensive trip (Fort Benton, in what is now northwestern Montana, the head of navigation on the upper Missouri river, was, according to Brown's computations, some twenty-seven hundred miles up the Missouri from St. Louis; $100 in 1861 had the purchasing power of more than $2,500 in 2010), looking to kill game, eager to meet and interact with Indians, and happily unaware of how rigorous his trip was to be.

On both his trips, Brown and his fellow travelers killed large quantities of game, including buffalo, antelope, deer, elk, bear, duck, and even the occasional bald eagle. The steamboats to Fort Benton, which first reached that fort in 1860, served important commercial purposes, carrying upriver the annuity goods which the U.S. government was obliged by treaty to furnish to Indian tribes and bringing back down to St. Louis large quantities of buffalo robes and other furs. But the steamboats also carried sightseers from the United States and Europe who wanted to blast away at game as they traveled. On the second day of his 1861 trip, Brown described "an English gentleman . . . who with his wife, a young lady protégé, and two or three New Yorkers in company are making a pleasure excursion to Ft. Benton [carrying] baggage enough for a regiment and fire arms sufficient to arm a platoon of riflemen." That same day, the passengers decided to form a rifle company ("pour passer le temps," in Brown's words) and asked Brown, who had had some military training, to be its captain. The passengers may have wanted to be prepared to fight off Indian attacks, if need be—Brown put the rifle company through a drill or two—but the diaries also reflect an insatiable eagerness to kill animals.

Game not far from St. Louis was already scarce—partly because of hunting, but largely because of the ever-growing spread of farming, which increased after Sioux chiefs in 1858 entered a treaty ceding claims in what is now South Dakota, between the Big Sioux River and the Mississippi River, and after the Dakota Territory was created in March 1861. By 1861, the farming frontier already extended to Fort Randall in what is now southern South Dakota.[8] Not until *Spread Eagle* was almost twelve hundred miles upriver from St. Louis did Brown and fellow passengers see their first game: a large wolf and some turkeys. Farther up in Indian country, however, game could still reach awe-inspiring numbers—as reflected in Brown's description (June 6, 1862) when, north of Ft. Berthold, in what is now North Dakota, he saw "immense numbers of Buffalo blackening the Prairies to the Westward." Brown and his fellow passengers reduced the numbers of animals within reach of their guns. By my count, on the trip to Fort Benton in 1861 they killed, between June 7 and July 8, 23 buffalo, 11 antelope, 6 wolves, 5 elk, 2 beaver, and a bear. On the comparable trip to Fort Benton between June 2 and June 20, 1862, Brown and the other passengers killed 31 buffalo, 4 antelope, 2 elk, and 1 deer. The creatures they killed ranged in size from grizzly bears and buffalo down to doves and whatever lay between these extremes ("Killed a big horn and two rabbits"—August 15, 1861; "Shot a wolf and killed 4 prarie chickens with a revolver"—September 2, 1861).

The diaries also reflect the killing of enormous quantities of game—particularly buffalo—by Indians and white hunters. The Chouteaus had built what became Fort Benton in the 1840s as the uppermost fur trading post on the Upper Missouri. The fort's importance in the fur trade was evident in Brown's diaries. On June 21, 1861, at Fort Union, Montana, the *Spread Eagle*, before heading back down to St. Louis, took on board "24000 [buffalo] robes principally from Fort Benton brought down in Mackinac boats." Mackinac, or Mackinaw, boats were shallow-draft boats used by trappers and fur traders to carry their furs. May 27, 1862: "While sounding for the channel Jeff Smith's mackinac boat came down bound from the Gros Ventres to St Louis loaded with 1400 buffalo robes. Chas Chouteau purchased them and we took them aboard." June 7, 1862: "Just below Big Muddy met Bob Lemon with a mackinac loaded with Buffalo Robes." June 9, 1862: "Carroll down from Ft. Benton with 3 mackinacs full of robes."

Brown on his travels encountered many Indian tribes—among them the Pawnee, Omaha, Ponca, several groups of Sioux (Brulé, Hunkpapa, Minneconjou, Sans Arcs, Santee, Yankton), as well as Arikara, Mandan, Gros Ventre, Assiniboine, Crow, Blackfeet, Nez Perce, Pend d'Oreilles, Kalispell, Kootenay, Snake, Chinook, and Spokane. His diaries reflect his desire to learn as much as he could about each of these tribes. He liked many of the Indians he met. He got on well with the men and admired the beauty of many of the women. On June 13, 1861, among the Ree (Arikara), young Brown noted "A young Ree and his squaw, both very handsome" and "a girl of about 19 years known as the Belle of the Rees. Her proper name is 'The White Corn' and so distinguished is her beauty that a marriage settlement of 17 horses was a short time since vainly urged."

To understand and communicate with Indians, Brown, who throughout his life was good at languages, worked hard to learn words in the languages of many of the tribes he encountered. The Indians of the Plains spoke so many different languages that they had developed a sign language to overcome the language barrier. Because of its broad utility, Brown first devoted his attention to getting along in sign language. On June 3, 1861, barely a month into his first trip, Brown, after noting his ability to make out the gist of a "great talking and gesticulation" by two Sioux on board about a recent war party of the Arikara against the Sioux, added: "Have been putting in practice and augmenting my stock of signs for intercourse with the Indians. Can get along surprisingly well already. The sign language is common to all tribes on the Eastern side of the Rocky Mts. . . . The Indians use [the signs] even when talking." By August 16, in Fort Owen, Brown wrote that he had interpreted for a white man "in sign-language to a Snake Indian. Succeeded very well in making and comprehending the signs." He also noted: "Worked hard at night on a Chinook vocabulary. The dialect is easy of acquisition and is the 'Lingua Franca' so to speak of the Pacific slope." In addition to sign language and Chinook, he also had a number of words of Crow, Snake, and Blackfeet (August 9, 1861).

Brown spent more time with the Blackfeet than with any other tribe. It is likely that Father De Smet had told Brown much about them. Although over half of the Blackfeet had died in the smallpox epidemic of 1837, they were still a large and powerful tribe, greatly and rightly feared both by whites and by Indian tribes such as the Pend d'Oreilles and the Crow, among whom De Smet and his Jesuit colleagues had established missions, starting in the early 1840s.[9] In 1846, after a battle between Blackfeet and Crows, De Smet met with the Blackfeet, seeking to induce them to agree to peace with other tribes, and arranged for another Jesuit priest to found a mission among them. Brown was among the Blackfeet from mid-July to early September 1862, looking for gold, hunting, fishing, and rejoicing in the beautiful countryside in and near what are now Glacier National Park and Waterton Lakes Park in northwestern Montana and southwestern Alberta. He made friends with many Blackfeet, including the trapper Hugh Monroe and his son John. Hugh Monroe, born in Montreal in 1798, had lived among the Blackfeet since 1816, when he started trading with them for the Hudson's Bay Company. He married a Blackfeet, was adopted into the Piegan tribe of the Blackfeet Confederacy, and was given a Blackfeet name meaning "The Wolf's Word" (according to Brown) or "Rising Wolf" (according to others).

Brown set out to learn as much as he could from the Monroes and other Blackfeet about Blackfeet traditions and creation myths. Brown's August 7 diary entry included: "Became brother and Comrade with En-es-tayp'-o-ka—'The Little White Calf'—a really fine fellow. . . . Old Munro began the story of the Cosmogony of the Blackfeet but we were interrupted. Several horses were given me by Enestaypoka, Bull Head, Oliver and Rising Head but I was forced to decline them having nothing adequate to give in return." August 8: "Enestaypoka told me part of the story of the Old Man." The Old Man was how the Piegans referred to their creator. August 10: "The Piegans very well behaved and friendly. Do not beg or seem disposed to thieve. For the latter however I and Nep the dog watch very closely. Was feasted (on berries and meat) at 8 different lodges at night." August 22: "To-day, just as I was mounting my horse to hunt, saw a party approaching with what appeared to be a flag. Rode out to meet them and found them to be 8 Piegans under Kayo-Siecunum The 'Black Bear.' In the center of the party rode 'Tu-wi'-ber' or 'The Man Who Rushes' Head Chief of all the North Piegans who carried, with all due gravity a U.S. flag, about as large as a handkerchief, upon the end of a fishing pole. They had been informed by Istumaka [Bull Head, one of the Piegans who had given horses to Brown] of my whereabouts and dignity and came over to see me. Feasted them in the Lodge and they opened their presents—a bale of tongues and a parcel of dressed skins. . . . Spent the evening smoking and talking with my new friends."[10]

My father, a subsequent John Mason Brown, gave me two pipes, made of catlinite, the red pipestone quarried in Minnesota that was used for pipes throughout the northern plains (see figure 6.2). The pipes had belonged to his grandfather John Mason Brown. Perhaps these were pipes that, mounted on long feather-trimmed reed stems, passed between Brown and his Blackfeet friends as he learned more and more about them and about a way of life that he believed to be vanishing. Less than five years after becoming a brother of Enestaypoka, Brown wrote an article for a New York magazine about the traditions of the Blackfeet based on what he had learned on his trips. Brown described how Na-pi-eu, the Old Man, formed the men and women of the Blackfeet nation out of clay and why he decreed that "the men should hunt and sleep; the women must work for the men." The Old Man turned against the Blackfeet, who thereafter were protected by Na-tush, The Man-in-the-Sun, who gave them buffalo and other game and saved them from a flood. The Old Man lost his claim to the Blackfeet in a game of bowls that was played in Blackfeet land against Another Old Man, a spirit of unmixed evil. From that time on, the Old Man transferred his powerful support to the whites, while Another Old Man has sought to extinguish the Indian race. The Blackfeet, in Brown's account, believed that The Man-in-the-Sun could only delay, not avert, the ruin which impended over their people. Brown ended his article by describing the Blackfeet as

the purest type of the aboriginal Indian. They have all the good and bad traits of the native Indian in unalloyed simplicity. As their native fierceness is unsubdued, so are their legends still untinged with the white man's religion or allegory. Such will not long be the case. The lapse of a few years will reduce the Blackfeet to insignificance in numbers, and degradation in character. Instead of seven thousand bold and hardy warriors, feared by whites and Indians, they will number but a remnant of diseased wretches, dependent on the grudgingly-given annuities of the Government, and with but one aspiration in life—*rum*.[11]

Fig. 6.2. Catlinite (pipestone) pipes that belonged to John Mason Brown. *Author's collection.*

Fortunately, the future of the Blackfeet, while challenging, proved to be less grim than Brown foresaw. But he was right that the Blackfeet—along with the other tribes he encountered in his travels—were undergoing a drastic transition. Their game was being destroyed (in part by the Indians themselves). They were being forced by the U.S. government to live on reservations. Instead of endless buffalo and other game, they were already dependent on annuities the government had promised in exchange for Indians' restricting themselves to reservations. They were increasingly being converted to Christianity. Alcohol was destroying many. Yet some still engaged in intertribal raids, and some still killed whites.

American Fur Company for decades had sought—in most years successfully—to win the bidding for U.S. government contracts to deliver treaty-required annuity goods to the tribes up the Missouri River—in part to receive the contractual payments, but more to keep for the company, and to deny to the company's competitors, control of the annuities (and the resulting influence over the tribes and access to their valuable robes and furs). The company had won the annuity contracts for 1861 and 1862, the years of Brown's trips.[12] On his first trip, Brown noted 12 or 15 tons of U.S. annuity goods being loaded on the *Spread Eagle* at St. Joseph, Missouri. On both trips, he saw the unloading and distribution of annuities to different tribes— Omaha, Ponca, Sioux, Arikara, Mandan, and Blackfeet. The Indians closest to St. Louis appeared to Brown to be most desperately in need of the annuities. Describing the landing at Omaha of freight for the Pawnees, he wrote:

"The Govt. annuities are to them indispensable, for aside from their thievish propensities, which they retain in unimpaired vigor, they possess but little that they can turn to practical account," the Pikes Peak trade having largely driven the buffalo and the Pawnees from their former hunting grounds on the Platte. Brown also recorded large groups of Indians much farther upriver who had gathered to wait for their annuity goods. Examples: May 31, 1861, at the Yankton Agency (in what is now South Dakota): "Found here the entire Yankton band of the Sioux Nation numbering 300 or more lodges and about 2500 souls, collected to receive their annuity"; May 27, 1862, Fort Pierre (in what is now South Dakota): "A good many Sioux here perhaps 1800"; May 28: annuities landed for "the Minne Kanjous, Brulés, Unk-Pa-Pas, Yanktonaise and Blackfoot Sioux tribes"; the Sioux (to Brown's disgust) also successfully demanded that the Indian agent turn over to them all Arikara annuities, "the Sioux being at war with that tribe."[13]

Although Brown sought to record the traditional beliefs of the Indians, his diaries reflect the increasing number of missions, many founded by Father De Smet and his fellow Jesuits, spreading both Christianity and farming. Brown delivered letters of introduction from De Smet and was warmly welcomed by the Jesuit priests. On August 1, 1861, outside of St. Ignatius Mission, north of what is now Missoula, Montana, he saw Father Menetry's "90 a. of wheat *very* flourishing," averaging 40 bushels per acre. "A choir of Indian children, under direction of F. Imoda, sang quite well at vespers in Latin and Kalispelm. As yet there is no organ." August 2: "Rose early and attended matins. Some 135 Indians were present; decorous and accurate in the ceremonials." August 4—"Sunday.—All the neighboring Indians came in to the church, to the number of three or four hundred. Father Menetry preached to them in Kalispelm, the language of the Flatheads and Pend d'Oreilles." June 29, 1862, at Fort Benton: "Sunday—Service by Father Giorda with a short sermon in English which he translated into French and Blackfoot. In afternoon Malcom Clarke [employed by the American Fur Company] and Ahksenikè (The Soft Low voice) were married by F De Smet." July 24, 1862, near Upper Chief Mountain Lake, trading with a camp of Kootenays: the Kootenays are "nearly all are devout Catholics. Carroll saw in their camp some Mt. Assinaboins, who are all zealous Protestants and have books written in their own language, which they all read & write fluently." August 18: the Big Weasel [a Blackfoot] "kept us all awake with hymns and chants. I rose up wide awake at hearing that old tune 'Am I a Soldier of the Cross.' The Indians sang it very well." September 15, Sunday: stopped at the Coeur d'Alene Mission "and there saw and took a final adieu of my very good friend Father Menetry who is there for a few days. This Mission has been established for a long time among the Lower Pend d'Oreilles."

Federal law forbade importation into Indian country of intoxicating beverages, but plenty of alcohol found its way to the Indians. American Fur Company steamboats often carried liquor, believing that was necessary to compete with small traders who regularly sold it to Indians.[14] Brown witnessed heavy drinking, among Indians and among whites. May 31, 1861, above Niobrara, Nebraska: "Passed a band of Ponkas who lined the bank as we came in sight, and invited us by signs to land. Several ran along the shore shouting their only English word *Whisky*." June 24, 1861: "A man came in from the river bringing word that a good deal of liquor had fallen into the Indians hands and they were becoming troublesome." One "horse was ridden off by a drunken Indian." "Were annoyed by a drunken Indian who about dark came up to the Fort [Fort Nolan] and being admitted made himself particularly disagreeable with his tomahawk." But Brown also saw heavy drinking among whites. September 28, 1861, at an army garrison outside of Walla Walla: "Had much trouble taking care of a Dragoon Captain who has constituted himself my chaperone and gets drunk from the purest promptings of hospitality." He noted that July 4, 1862 was "Generally observed by all who could procure ardent spirits." September 1, 1862: "Jerry & Isidore drunk and very troublesome."

The diaries also are a window into violence: violence within communities, continuing intertribal raids, and Indian killings of whites. A few intracommunity examples: On June 14, 1861, a cook on the *Spread Eagle* "was shot through the head and instantly killed by one of the Negro cabin-boys. Supposed to have been accidental." On July 12, Brown noted that "The Little Dog," head chief of the Blackfeet, was not visible on his farm, because he was "secluding himself in grief at being obliged to shoot 3 of his own warriors last week." June 27, 1862: "A gentleman from Quincy Ill accidently shot his son. He was buried at the Coulée." July 1, at Fort Benton: "Grand dance at night winding up with a free fight between the cis and transalpine mountaineers." August 31, at Fort Benton: "Heard of Frank Goodwin's death. He was shot on Wednesday by Menace the Greek in the Fort yard."

Intertribal fighting was a constant source of concern. In early September 1861, near St. Ignatius Mission, Brown received a report of "a general war among the Blackfeet, Crows, Crees, Gros Ventres and Assiniboines. Per consequence a boat voyage down the Mo. would be foolishly hazardous." Instead of going back to St. Louis by steamboat, he arranged to go "to Walla Walla and thence via San Francisco home to Ky." On June 4, 1862, when Brown's steamboat arrived at Fort Berthold, there were "Gros Ventres cele-brating a Scalp Dance over a Sioux killed a few days since." On June 9, the American Fur Company's head man at Fort Union reported troubles between Crows and Assiniboines. On August 15, 1862, at a Piegan camp, the Indians were "wild with the news of a great battle just fought between the Piegans and Pend d'Oreilles." On September 1, at Fort Benton, "at midnight an attack was made on the lodges camped just at the Fort gate. Twelve shots were fired into Matsey's killing one of his wives and wounding another and a child. All hands rushed out and one of the assailants was shot badly judg-ing from the blood that marked his trail. The attack probably made by Gros Ventres as well as could be inferred from the arrows." September 2: "Buried the dead squaw. A Piegan war party danced the grand war dance and started out for the Gros Ventres." September 4: "It now seems certain . . . that the attack of Monday night was by North Blkfeet or Bloods, not by Gros Ventres as we at first supposed." September 7: "A runner brought in news of the hard battle between the Crows & Piegans and the Assinaboins or Sioux near Arrow River." Years after Brown's trips through Indian country, a nephew vividly remembered seeing in Brown's study in Louisville, among his collec-tion of Indian artifacts, "a round buffalo skin shield over which were crossed two long wooden spears tipped with sharp vicious-looking knife-like heads, from each of which hung a human scalp, one gray, the other black." The scalps on the lances may well have come from inter-tribal fighting during Brown's trips to Indian country.[15]

Brown's diaries also reflect Indian attacks on whites. Attacks of this kind grew in number between 1861 and 1862—perhaps because of Indian awareness of the reduction in the number of U. S. soldiers stationed west of the Mississippi as more and more troops were withdrawn to the east to fight in the Civil War and also because of the bloody uprising of the Santee Sioux in Minnesota that started in August 1862. On August 18, 1861, Brown, at Fort Owen, reported rumors "that 16 or 18 whites have been massacred by Spokans &c near Collville [Colville, in northeastern Washington]." On September 6, 1861, just as Brown and a man named Blake were mounting up to start for Walla Walla, "a runner brought in word that 4 whites had been killed at the head of the valley. Instead of pursuing our journey, rode to the spot indicated and found Capt. De Lacy, Beaver Dick Smith, Andw. Livingston and Hudson shot with arrows and scalped. Blake recognized the bodies which we buried. . . . The murder committed by Snakes or Nez Perces. Very tired, got to the Fort late at night after a ride of nearly 90 m."

The most overt risk to Brown's life from Indian attack was in September 1862, when he and his companions were repeatedly shot at as they made their way back to St. Louis on a boat they had built. September 17: "Got up our sail and were making fine time when we were hailed from the bank by a War Party. We at first thought to keep on but they leveled their guns and hailed in Blackfoot "Nappa' pok-sa-pote" and we pulled in. To our dismay we found them Assinaboins. More than half our guns were useless from rain but we had them all capped and made a good show or they would have plundered us of everything as they did Neil who landed just below us. For half an hour we were in great danger. Mc[Cullogh] and I who took charge of matters had several arrows pointed at us and guns cocked at our heads. Finally ordering the men to cock their guns Mc[Cullogh] gave presents of Tobacco & flour and I and Howard jumped in the water and pulled the boat out of the Indians hands. We had not gone 15 miles when 2 Indians (Crows probably) hailed us from the S bank and as we did not land they fired—the balls striking the water and ricocheting over the boat. No damage done and the men all perfectly cool. 20 m on met a Crow war party 30 strong, 2 of whom swam over and received the small present we had to give them. But the remainder, angry that we did not come in and surrender unconditionally took dead aim at us at about 80 yds. The office of pilot, I now found a most unenviable one. Standing on an elevated bench, the better to manage the great steering oar, he offers a most conspicuous mark. Eight bullets whistled (as it seemed to me) within a foot of my head and one grazed the oar near my hand. One man of Neil's party whom we had taken in above was pulling the bow oar and skulked. The rest all showed true grit. We did not return the fire, from motives of policy. Got out of this, our 3rd scrape to-day, all right."

October 1—"Heard of the troubles between the Santee Sioux and the whites." The "troubles" Brown heard of was the uprising in Minnesota by the Santee Sioux (now often known as the Dakota), provoked when the treaty annuities to the Santees were late, the Indians were desperate with hunger, and a white trader named Andrew Myrick reportedly said "If they're hungry, let them eat grass or their own dung." On August 17, after Santee hunters killed five whites, the tribe decided to attack whites throughout the upper Minnesota River valley. One of those killed on August 18 was Myrick, who was found with his mouth stuffed with grass. In all, between 400 and 800 whites were killed before the Santees were defeated in late September.[16] More than three hundred Santees were sentenced to death, but President Lincoln approved the killing of only 39 of them. On December 26, 38 Santees were hanged in Mankato, Minnesota, in the largest mass execution ever in the United States. News of the Santee uprising caused panic not only in Minnesota but also in Iowa and elsewhere in the West. Brown's diary, October 8: "Left Yankton in the mail wagon for Sioux City. . . . Passed numerous little farms in the fertile praire, but the houses have without exception been abandon'd through fear of the Sioux Santees, now at war with the Whites."[17]

Brown's diaries also record violence by whites against Indians. On September 18, 1861, Brown and his companions rode out on the Spokane plain. Near a ford used by Colonel George Wright and the 9th Infantry in their 1858 campaign against the Spokane Indians, Brown found "a huge mound of bones, the skeletons of 900 horses captured by Col. W. from the Spokans, Yakamas &c and shot here. The policy was excellent as events have proved. It crushed the Indians effectually."

In brief, traveling in Indian country in 1861 and 1862 was far from risk free. The inscription on the opening page of Brown's 1862 diary (see figure 6.1) suggests Brown's awareness of the risks of his travels in Indian country:

> If any accident should happen to me and this memorandum come into any white man's hands, let him please communicate with my Father, Hon. Mason Brown, Frankfort, Kentucky, U.S.
>
> Chief Mountain Lake
> British America
> July, 1862

Another recurrent theme in the diaries is the search for gold by whites, including Brown himself, who had experience as a geological surveyor. Gold fever had swept the United States after gold was discovered at Sutter's Fort in California in 1848, and fortunes were made and lost in the California Gold Rush of 1849. When that rush died down, and panning and other placer mining had been replaced by much more capital-intensive hydraulic mining, Americans looked for gold elsewhere in the West. As early as 1854, some gold particles were taken from the mountains west of Fort Benton but not in amounts sufficient to trigger a gold rush. In 1861, a gold mining camp was started in Orofino, Idaho. By the spring of 1862, gold worth panning for was found in what is now western Montana, and the gold rush had spread from Idaho into Montana.[18] Even in 1861, Brown was looking for gold in western Montana. He first mentions his quest on August 14, 1861, at Fort Owen: "Prospected the head of the creek running by the Fort but found no 'color', though worked industriously almost all day." August 19, still at Fort Owen: "Prospected with but poor success, merely raising color." August 21: Blake, in from Orofino, "reports 'big diggins' at the Nez Perces mines and Rhodes Creek." Brown saw more of the impact of gold mining as he passed through Washington, California and Nevada in the fall of 1861. September 24: "Found W.W. [Walla Walla] a very brisk town, flourishing on the Nez Perces mines excitement. Every other house a drinking shop or gambling house." October 9: "Extensive flumes & other mining arrangements, particularly numerous around Cottonwood [California]." October 10 into Scotts Valley "where saw extensive mining operations in progress." October 11 into Oroville "after threading a labyrinth of sluices, flumes &c." October 15 stage into Placerville [California]: "quite a town, active mining operations going on on all sides."

Brown focused more on gold prospecting in his 1862 trip. The diary for that year, in listing what he brought with him, includes a considerable amount of gold mining equipment, including:

4 Gold Pans
3 Picks & Shovels
Xtra handles
2 Rockers
2 Dipper

Crevicing spoon
Blower

The list indicates a desire to go beyond hand panning for gold into sluic-
ing and setting up rockers for separating out the gold. At Fort Benton,
which had become an outfitting center for gold prospectors, Brown had
one rocker assembled between June 30 and July 1 and another one built by
July 9. On July 10, his party, with horses and an ox wagon to carry mining
gear and other freight, set out for St. Mary's or Chief Mountain Lake, on
the eastern side of what is now Glacier-Waterton Park, some 200 miles
northwest of Fort Owen. Brown may have been following an imprecise
tip as to where gold could be found.[19] By July 28, he was on a creek on the
Belly River (in what is now southwestern Alberta) "named in honor of me
'Captain Brown's Creek.'" July 29: "Examined the country about the Creek.
Found Gold in the creek bed and bars, also in Coulees pulling down from
N." Brown's findings reflect his interest in gold—an interest shared by tens
of thousands in western America—but did not include enough "color" to
trigger a gold rush. Brown was not far off, however. In July 1862, when he
was prospecting just north of what is now western Montana, gold strikes
were made at Bannack, in southwestern Montana, and in September, a
newspaper reported that a steamboat had brought to St. Louis $100,000
of gold dust, presumably from Gold Creek near the middle of western
Montana. In 1863, about $8 million in gold was produced in Bannack and
nearby Virginia City. Montana's total gold yield from placer and quartz
mining in 1862–1868 was estimated to be $94 million—about $1.3 billion
in 2010 dollars. The rush for gold (and later for silver and copper) brought
many thousands of immigrants into Montana.[20]

The diaries make clear how rigorous travel in Indian country was. Brown
found the steamboat *Spread Eagle* "very roomy and comfortable" when he
boarded it on May 1, 1861. The following day, Brown, who loved to play
and hear music, was delighted to find on the ship "Piano, Melodeon, flutes,
violins and banjos, and, what is an important accessory, persons on board
who play them well." But by May 7, the boat underwent the first of what
proved to be a series of groundings. The Missouri was known for its frequent
shallowness and shifting sands. To cope with this, *Chippewa* was built to
draw only 31 inches. *Spread Eagle*, however, a much larger boat, drew six

feet. Moreover, steamboats going up the Missouri often were damaged or destroyed by snags from fallen trees. The boats typically did not last many years.[21] Frequently, to enable a steamboat to get around a shallow bend, the freight had to be taken out of the boat on one side of a bend, carried to the other side, and reloaded. On September 17, 1862, Brown and his men were taking the boat they had built down the Missouri in the darkness, because the risk of Indian attack had made the country "eminently hazardous": "Had gone on well till 9 o'clock when we ran in the dark with our bow upon a snag and the rapidity of the current swung the stern round upon another. Nothing but God's mercy prevented the instant destruction of our boat and the death by drowning of all aboard. Made some ineffectual efforts to get off. Thinking that the violence of the water would inevitably cause her to go to pieces, I caused those who could not swim to 'coon out' upon the snags and the rest of us waited cold and wet and terribly anxious for daylight." They managed to work their way off the snags the next day.

On the 1861 trip, well up the Missouri, after men and freight had transferred from the *Spread Eagle* to the *Chippewa*, something worse than a snag happened to *Chippewa* near what is now Poplar, Montana: "June 23rd, Sunday. . . . We were smoking our after-supper pipes when the cry of *Fire!* was raised below. The rush and excitement was terrifying but the boat being near shore a hawser was gotten out and after some delay the human freight was safely landed. I managed to save my gun, pistol, overcoat, valise and blankets, besides various property of others. 200 kegs of Powder were aboard, fire in the hold. The knowledge of this deterred us from making exertions that might have saved a great part of the cargo. The boat floated down after the hawser burned and the powder exploded with a tremendous noise. Boat and cargo a total loss." The fire may have been started by a deck hand carrying a candle going down into *Chippewa*'s hold to draw illicit alcohol from one of many barrels hidden not far from gunpowder in the hold.[22] Brown and the other passengers had to proceed by foot and horse, driving oxen, some three hundred miles to Fort Benton. Thanks to the cattle and the nearness of buffalo, Brown and his fellow travelers were often plagued by clouds of mosquitoes. For example, July 16, 1861, on the Dearborn River: Camped "in a spot litteraly swarming with mosquitoes. The Cattle almost frantic, ran to the ridges but could not escape the pests. It was not until 2 in the morning that the cold gave us some rest from them. Was forced to sleep with head covered by an India Rubber blanket." Perils continued as Brown made his way to the Pacific Coast. On October 3, 1861, taking a small steamer down the Columbia, he wrote: "The navigation of the Columbia is hazardous beyond any that I have ever seen. Great skill in the pilots . . . [is] necessary to avoid the numerous rocks that obstruct the channel and thread the rapids." He then undertook a portage of 15 miles over bad road to "avoid the dangerous channel known as the Des Chutes." Nor was it easy to trek east across the desert later in October 1861. Taking a stage coach into Utah Territory on October 19, he found "The whole country alkaline & the waters so strongly impregnated as to chap the face & hands making them very tender and sore." In his 1862 diary, he described the grinding work involved in taking downriver the 30-foot boat he and his companions had built at Fort Benton. October 5: "Our supplies laid in at Ft. Pierre beginning to run short, made a forced run against a head wind all day. Very hard pulling but kept it up, not withstanding, till 4 o'clock at night or rather next morning when the men gave out and we had to stop for a few hours rest. River in good order and but for the wind we would run splendidly. Never was so fatigued in my life—having now been 36 hours without sleep, with insufficient food and hard at work all the time."

A constant background theme in the diaries is Brown's increasing knowledge, from news often many weeks or months out of date, of the Civil War. The war was just starting when Brown left on his first trip, and there was little or no fighting in Kentucky at the start of his second trip— but a full-scale Confederate invasion of Kentucky was underway by the time he went back to Kentucky in October 1862. Through the diaries, we see the war grow in importance in Brown's eyes until Brown is racing to get back to Kentucky and to take part in the war. We also see how erratically and slowly news traveled. On July 26, 1861, while in the Bitterroot valley in western Montana, Brown reported that someone had come in from the Columbia River settlements to the west, "with news from the States, which had great interest for us all. Felt very much as if I were not doing exactly right in absenting myself from the States at this time." August 12, at Fort Owen: "Owen's express from Walla Walla came in in afternoon with news from the States to 5th July. All very unhappy at the aspect of affairs." That entry reflects a delay of close to 40 days in dissemination of the news. By July 5, 1861, Lincoln had imposed a blockade on the

South, Lee had resigned his U.S. Army commission and had become a Confederate commander, and the U.S. Congress on July 4 had authorized a call of 500,000 troops. September 2, 1861, at Fort Owen: "A miner from Nez Perces brings a rumor of a terrible battle in Va, but so exaggerated that I cannot credit it. 15 yrs since my hurt leg." The "terrible battle in Va" was presumably was the defeat of the Union forces at First Bull Run, fought on July 21, 1861, only twenty-five miles from Washington. September 25, 1861, in Walla Walla: "Exciting news from the States and particularly from Ky. This makes me more anxious than ever to hurry home." October 1: "A rumor current that Jeff Davis has captured Arlington heights—discredited." October 24, at Fort Bridger: "The garrison consists of 3 officers and 1 private. Got news from the States here. Telegraphic communication now complete between San Francisco and St. Louis." October 28, Fort Laramie: "Got here news from States to 18th." The news now is only ten days old—but Brown is much farther east than he had been. By this time, it is likely that Brown has heard of some of the Civil War developments in Kentucky during September 1861: Confederate troops had seized the Mississippi River port of Columbus in western Kentucky; Grant's Union troops had taken Paducah, in western Kentucky; Unionist majorities in both houses of Kentucky's legislature, despite the governor's pleas for continued neutrality, had voted overwhelmingly to demand a Confederate unilateral withdrawal from the state; and a Confederate army commanded by General Simon Bolivar Buckner had established its headquarters in Bowling Green in south-central Kentucky.[23] By November 2, Brown crossed the Missouri River from Atchison, Kansas, and took a train to St. Joseph that was "crowded with a detachment of Illinois 16th Regt returning with their wounded from a skirmish at or near Platte City." He went on to St. Louis by November 4, the date on which his 1861 diary ends.

A little more than six months later, on May 13, 1862, Brown once again left St. Louis to go by steamboat up the Missouri into Indian country. In the intervening six months, Grant's drive south had caused the Confederates to retreat from Kentucky and Tennessee, and the lethal two-day battle of Shiloh had been fought in southern Tennessee—but enlistments by Kentuckians in the armies of either side had been relatively small, and the fighting in Kentucky had been modest in scale.[24] Brown's 1862 diaries reflect more Civil War news, eventually including distressing news from

Kentucky. September 4, 1862, at Fort Benton: "Meldrum brings dates from the States to 13 July. At night Mr Haggard arrived from Pacific slope. He is establishing an Express to this point, to connect ultimately with the East. He gave us papers with Washington dates of 11 Aug." Haggard's news was 24 days old; the news borne by Meldrum, who was based in Fort Union, was over 50 days old. October 6, at Fort Randall, in what is now southern South Dakota: "Got late papers containing very alarming war news from Ky. Am exceedingly impatient to get along." October 7: "Was so uneasy at the news I read yesterday that I could not sleep last night."

The "very alarming war news from Ky" presumably was not only of the successful raid into Kentucky in July 1862 by Confederate cavalry commanded by Colonel John Hunt Morgan but also that Kentucky had subsequently been invaded by two Confederate armies. One, commanded by General Edmund Kirby Smith, took Barboursville (August 18), Richmond (August 30), Lexington (September 1), and Brown's home town of Frankfort, the state capital (September 2). The other, under General Braxton Bragg, was in Bardstown, in central Kentucky, by late September. Spurred by the news, Brown pushed his boat quickly to Yankton, where he joined with a Union officer, a Major Hoffman, to go by stagecoach to Sioux City and on to St. Louis in order to cut a week off the trip. At Sioux City on October 8, he received news from the States up to October 4 before going by stage on to Council Bluffs and by steamer to St. Joe.

The 1862 diary breaks off on October 12 with a short entry of two sentences. The first records the day's trip to 7 miles above St. Joe; the second says merely: "Laid by until the moon rose." On the back pages of the diary, Brown records three undated bets on Civil War developments placed by companions on the trip (see figure 6.3):

> Smith bets Clarke a hat that before the 24th May 1862 Genl. Halleck will have been defeated by Beauregard
>
> Bailey bets Risley that on the 24th May Richmond will be in the possession of McClellan's army—
>
> Geo Parker bets Bailey a suit of clothes that up to the 5th June 1862 the "Merrimac," Rebel Steamship, has not been destroyed—

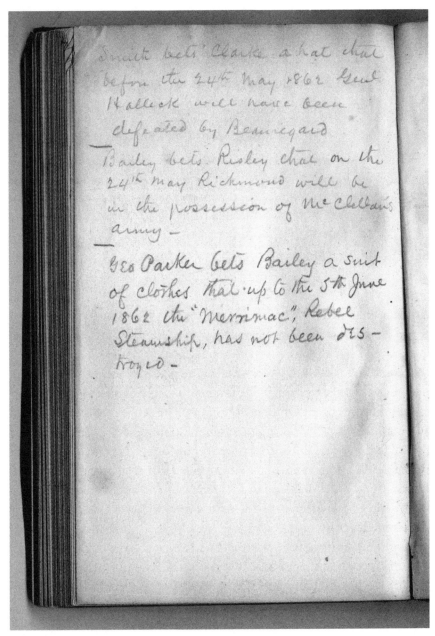

Fig. 6.3. Last page from the 1862 diary of John Mason Brown, recording bets on Civil War events. *Collection of Filson Historical Society. Gift of the author.*

Smith, Risley, and Parker were clearly rooting for the Confederates, Clarke and Bailey for the Union. Out in Indian country, instead of trying to kill each other, the polarized Americans were making friendly wagers. If the bets were paid off, Clarke got his hat. Beauregard did not defeat Halleck before May 24; Halleck laid siege to Beauregard's army at Corinth, Mississippi, until Beauregard retreated from the town on May 25. Bailey would have lost at least one of his bets: Richmond did not fall to the Union forces until April 1865. The *Merrimack* (which the Confederates renamed the *Virginia*), however, was destroyed before June 5, 1862—but not by Yankees. She survived a duel with the Union ironclad *Monitor* on March 9, 1862, but after McClellan's advance in May 1862 left her stranded, her crew, on May 11, 1862, blew her up rather than have the ship fall into Federal hands.

Within less than a month of the last entry in his 1862 diary, Brown was an officer in a Kentucky Union regiment. According to a family story, on the date of his arrival home, Brown's mother told him he had to join the army of one side or another the next day—and Brown chose to fight for the Union.[25] It is likely, however, that Brown was already eager to fight against the Confederacy. Brown, like his father and grandfather, had slaves, and a number of his relatives fought for the South (among them Generals John Cabell Breckinridge, John Buchanan Floyd, Albert Sidney Johnston, and William Preston). But none of his Confederate relatives were as closely related to him as the kinship in many Kentucky families of split allegiance (examples: John J. Crittenden's sons included a Confederate general and a Union general; four of Henry Clay's grandsons fought for the Confederacy and three for the Union; one Breckinridge, a Union soldier, imprisoned his Confederate brother). Moreover, in Brown's immediate family, his grandmother Margaretta Mason Brown, a New Yorker by birth, was an emancipationist and opponent of what she referred to as the "Monster Slavery." Brown's half-brother and close friend Benjamin Gratz Brown was, as earlier noted, an emancipationist and a founder of Missouri's Republican party. He had been shot in the leg in a duel in 1856 with the pro-slavery St. Louis district attorney. Early in the Civil War, Gratz raised a regiment of pro-Union volunteers in Missouri and served as that regiment's colonel. Brown's first cousin Orlando Brown, Jr., had joined a Union regiment in December 1861 ("the first young man in Frankfort to take up arms in defence of the Union," according to his father, also a Unionist). These close family ties would have added to Brown's inclination to the Northern side—but that inclination was already manifest by his hurrying to Kentucky as soon as he heard of the Confederate invasion of his native state. The Browns were not alone in their support of the Union. At least twice as many white males from Kentucky joined the Union side as fought for the Confederacy—although 71% of Kentucky's white males of fighting age, as William Freehling put it, "settled for inertia, a Southwide record for disinclination to fight for either army."[26]

As of October 27, 1862, Brown was commissioned a major in the 10th Kentucky Cavalry regiment, which had been organized during that summer (see figure 6.4). He joined the regiment soon after the Battle of Perryville, the largest Civil War battle in Kentucky, fought on October 8. Although inconclusive in itself, the battle led to the end of the massive Confederate invasion of Kentucky, as General Braxton Bragg retreated south through the Cumberland Gap, with the 10th participating in the pursuit. In December, Brown led a battalion through London and Barboursville to Big Creek Gap, engaging in a number of skirmishes. In the early spring of 1863, Brown spearheaded a defense against an attack by Confederate cavalry under Colonel Roy S. Cluke. Later that spring, Brown's forces and other Union troops blocked Kentuckian General Humphrey Marshall's drive into eastern Kentucky from Virginia. This was Marshall's third and final drive into Kentucky. He was a man whose hopes and ambition were as large in scale as he was (six feet tall and well over 300 pounds). Marshall in August 1862 had assured the Confederate vice president that Kentucky was a "region inhabited by my friends" and that if he invaded the state "the people will flock around my banner as the Italians did to that of Garibaldi," since Kentuckians "have been looking for me as their deliverer from accursed bondage." It did not happen.[27]

Despite his achievements, Brown was restive in the 10th Kentucky Cavalry. Perhaps Brown found that regiment to be insufficiently active in seeking out engagements; perhaps he wanted to command his own regiment. In any event, on April 3, 1863, Colonel Charles J. Walker, commander of the 10th, transmitted Brown's resignation to the division adjutant general. According to Walker, "Maj Brown has heretofore been regarded as an excellent officer, and as far as I have seen, is fully entitled to

Fig. 6.4. John Mason Brown as a major in the 10th Kentucky Cavalry Regiment.
Author's collection.

the reputation. For reasons which, he did not deem proper to state in the enclosed communication, he now offers his resignation. He is 'dissatisfied with' somebody's 'management'(possibly my own) 'of affairs' and is desirous of changing the field of his operations. Though I dislike to loose Maj Brown's services whilst, my Regt is in its present crippled condition, . . . Maj B's longer continuance, especially whilst he remains in his present state of mind, can be conducive of but little good." An undated, unsigned endorsement directed Brown to be detached from the 10th and ordered to report to the Governor of Kentucky. On August 3, 1863, Brown wrote to Major General Ambrose Burnside, noting that the governor of Kentucky had designated him to "recruit and Command a Regt of Cavalry" and asking to be detached on that duty. By October 1863, Brown had raised enough recruits to increase what had been a battalion of Kentucky volunteers to a regiment, the 45th Kentucky Mounted Infantry, which was mustered into the United States's service in January 1864 under his command.[28]

Brown may have been looking forward to the challenges of leading a regiment into battle. One of his first tasks as a colonel, however, in January 1864, was to forward to Captain W. P. Anderson, assistant adjutant-general of the Department of Ohio, charges against a major in the new regiment for being drunk on duty and conduct unbecoming an officer and a gentleman, "in that he did grossly insult an unprotected female using towards her words and actions of the most obscene and disgraceful character." The major was dishonorably discharged. A letter from the same W.P. Anderson to an army chief of staff in February 1864 records a greater role for Brown, fighting against the Confederate guerrillas who were looting and terrorizing eastern Kentucky. Anderson wrote "the guerrillas are very troublesome, murdering Union men every day, and continually running off stock. Within the last two weeks, Col. J. M. Brown, 45th Kentucky, stationed at Mount Sterling, has killed upward of 30 of these guerrillas, and taken 22 prisoners; he has been very energetic. Five of the guerrillas sent in by him were captured immediately after having murdered one Union man and while in the act of hanging another."[29]

The main achievement of the 45th, under Brown, was its role in defeating the cavalry and foot soldiers commanded by John Hunt Morgan, the celebrated Confederate raider, and driving those forces out of Kentucky in June 1864. In May of that year, Brown was in charge of a brigade including the 45th that was en route to the Virginia border as part of an expedition led by General Stephen G. Burbridge, who commanded the District of Kentucky, to attack the salt works and lead operations in southwestern Virginia. The targets were important ones. The salt works produced over half of the Confederacy's salt, and the Wytheville lead mines yielded up to 150,000 pounds of lead per month.[30] In early June, Brown learned from one of his scouts that Morgan, who was from Lexington and who had raided Kentucky repeatedly before, had once again invaded Kentucky. Morgan intended to sever the railroad connecting Lexington and Cincinnati and then disable the Louisville & Nashville Railroad. As Morgan's force moved toward Mount Sterling, Brown turned his brigade back to pursue Morgan, sending a courier to inform General Burbridge while Brown pushed his men and horses as fast as they could go to surprise Morgan. As Brown put it, "The march conducted in this way was very exhausting both upon men and horses—The labor necessary to prevent information getting ahead of my column was of a kind that taxed both the sagacity and endurance of my officers and men to the utmost. It was performed however with unvarying thoroughness and alacrity." By the night of June 7, Brown "found the trail of Morgan's entire force. From this point I made frequent captures of stragglers but strictly prohibited any firing, intending to surprise the Enemy if possible." On June 8, Brown's careful scouting of a formidable pass showed it to be "entirely unguarded," which convinced him that "the Enemy was entirely ignorant of our pursuit." That made Brown believe that his men and the rest of Burbridge's division might be able to surprise Morgan's forces at Mount Sterling. Brown rode back to tell Burbridge, who "at once resolved on an attack," led by Brown's brigade, the unit that was closest to Morgan's men.

Morgan captured Mount Sterling on June 8 and moved on with part of his men to take Lexington, leaving troops behind to hold Mount Sterling, destroy Union supplies, and look for fresh horses. Early in the morning of June 9, Brown's brigade, augmented by the 11th Michigan Cavalry, charged through the rebel camp at Mount Sterling. "The enemy were completely surprised," Brown later reported. "All their pickets killed before they could reach their camp and the infantry completely routed with great slaughter." Burbridge's forces and Brown's brigade overran the Confederates at Mount Sterling. Morgan, with horses from Lexington, rode for Georgetown and on to Cynthiana. Morgan's men took and largely burned Cynthiana on June 11 and captured thirteen hundred Union troops under General Edward Henry Hobson. On June 12, Burbridge's forces, including Brown and the 45th, stormed the Confederate troops near Cynthiana, killing and capturing many of Morgan's men and freeing the Union troops Morgan's men had taken captive. A remnant of Morgan's invading force straggled back to Virginia.[31]

The 45th continued fighting, notably as part of an operation into southwestern Virginia that destroyed the salt works, the lead works, and the ordnance stores there, before being mustered out in December 1864 and February 1865. Brown also continued to be involved in continuing efforts to quash pro-Confederate guerilla attacks on Union troops and Union supporters in Kentucky. In August, when Brown was commanding the 3rd Brigade, he was advised by headquarters of the First Division that he would be "fully sustained by the Gen'l [N. C. McLean] in carrying out the order of Gen'l Sherman in regard to guerila's Viz. 'treat them as wild beasts.'" Brown was directed "to shoot well-known guerillas any where and at any time and will be doing a service to the citizens and the army by this course."[32]

On November 8, 1864, Americans voted for president. Brown was part of a widespread effort by the Union military to get out the vote for Lincoln's re-election. Headquarters of Kentucky's First Division—the same headquarters that had directed Brown to shoot secessionist guerrillas—on November 4 directed him to report "at once" how many soldiers from the 45th Kentucky wanted to vote, and on November 5 he wrote: "The General Commanding directs that the officers and men of your Command who desire to vote at the approaching Presidential Election march to Sanderville Precinct by 10 oclock am on the day of Election & there record their votes—Officers must accompany their men & be held responsible for their good conduct." Nationwide, the effort paid off: Union soldiers gave Lincoln over 70% of their vote. Brown also, through the governor of Kentucky, sought permission to organize a regiment of veteran Kentucky troops so that the state could be represented in the First Army Corps, but the War Department in December wrote the governor that the regulations under which the First Corps was organizing did not "contemplate recruitment by regiments raised in the respective states."[33] Brown was mustered out of service on December 24, 1864.

After the war, Brown went back to the practice of law, first in Frankfort, then in Lexington, and from 1873 on in Louisville. He flourished as a lawyer. He studied and wrote history, especially Kentucky history, and in 1884, he became one of the founders of The Filson Club (now The Filson Historical Society), a Kentucky-focused historical society in Louisville. Brown kept up his language skills, grilling his children in Latin and Greek, keeping up his French, learning Spanish so as to be able to translate documents about Spain's efforts to win over Kentucky before it became a state, even wrestling with Mayan hieroglyphics and learning some Arabic. He also was active in politics. He was a strong supporter of the Republican Party, although he lived, as his son put it, "in a state that was overwhelmingly committed to a contrary political belief." Some have said that Kentucky joined the Confederacy after the Civil War was over. It is true that both houses of its legislature in 1865 voted against ratifying the Thirteenth Amendment that abolished slavery and that Kentucky voted with the Southern Democrats for decades after the war. Brown, in the meantime, campaigned for Republican candidates, among them his long-time friend Benjamin Harrison of Indiana. After Harrison was elected in 1888, Brown went so far as to send to him in the White House his own cook, whom Brown's son described as "a family treasure beyond price." Brown's combination of legal skills and Republican loyalty probably were factors that led him to be a leading candidate for the United States Supreme Court when he died of pneumonia on January 29, 1890, at the age of 52. Brown's strong Republican leanings, however, did not bar him from marrying, in November 1869, his cousin Mary Owen Preston, the daughter of General William Preston, C.S.A., a Kentuckian who fought for the South in some of the bloodiest battles in Mississippi and Tennessee.[34]

7

Travels of an English Pistol

In October 1861, while John Mason Brown was between his two long trips to Indian country, his relative and fellow Kentuckian William Preston joined the Confederate army. Preston, who had been a lieutenant colonel in the Mexican War, a U.S. congressman, and the United States minister to Spain, served the South first as a colonel and then as a general, fighting at the crucial battles of Shiloh and Chickamauga. My father gave me Preston's revolver (see figure 7.1), which he had been given by Preston's grandson General Preston Brown. The pistol, a British-made Adams revolver from the 1850s, calls to my mind Preston's pugnacity, the Southern code of honor, how the Confederacy at Shiloh lost its best chance to win a decisive battle in the West, and how relative fought relative in the Border States during the Civil War.[1]

General William Preston was a grandson of Colonel William Preston, who had played a leading role in opening up Kentucky to American settlers before and during the Revolution.[2] Primarily as a result of the large tracts of land in Kentucky surveyed for and claimed by his grandfather, General Preston and other descendants of Colonel William Preston were among the largest landowners in Kentucky. In the words of General Preston's biographer Peter J. Sehlinger, "the Kentucky frontier was never a democratic one, as the early landowners occupied large tracts of the most valuable land."[3] General Preston's father, Major William Preston, who, as a captain in the United States Army, had taken part in the army's decisive victory over a coalition of Indian forces at the Battle of Fallen Timbers in

Fig. 7.1. Deane Adams and the Deane 5 shot .44/.450 caliber double-action percussion revolver. *Photograph courtesy of Reed Radcliffe.*

northwestern Ohio in 1794, had moved with his family in 1814 from his plantation in western Virginia to develop a large plantation he owned at Middletown, east of Louisville, and to build a home on a thousand-acre tract, then just east of Louisville, that had belonged to Colonel William Preston and that became known as the Preston Plantation. There, the William Preston who was to become a Confederate general was born on October 16, 1816, the seventh of eight children. His father the major died in 1821. Young Preston became the sole male in the family in 1827, when his only brother was killed by a fall from a horse.[4]

William Preston grew up quickly in a family that was rich in land and connected by kinship or marriage with many of the other leading families in Kentucky, including the Breckinridges, Wickliffes, and Browns. His mother, Caroline Hancock Preston, saw to it that he was well educated, first at Augusta College and St. Joseph's College in Kentucky and then studying Latin and Greek classics at Yale and law at Harvard. He often spent far more than his allowance, in part on gambling, and went to rounds of dances and dinner parties in Boston, Louisville, and Washington, developing an eye both for the looks and for the fortunes of young ladies. Writing to his sister Susan of a dinner party at the White House in December 1839 with President Van Buren and twenty guests, Preston said he was taken by a "very pretty belle" who was "worth some $250,000. Can she be otherwise than irresistible?"[5] Preston himself was well equipped to flirt. He was six feet tall—tall for those days. Contemporaries described him as "a powerfully built man," "well proportioned" and of "magnificent personal appearance." He had not yet developed the thinning hair that caused him in later years to comb his remaining hair carefully over his increasing baldness.[6]

On December 9, 1840, one year after his pleasant dinner at the White House, Preston, aged 24, married his remote cousin Margaret Preston Wickliffe. She had been remarkably well educated in private academies in Lexington (where one of her classmates was Mary Todd, Abraham Lincoln's future wife, who considered Margaret to be "the best friend of my earlier days") and in Mme. Sigoigne's school for young ladies in Philadelphia. Margaret was nearly as tall as Preston and strikingly good-looking, in a well-rounded way. Preston found in her "the most charming en bon point imaginable, the freshest and most delicate complexion, the fullest and finest development of a person." She was not made less attractive by being the daughter of Robert Wickliffe, Sr., known as the "Old Duke," one of the richest men in Kentucky, an outstandingly successful real estate lawyer and the state's largest slaveholder, who in 1839 owned 180 slaves valued at $73,000 (about $1.5 million in 2010 dollars). Wickliffe gave Preston, as a wedding present, 300 acres of land in Jefferson County (the county in which Louisville sits).[7]

Preston's net worth grew as the value of his real estate holdings in or around Louisville soared with Louisville's growth. Preston's grandfather Colonel William Preston and his surveyor John Floyd had chosen wisely by laying claim to land near what was to become Louisville, as the Preston family did by adding on to their holdings in that region. The site's future commercial importance was clear from its location just southeast of the Falls of the Ohio, the only impediment to shipping on the Ohio River's long journey from Pittsburgh to the Mississippi. Before a canal with locks was built around the falls, freight had to be handled and transshipped in or close to Louisville. The building of a canal and locks in the 1820s enabled year-round navigation around the falls, increasing the commerce that passed by or was shipped out of Louisville. The town's population, only 1,600 when Preston was born in 1816, rose to 4,000 in 1821, more than 10,300 in 1830, over 21,300 in 1840, and 43,000 in 1850, when

Louisville was the tenth most populous city in the United States. The city limits also expanded, growing in 1827 to include much of the Preston land that had been east of Louisville. The city's growth increased real estate values, enabling Preston's widowed mother, as early as the 1820s, and later, William Preston and his wife to generate large amounts of income by selling or leasing lots subdivided from their land.[8]

Preston was admitted to the Kentucky bar in 1839. He devoted most of his efforts as a lawyer to matters involving land claimed by him or his family and social connections. One of his closest connections, although 23 years older than him, was Albert Sidney Johnston, a Kentuckian by birth, who married Preston's oldest sister Henrietta in 1829. Johnston, a West Point graduate, resigned his U.S. Army commission after eight years of service and moved in 1836 to Texas, then an independent republic, where he became the commander in chief of the Texas army (in the process fighting a duel with a rival claimant to the post, during which Johnston was badly wounded in the right hip) and then the republic's secretary of war. By 1839, Preston, then in his early 20s, knew Johnston well enough to borrow money from him to pay some of the gambling debts Preston had run up at Yale and Harvard, and to write to him grandly, after being admitted to the bar, that "my fortune is sufficiently large to supersed the necessity of severe professional exertion at the present time." Preston also asked Johnston's help in being named to a diplomatic mission from Texas to Paris—saying that he was willing to become a citizen of Texas, because he never intended "to let an unvalued adherence to my own country interfere with my prosperity in another."[9]

As with many well-born antebellum Southerners, Preston was under sustained pressure from his close female relatives to bring honor and glory to the family. "The eyes of many are on you," his mother wrote him. His younger sister Susan—to whom he was extremely close—urged him to "do credit to our family." His older sister Henrietta, when he was 16, reminded him, "You have received a rich inheritance of all the manly virtues from your honorable father." His wife, during the Mexican War, was to remind him that since 1753 his paternal ancestors "had taken part in every war the country has been engaged in"; to urge him to garner "some military glory to bequeath to your children"; and to warn him not to return "Disgraced and Degraded—Great God—Death, anything but that." She wrote him forthrightly: "If you distinguish yourself, the future seems all too bright—If the reverse, I have nothing to hope for in life."[10]

Preston did seek to garner honor, as well as money. His accumulation of wealth depended in large part on the fruits of slavery and on the value of slaves. By 1840, he had 14 slaves—less than a tenth of the number held by his father-in-law, but sizable by Kentucky standards. Preston viewed slaves as chattels. At the 1849 Kentucky convention to consider a revision in the state's constitution, he proclaimed: "If a difference exist between slaves and other property, I defy any man to show the difference." In 1853, he spoke of the need to hold Africans "in bondage, because we prefer that their untutored labor should be directed by the superior intelligence of our race to useful industry."[11]

Preston also sought honor in traditional ways: military office and political position. In May 1846, after the United States Congress overwhelmingly approved the declaration of a state of war with Mexico, Preston, who captained a company of volunteers in the Louisville Legion, led a successful effort to raise $50,000 to transport troops from Kentucky to Mexico. Apart from patriotic fervor, Preston was presumably motivated by his interest as a slave owner in protecting slavery by preserving Texas (which had become a state in December 1845) as part of the United States, because Texas permitted slavery and its statehood helped offset the political power of antislavery northern states. Moreover, Preston owned land in Texas, acquired in 1841 (some in South Texas, bought with Albert Sidney Johnston's help), and had an interest in a huge tract of twelve thousand square miles just north of where Dallas was built. Preston also believed that America needed to acquire Mexican land from Texas to California so it could build railroads linking Kentucky to the Pacific. Most other Kentuckians enthusiastically supported the war effort. More than ten thousand volunteers sought to fill the twenty-five hundred places in the three regiments President Polk had asked Kentucky's governor to raise to fight Mexico. Preston was not in this first wave of soldiers from Kentucky. He was mustered into service in October 1847, when the Louisville Legion, in which Preston had become a lieutenant colonel, was incorporated into the Fourth Regiment of Kentucky Volunteers, which did not land in Veracruz until November 19, 1847, two months after the U.S. Army under General Winfield Scott had captured Mexico City.

So Preston's Mexican War was not a shooting war. Instead of fighting, Preston, at his wife's suggestion, kept a "Journal in Mexico," which he filled with writing as lush as the tropical vegetation and birds he noted in it, or as the interior of Puebla's cathedral, which he found "richly decorated with the gorgeous, but barbaric taste manifested in the ecclesiastical edifices throughout Mexico." He became convinced that the lowering of "the barriers which separated the races" in Mexico had caused "the horrid results of a debased, amalgamated race." During his five months in Mexico City, where he was waited on by two slaves he had brought from Kentucky, he attended bullfights, the opera, and the ballet. More relevant to his future career was his election to membership in the Aztec Club, a group of American army officers that included many who would become famous generals in the Civil War—among them Robert E. Lee, Ulysses S. Grant, Joseph E. Johnston, Joseph Hooker, and George B. McClellan.[12]

The war ended in February 1848 with the signing of the Treaty of Guadalupe Hidalgo. By July 1848, Preston was back in Louisville and out of the army. He turned to politics and was elected as a Whig in Kentucky's 1849 constitutional convention, then to the state general assembly in 1850 and the state senate the following year, and to the U.S. Congress in 1853. He was consistently pro-slavery. When Congressman Gerritt Smith of New York (later a principal supporter of John Brown, leader of the Harpers Ferry raid) spoke in December 1853 in support of abolition, Preston, in a speech later widely circulated as a pamphlet, defended slavery as part of the natural hierarchy of humanity. "Slavery," he said, "seems to be the price that ignorance pays to intelligence for its tuition in the arts of civilization." In 1854, Preston worked hard in support of Senator Stephen A. Douglas's bill, which became the Kansas-Nebraska Act, permitting the settlers in Kansas and Nebraska to decide whether or not to permit slavery. In effect, the act repealed the Missouri Compromise of 1820, which had prohibited slavery north of latitude 36°30′. The result was that Kansas became a bloody battleground, as pro-and anti-slavery factions fought for control of the territory.[13] Preston as congressman also successfully lobbied Jefferson Davis, then secretary of war, to promote Albert Sidney Johnston from major to colonel.[14]

Politics in Kentucky was often violent in Preston's day. During the campaigning for delegates to the 1849 constitutional convention, when feelings were already running high on the issue of slavery, Cyrus Turner, the son of a pro-slavery candidate in Madison County, infuriated at an abolitionist speech made by Cassius M. Clay at a meeting not far from Lexington, lunged at and stabbed Clay. Another relative of the pro-slavery candidate put a pistol to Clay's head and pulled the trigger several times, but the percussion caps did not fire. Clay, a noted fighter with a Bowie knife, stabbed Turner fatally in the abdomen.[15] In 1855, Preston faced a bitter fight for re-election against Humphrey Marshall, candidate of the Know-Nothing or American Party, which opposed foreign immigration and the voting rights of foreign immigrants, including the large numbers of German and Irish Roman Catholic immigrants in Louisville. Preston, for all his racist sentiments about African Americans, was not anti-immigrant or anti-Catholic, having attended a Catholic school and having sold or rented many properties to German and Irish immigrants who were Catholics. On election day, August 6, 1855—a day marked by so much violence it became known in Louisville as "Bloody Monday"—American Party operatives took control of polling places in predominantly German American and Irish American precincts and permitted only voters displaying the Know-Nothing ticket to vote. Preston went from voting station to voting station encouraging the foreign-born to vote. At one polling place, a man threatened Preston with a pistol, which Preston kicked out of his hand. On the same day, Know-Nothings set fire to a number of houses of German Americans and a brewery in Louisville's East End, killing 10 German Americans. Nativists also burned houses in an Irish district and killed a Catholic priest. Preston was soundly defeated by Marshall.[16]

Ousted from Congress, Preston and his family moved back from Washington to Louisville. The Whig party was dead, shattered by the split over slavery. Preston joined the Democratic Party and in 1856, as a delegate to the Democratic National Convention in Cincinnati, played a large role in the choice of James Buchanan of Pennsylvania as the Democrats' presidential candidate and of Preston's cousin John C. Breckinridge as the vice presidential candidate. Preston campaigned for Buchanan in several states, and the Buchanan-Breckinridge ticket was elected. The violence associated with Louisville politics continued. In 1857, when a Democrat-backed candidate was running against a Know-Nothing for an appellate judicial position, Preston went, with the Democrats' candidate, to observe

the voting in a largely German American ward. Preston and a Know-
Nothing supporter yelled insults, shoved, and pointed their pistols at each
other. I like to think Preston's pistol was the one my father gave me. The
Know-Nothings pressed charges against Preston for carrying a concealed
weapon and drawing his pistol inside the polls, but the case was dismissed
after the jury failed to reach a verdict.[17]

In 1858, President Buchanan appointed Preston United States envoy
extraordinary and minister plenipotentiary to Spain. Apart from wanting
to repay Preston for his help in the 1856 election, Buchanan knew that
Preston favored America's acquiring Cuba from Spain. Buchanan sought
the same objective, partly because of his belief in Anglo-Saxon superiority
and partly because he thought that building an American empire would
reduce the growing sectional tension in the United States over slavery.
General Winfield Scott predicted to Margaret Preston that if Cuba became
an American colony, Preston could become secretary of state. Preston's
wife, who was not moderate in her aspirations, believed that the ministry
to Madrid would help her husband to become president.[18]

Many in America—including Buchanan—had been backing an
American acquisition of Cuba for years, without success. In 1848, Spain
declined an offer by Buchanan, then secretary of state under President
Polk, of $100 million for the island. In 1851, 150 Kentuckians volunteered
to support the efforts of a Venezuelan-born filibuster to seize Cuba by force.
The Spanish captured the invaders and executed 51 of the Kentuckians.
In 1854, Buchanan, then American minister to Great Britain, joined with
two other Democrats, the ministers to France and Spain, in the Ostend
Manifesto, which urged the United States to purchase Cuba and strongly
suggested that if Spain did not agree, America would be justified in "wrest-
ing it from Spain." The manifesto accomplished little but to stir up a storm
of protest from Northerners, who saw it as part of a Southern plot to extend
and perpetuate slavery. In 1858, however, Buchanan hoped that Spain, to
help pay off the crushing load of debt it owed to international banking
houses, would be willing to sell Cuba. The hopes of Buchanan and Preston
were shattered, both in Spain and in America, before Preston arrived in
Madrid and presented his credentials to Queen Isabella II on March 13,
1859. The deputies in Spain's legislature, led by a government that used
the threat of an American acquisition of Cuba to build support for their

administration, went on record in December 1858 opposing any discussion of ceding Cuba and in January 1859 voted unanimously never to transfer the island. Also in January 1859, soon after the Prestons took ship for Europe, Southern congressmen introduced in the Senate and the House proposals to appropriate funds to buy Cuba. Republicans were outraged, and the proposals were blocked in both houses.[19]

Preston kept hoping that somehow Cuba would become American, but he recognized that "all attempts to buy without ready money would be idle, and as Congress has not thought to grant that, any attempt to negotiate would be useless." Instead, the Prestons devoted themselves to extravagant entertaining and to fixing up the house they leased, until by 1861, Preston was able to boast that it "is now very handsome and by far the most comfortable in Madrid." He bought a gold table service after Margaret wrote that she would be "humiliated" if he did not do so. The lavish entertainment increased the Prestons' girth. Preston became a full-figured man. Margaret, whom Preston in 1840 had found to have "the most charming en bon point imaginable," was described in 1860 by an acquaintance as "immensely large."

After Lincoln was elected, Preston submitted, in January 1861, a letter of resignation, dated March 5, a day after Lincoln was to be sworn in. In February 1861, Preston reported with pride that "the Queen thanked me on behalf of the society here for the addition we had made to the social engagements of her capital" and assured him of "the universal esteem that you have acquired and the special regard that my Husband and I always shall have for you." Preston in turn, in his final audience with the queen in May 1861, proclaimed ornately: "The remembrance of the distinguished kindnesses of Your Majesty and of His Majesty the King will accompany me across the Atlantic; and engraved indelibly in my memory, it always will be nurtured by me with effusiveness and affection."[20]

How special was the queen's regard for William Preston, and what sorts of queenly kindnesses were engraved in his memory? A photograph of Isabella II from William Preston's album shows a dumpy, plump-armed lady, with a physique resembling that of Margaret Preston's friend Mary Todd Lincoln. But Preston had found Margaret's "en bon point" to be "charming," and by now Margaret, who was eleven years older than Isabella, was "immensely large." Isabella, who had not turned thirty when Preston met her, may have looked good in comparison with Margaret. A German diplomat in Spain said of Isabella in 1854: "Without being handsome, she is certainly a fine looking woman, and though very large for her age, yet being tall and with a very regal port, carries it off well." Around the time when Preston met her, the Italian historian Marquis Beramendi wrote that he had "never seen any woman more attractive . . . nor any woman who possesses finer qualities for charming the mind," with manners that are "in perfect harmony with her blue, knavish eyes." Moreover, Isabella was a queen, and Preston was impressed by rank and title. For his part, Preston was tall and good-looking ("a notably handsome man, with accomplishments to grace any station," according to a soldier who served under him in the Civil War) and had had a military career of sorts, like many of Isabella's lovers (including, later in her life, American Minister to Spain Dan Sickles, who was a Union general in the American Civil War). Isabella gave birth to 12 children, even though her husband, her double first cousin Francisco de Asís de Borbón, was reputedly impotent, homosexual, or both. One of Isabella's biographers reported that Francisco and Isabel both "burst into tears when declared man and wife." As Isabella said years after her arranged marriage to Don Francisco, which took place when she was only 16: "what shall I say of a man who on his wedding night wore more lace than I?" Isabella turned elsewhere for lovers and fathers of her children. Did Preston sire any of them? I have no proof of this. Preston's biographer Peter Sehlinger told me he had heard rumors to this effect but had seen no evidence. It is noteworthy, however, that two of Isabella's children were conceived in years when Preston was in Spain: Maria de la Concepción (born December 26, 1859) and Maria de Pilar (born July 4, 1861). In biographies of the queen, I have seen no reports that Preston fathered these children. My only evidence of Preston's paternity of the children is hearsay. When I was a child, my great-aunt Mary Mason Brown Waite, Preston's grand-daughter, came to our apartment for lunch most Sundays. Aunt Mary and my father often exchanged accounts, many of them scurrilous, about the sexual activities of long-dead relatives. I remember one woman was said to have slept with a stable boy, another with a Great Dane. At one point during a Sunday lunch, my father said that William Preston had sired a child by Queen Isabella of Spain. Aunt Mary held up two fingers. "Two," she said, proudly.[21]

By September 1861, Preston was back in Kentucky. In January, he had described South Carolina's movement to secede as a "wild and immeasurable remedy," but after the shelling and surrender of Fort Sumter in April 1861, he was convinced that separation of North and South was inevitable and that "a great struggle is upon us." Union supporters in control of Kentucky's general assembly declared Kentucky's allegiance to the North, while pro-Confederate troops controlled western Kentucky under the command of General Simon Bolivar Buckner, whose headquarters were in Bowling Green. Preston and his cousin John C. Breckinridge decided to join the Confederate army. On November 3, Preston was made a colonel. His brother-in-law Albert Sidney Johnston, commander of the South's sprawling Confederate Department Number Two (extending from the Appalachian Mountains in the east to the Indian Territory in the west), made Preston his "volunteer aide-de-camp to the General commanding." Later that month, the Confederate Sovereignty Convention, with representatives from 65 Kentucky counties, passed an Act of Secession and appointed Preston and two others as commissioners to go to Richmond and seek Kentucky's admission to the Confederacy. This the Confederate Congress approved in December 1861. That act proved meaningless, however, since Confederate forces soon withdrew from Kentucky, and the Southern supporters in Kentucky were unable to form an effective de facto government.[22]

As Lincoln recognized, it was critical that Kentucky not be part of the Confederacy. Lincoln reportedly said "I would like to have God on my side—but I must have Kentucky." Kentucky's importance came in part from geography. Northern Kentucky bordered much of the Ohio River, through which goods were carried from the Alleghenies to the Mississippi. In Western Kentucky, two key rivers flowed into the Ohio—the Cumberland, which flowed through much of northern Tennessee before turning north into Kentucky, and the Tennessee, which rose in Tennessee and flowed west through northern Alabama before turning north through Tennessee into Kentucky. To control the mouths of these two rivers was to control much of access to Tennessee and northern Alabama. Part of Kentucky's importance was fear of a domino effect. If the large and populous state of Kentucky went with the Confederacy, wouldn't the other Border States be likely to follow? Lincoln wrote a friend in September 1861: "I think to lose Kentucky is nearly the same as to lose the whole game. Kentucky gone, we cannot hold Missouri, nor, as I think, Maryland. These all against us, and the job on our hands is too large for us. We would as well consent to separation at once. Including the surrender of the capital."[23]

In May and June 1861, the Confederacy, recognizing the importance of controlling access to the Tennessee and Cumberland rivers, built forts in northern Tennessee near the Kentucky border—Fort Henry on the Tennessee, Fort Donelson on the Cumberland. On February 6, 1862, Brigadier General Ulysses S. Grant and a strong U.S. Navy force of ironclads and timberclads captured Fort Henry. Grant and the U.S. Navy then turned to Fort Donelson. After commanding Confederate general John B. Floyd (who had been secretary of war under President Buchanan) seized the only available steamboat and fled, the remaining Confederate forces—at least twelve thousand men—surrendered Fort Donelson to Grant on February 16.[24] With the two key forts in Union possession, U.S. ships were able to push up both rivers. Grant and the U.S. Navy began to move their forces south on the Tennessee River, to the little hamlet of Pittsburg Landing in southwestern Tennessee. Flanked, General Johnston pulled the Confederate forces out of Kentucky and out of most of Tennessee, gathering many of his troops at the key railroad junction town of Corinth, in northeastern Mississippi—perhaps fifty miles south of Pittsburg Landing. If the Confederacy lost Corinth, the Union could block rail traffic both on the east-west line between Memphis and Charleston and on the north-south Mobile and Ohio line. Corinth was, as Grant said, "the great strategic position at the West between the Tennessee and the Mississippi and between Nashville and Vicksburg."[25]

Within a few months, the Confederacy had lost control of vital areas under Johnston's overall command—including western Kentucky and Tennessee. Johnston, a fine-looking man who had led the army of the Republic of Texas and served with distinction in the Mexican War, had been hailed as the Confederacy's finest general when he was appointed to his command. He now came under vituperative attack from Southern newspapers and politicians who blamed him for the Confederate losses of territory.[26] Johnston saw an opportunity to recoup his command's reverses when his men were joined at Corinth by tens of thousands of other southern troops, including about ten thousand men sent from Pensacola, Florida, under General Braxton Bragg and thousands of troops assembled from west

Tennessee and elsewhere by General Pierre Gustave Toutant Beauregard, West Pointer, veteran of the Mexican War, and hero of the Confederate victory at Manassas (the first battle of Bull Run). Together, the Southern forces assembled at Corinth by the beginning of April nearly equaled in number the Union troops under Grant at Pittsburg Landing. Johnston, like the Confederacy's President Jefferson Davis, believed that the South's best chance to repel the Union drive in the west was to attack Grant's men before they could be joined by another Union army—some eighteen thousand men under General Don Carlos Buell, who were marching to Pittsburg Landing from Central Tennessee.

On April 3, Johnston gave the gathered Confederates the order to march to attack the Union forces near Pittsburg Landing and issued a circular to encourage his men: "I have put you in motion to offer battle to the invaders of your country. With the resolution and disciplined valor becoming men fighting, as you are, for all worth living or dying for, you can but march to a decisive victory over agrarian mercenaries, sent to subjugate and despoil you of your liberties, property, and honor. . . . Remember the dependence of your mothers, your wives, your sisters, and our children on the result."[27]

Although the march was slow, by the night of April 5, Johnston's troops were within two miles of Grant's men. The war was still young, and many on either side were ill-trained and inexperienced—but the numbers on both sides meant that the clash was by far the largest up until that time in the Civil War, involving close to fifty thousand Union troops under Grant (not counting the eighteen thousand under Buell), and more than forty-four thousand Southern soldiers in Johnston's Army of the Mississippi. If the Confederate advance was ill coordinated, at least the Southern troops knew they were to attack the Northern troops. The Union forces were dispersed, without adequate pickets and scouts before them, with minimal warning that a Confederate attack was imminent, and with little or no protective entrenchments or fortifications. Grant later admitted he had believed that the Federal army was engaged in an offensive campaign and "had no idea that the enemy would leave strong entrenchments to take the initiative when he knew that he would be attacked where he was if he remained." Even after skirmishing began before the battle, Grant did not believe that the Confederates "intended to make a determined attack, but simply that they were making a reconnaissance in force."[28]

Many of the Union troops were scattered about Shiloh Church, a small log cabin Methodist church about three miles southeast of Pittsburg Landing, on the road from Corinth. The ensuing battle (though some-times referred to as Pittsburg Landing) is most commonly known as Shiloh, after the church. Shiloh was hardly a warlike name. It recurs in the Old Testament—among other things, as a town that for a long time was the seat of the tabernacle, a center of Israelite worship, and where the Lord spoke to young Samuel. Some think "Shiloh" is a Hebrew word referring to Peace, or Place of Peace, but the etymology is obscure.[29]

Nothing was peaceful about what happened near Shiloh Church on April 6 and 7. Fighting started at 5:00 AM on April 6, when a Union reconnaissance patrol encountered Missouri infantry. Johnston ordered a general advance for 6:30 AM, and the Confederate army charged largely unopposed through the Union tents. Although there had been reports of Rebel troops nearby, they had been disregarded. "My God, we are attacked!" Brigadier General William Tecumseh Sherman reportedly said when he saw the glistening bayonets of masses of Rebel infantry advanc-ing on a Union camp. Johnston, who had ordered Beauregard to stay in the rear and steer Confederate troops to the front, led his men, riding his horse Fire Eater back and forth along the Confederate line. By 2:00 PM, the Southern troops were faltering in the face of heavy resistance, including a determined Union line with ample artillery support in a place that came to be known as the Hornets' Nest (see map 7.1). Johnston rallied tired regi-ments to charge by leading them himself, and the men carried the Federal position in front of them. Johnston fell back. In the charge, Fire Eater was wounded, and a bullet tore the sole off one of Johnson's boots. Around 2:30 PM, Governor Isham Harris of Tennessee saw Johnston almost alone, reeling in his saddle. Asked if he were wounded, Johnston said, "Yes, and I fear seriously." Harris and others led Fire Eater to a sheltered ravine, helped Johnston dismount, and looked for the wound. Preston, coming to the scene with other staff members, knelt and supported Johnston's head in his arms. "Johnston, do you know me?" Preston cried. Johnston "smiled faintly, but gave no other sign of recognition." Preston called for whis-key. A captain tried to pour some bourbon down Johnston's throat, but he couldn't swallow it. Within minutes he died from loss of blood. A minié ball had ripped into an artery below his right knee. It may be that Johnston

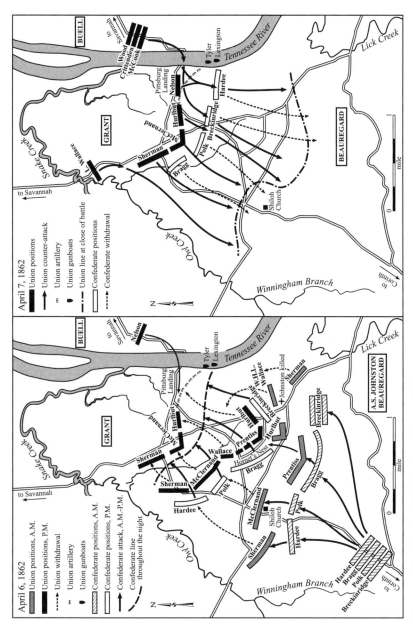

Map 7.1. The Battle of Shiloh, April 6–7, 1862

was not immediately aware of the seriousness of the wound, because the ball had struck Johnston's right leg, which had been numbed by a bullet wound to a nerve some years before in the duel Johnston had fought in Texas. Neither Preston nor any of the others thought to apply a tourniquet to stop the loss of blood—even though Johnston had a tourniquet in his pocket.[30]

Preston recorded in his diary that he wrote to Beauregard, "instantly informing him" of Johnston's death "at the moment of victory, after routing the enemy at every point" and "that the completion of the victory would devolve upon him." Beauregard pressed forward as the afternoon continued, but his men were exhausted and had borne heavy casualties, the fire from the Union artillery and the big guns on the Union timberclads was heavy, and the Confederates had been fighting since early morning. Some Southern units began to retreat without any orders to do so. The Hornets' Nest had finally been taken around five PM; twenty-two hundred Northern soldiers were captured. The battered Union troops had been driven back all along the line, and Beauregard hoped they would all go down to Pittsburg Landing, board boats, and leave. Around six o'clock, Beauregard ordered the troops to discontinue the attack and fall back from the enemy guns. That evening, he sent a telegram off to Richmond, reporting: "We this morning attacked the enemy in strong position . . . and after a severe battle of ten hours, thanks to the Almighty, we gained a complete victory, driving the enemy from every position." Beauregard told Preston, with other members of Johnston's staff, to take Johnston's body to New Orleans.[31]

But the battle was not over. Grant and his men had been strengthening the Union position throughout the afternoon, and by five PM, the first units of Buell's army had arrived. The Union artillery and the heavy Navy guns kept up a deafening barrage of shells throughout the night. According to a Union infantryman, "The terrible shrieking of the large navy shells had a demoralizing effect upon the enemy, causing him to change his position several times during the night, besides depriving him of much needed sleep and rest; while it was soul-stirring music to our ears." Rebel soldiers recorded the effect of the guns. One wrote in his diary: "the gunboats' horror has seized on both men and officers." During the rainy night, Sherman said to Grant, who was chewing on a cigar, "We've had the devil's own day, haven't we?" "Yes," Grant said, "lick 'em tomorrow, though." Grant acted on his belief "that a great moral advantage would be gained by becoming the attacking party." When day broke, the Union army, over forty thousand strong and buttressed by fresh reinforcements, including some five thousand under General Lew Wallace and more than ten thousand of Buell's troops, attacked perhaps half as many ill-prepared Confederates, who gave ground until they were able to stabilize a line around eight AM Despite numerous bloody counterattacks, Grant's army pushed ahead. About 2:30 PM, Beauregard, to save what was left of his army, ordered a retreat back to Corinth. After a charge organized by Grant around three o'clock, the retreat became a chaotic rout, although Grant's troops were too fatigued from two days' hard fighting to pursue them.[32]

Beauregard left behind him a stinking battlefield of corpses and wounded men. Grant was to call Shiloh "the severest battle fought at the West during the war" and to remember a field recaptured by his army the second day "over which the Confederates had made repeated charges the day before, so covered with dead that it would have been possible to walk across the clearing in any direction, stepping on dead bodies, without a foot touching the ground." Sherman wrote his wife describing the wounded and "the piles of dead soldiers' mangled bodies . . . without heads and legs." In all, almost one in four of the roughly 100,000 who fought at Shiloh were killed, wounded, or missing—far more than the casualties in any previous Civil War battle, and more than the total number of casualties in the Revolutionary War, the War of 1812, and the Mexican War combined.[33]

Shiloh was a turning point, as well as a slaughterhouse. In the words of the great Civil War historian Bruce Catton, it was "a battle the Confederacy simply had to win. For it had been a blow struck to restore a disastrously lost balance, a desperate attempt to re-establish the Confederate frontier in the Kentucky-Ohio valley. It had failed." The defeat at Shiloh left the Union army strong in the West and led to the fall of Corinth in May and of Memphis in June. As the New Orleans writer George Washington Cable put it, "The South never smiled again after Shiloh." From the Northern perspective, Shiloh led to the unhappy realization that the war would be long, hard, and bloody. Grant wrote: "Up until the battle of Shiloh I . . . believed that the rebellion against the Government would collapse suddenly and soon, if a decisive victory could be gained over any of [the

Confederate] armies," but after the Confederacy, despite the loss of Forts Donelson and Henry, took the offensive in "such a gallant effort to regain what had been lost, . . . I gave up all idea of saving the Union except by complete conquest."[34]

Would the outcome have been different if Johnston had not died on the afternoon of the first day of the battle—if, for example, William Preston or someone else on Johnston's staff had stopped the loss of blood by applying a tourniquet soon after Johnston had been wounded? Would Johnston have been able to drive Grant's battered forces down to Pittsburg Landing before Buell and Wallace brought fresh strength to the Union forces during the late afternoon and night of April 6? Or, if Johnston had been unable to continue to lead, could Beauregard have beaten Grant if he had continued the fight into the night of April 6, rather than pulling back from the Federal guns? Much ink has been spilled since 1862 exploring these "ifs." Generals Braxton Bragg and Leonidas Polk, along with William Preston and Johnston's son and biographer William Preston Johnston, believed that Johnston would have continued pressing Grant's troops back to the Tennessee River and that Beauregard, by withdrawing, lost a precious opportunity to destroy Grant's army and then defeat Buell's troops. A Confederate private named Sam Watkins remembered vividly how harshly the order to halt sounded on the ears of the Southern soldiers. "What! Halt after today's victory? . . . The victory was complete, but the word 'halt' turned victory into defeat." Others, including Grant himself, believed that the Confederates were totally "fought out" by late afternoon on April 6 and could not have taken the Union position on the bluffs near Pittsburg Landing, given the strength of the shortened Northern lines, the power of the 56 cannon supporting the Federal position, the heavy guns of the timberclads, and the fresh troops (notably Lew Wallace's and the first units from Buell's army) that had already arrived before Beauregard ordered the pullback. Grant did not believe that Johnston "could have done any better under the circumstances" than Beauregard did, there having been no hour of the day when Grant "doubted the eventual defeat of the enemy." But even if Johnston's death did not prevent the South from winning at Shiloh, it did deprive the Confederacy of a leader who might well have been its most effective general in the west, a man Jefferson Davis called the "great pillar of the Confederacy."[35]

Preston kept fighting for the Confederacy after Shiloh. Within two weeks of the battle, on Beauregard's recommendation, he was promoted to brigadier general. He presided over the Rebel rear guard in late May 1862, when the Confederates, faced with an overwhelming Union force, abandoned Corinth. In June, Bragg became commander of the Army of Tennessee, replacing Beauregard. To prevent the Rebels from retreating farther south, Major General Edmund Kirby Smith urged a drive into Kentucky, with the hope that Kentuckians would rally around the Confederate flag. Preston, through his nephew William Preston Johnston, urged Jefferson Davis to support this plan. "I wish to help secure Kentucky forever for the South," Preston wrote Johnston in September 1862—and added his hope for support by the Kentucky aristocrats: "I wish on returning to get the men of influence to espouse our cause and enlist their children in our own ranks." So the Confederates marched into Kentucky, as far north as Lexington and Frankfort. General Bragg, after proclaiming, "Kentuckians! I have entered your state with the Confederate Army of the West and offer you the opportunity to free yourself from the tyranny of a despotic ruler," installed a secessionist as the governor of Kentucky on October 4 in Frankfort. During the South's invasion of the state, the Confederate private Sam Watkins took heart at the warmth of Kentucky's reception: "I remember how gladly the citizens of Kentucky received us. I thought they had the prettiest girls that God ever made. They could not do too much for us. They had heaps and stacks of cooked rations along our route, with wine and cider everywhere, and the glad shouts of 'Hurrah for our Southern boys,' greeted and welcomed us at every house" while "the bands played 'Dixie' and the 'Bonnie Blue Flag.'" "The Kentucky girls made cockades for us, and almost every soldier had one pinned on his hat." Preston was able to see his family in Lexington, and William and Margaret arranged "brilliant festivities" for Generals Bragg and Kirby Smith while they were in Lexington.[36]

The South's deep thrust into Kentucky was short-lived. Only a few hundred Kentuckians joined the Confederate army—far fewer than the number of Confederates lost in the fighting in Kentucky. On October 8, while Preston was with Kirby Smith's army to the north, some fifteen thousand of Bragg's men fought a larger number of Buell's Federals to a bloody standstill near Perryville, not far from Danville—at a cost to each side of

over thirty-four hundred killed, wounded, or missing. "I do not remember
of a harder contest and more evenly fought battle," Sam Watkins was to
write. But the Rebels, not the Yankees, retreated—and soon abandoned
Kentucky, except for occasional raids.[37]

Preston kept fighting for the Confederacy as Bragg's army was forced
farther and farther south. Preston had never warmed to Bragg, a man who
was generally detested by his troops as a tyrant who slaughtered troops by
ordering them to undertake doomed frontal charges against overwhelming Union positions. The fighting in Tennessee increased Preston's dislike
of Bragg to hatred. From December 31, 1862, through January 2, 1863, at
Stones River, just outside of Murfreesboro, Tennessee, Bragg, with some
thirty-five thousand Confederates, tried to block about forty-two thousand
Federals marching south from Nashville under Major General William S.
Rosecrans. On the morning of New Year's Eve, after his brigade "fell into
confusion under a crushing fire," Preston himself "seized the colors and
rode before the line toward the enemy," encouraging his men, who took
a Yankee position (although at the cost of 438 killed or wounded out of a
brigade of 1,951 soldiers). Rosecrans did not retreat, despite large casualties. On January 2, Bragg ordered General John C. Breckinridge's corps,
including Preston's brigade, to take a high ridge manned by a Federal division with 57 cannon—despite Breckinridge's protest that the effort was
doomed to end in failure and a senseless loss of Confederate lives. The
Rebel attack failed, with Preston's brigade suffering another forty-one dead
and 245 wounded. Preston, in his formal report of the action, attributed the
repulse "to the manifest hopelessness of the attempt to hurl a single division, without support, against the cardinal position of the whole hostile
army"—something he said "was apparent to the least intelligent soldier."
In all, the casualties at Murfreesboro (more than thirteen thousand for the
Union and more than ten thousand for the Confederacy) were higher in
percentage of troops engaged than at any other major battle of the Civil
War. Preston described Murfreesboro as a "concentrated Shiloh, with
shorter rushes, and bloodier struggles, and the same results." In a letter to
William Preston Johnston, he described "the winter scene, the frost, the
dead and dying" as a stark memento mori, "wild enough for a Banquet
of Ghouls." As at Shiloh, Southern advances were ultimately followed
by retreat. Starting on January 3, Bragg began to move his army south,

to Tullahoma, Tennessee. Because of the ill will against Bragg borne by Preston and his cousin Breckinridge, Jefferson Davis removed the two Kentucky generals from Bragg's command.[38]

Preston was given command of a brigade in southwestern Virginia, in an army commanded by Simon B. Buckner. Nevertheless, in September 1863, Preston fought another bloody battle under Braxton Bragg—the battle of Chickamauga. In the late summer of 1863, Bragg had decided to launch an offensive to block the Union drive under Rosecrans to take Chattanooga, a major rail center. Bruckner's corps (including Preston) was sent to join Bragg's Army of Tennessee. In September, Bragg gathered his forces along Chickamauga Creek, in northern Georgia, twelve miles south of Chattanooga. About sixty-six thousand Confederate troops faced more than fifty-eight thousand Federal men. Once again, the Rebel troops initially broke the Union lines, but Major General George Thomas formed a new line on the high ridge of Snodgrass Hill, against which Rebel generals sent series of unsuccessful assaults. At the end of the day on September 20, after two Union brigades had abandoned the hill, Preston led a charge against the three remaining Federal regiments. Preston's men captured more than six hundred prisoners. His was a major contribution to a Confederate victory—in that Rosecrans retreated to Chattanooga—but Bragg did not follow up promptly with an attack on the Union forces there, and both sides had suffered losses, second in number only to Gettysburg among the Civil War battles. Preston, who, after Murfreesboro, had called Bragg "unfit for command," after Chickamauga said that Bragg "has a heart of ice and a head of wood" and joined other officers in petitioning Jefferson Davis for Bragg's removal from command. This did not endear Preston to Bragg, who still had the support of Jefferson Davis. Although General Buckner recommended that Preston be promoted to major general as "a simple act of justice" in light of the "skilful and gallant manner in which he conducted [his division] during the recent battle on the Chickamauga," Preston was transferred back to southwestern Virginia for several months.

Chickamauga was Preston's last battle. His Civil War career had been marked by brutal battles (Shiloh, Murfreesboro, Chickamauga) and perilous charges. At Murfreesboro, for example, one of Preston's staff was killed riding beside him; another, severely wounded, fell across Preston's horse, covering him with blood; and the visor of Preston's cap was shattered by a shell fragment. His war had also included amenities unknown to private soldiers, including tablecloths at dinner and trunks full of books, including ones in the Greek and Latin he had enjoyed reading since college.[39]

In January 1864, Preston was named the Confederate minister to Mexico. His mission to Mexico was as quixotic and unsuccessful as his mission to Spain had been. He had hoped that the Hapsburg archduke whom the army of French Emperor Napoleon III had installed as Emperor Maximilian I of Mexico would recognize the Confederate States of America as an independent nation and thus reduce the threat that the Southern states posed to Mexico. However, in light of the Union's growing strength and its string of victories over the Confederates, it made no sense for Maximilian or for Napoleon III to alienate the North by recognizing the Confederacy, as recognition could well be viewed by Lincoln's government as equivalent to a declaration of war against the United States. In April 1865, Preston sailed to the Rio Grande and joined with General Kirby Smith, who commanded the Confederacy's Trans-Mississippi Department. Smith promoted Brown from brigadier general to major general (see figure 7.2 for a portrait of Brown in two-star uniform)—but there was no longer a Confederate government in Richmond to confirm or disapprove the promotion. Although Lee had surrendered to Grant at Appomattox on April 9, the Trans-Mississippi southerners were determined to continue the fight. The soldiers themselves, however, were deserting and going home, and some mutinied. On June 2, Smith signed a surrender agreement, laying down the arms of the last Confederate army.[40]

The Civil War was over. The Prestons (like many ex-Confederates) found it opportune to move for a time to Canada. They returned only after Preston's parole had been approved by the attorney general (James Speed, a friend of Preston's from Louisville) in December 1865. Yet William Preston and his wife Margaret—despite federal laws branding Confederates as traitors whose property was to be confiscated—remained rich, although less so than in 1861, when he owned 54 properties in Louisville valued at $263,979, real estate in St. Louis at $100,000, and 27 slaves and other personal property at $34,500—not counting other properties in Kentucky, Indiana, Illinois, and Texas, or his wife's $238,000 (51 slaves, Wickliffe Place, and two farms in Kentucky). The couple's combined property valuation in 1861 was worth more than $15 million in 2010 dollars. Preston's

Fig. 7.2. "General William Preston." Portrait by H. Niemeier. *Courtesy Filson Historical Society, Louisville.*

legal training had helped keep him rich, even though the Thirteenth Amendment in 1865 stripped him of the value of his slaves. In December 1861—before he was indicted for treason in July 1862—he had conveyed all of his real and personal property to two trustees (one a relative of his) in Louisville. After the war, he was to crow that the "deed of trust . . . I drew baffled the thieves." In addition, Preston's sister Susan P. Hepburn and his wife Margaret had managed his property in his absence during the war. He was also helped by Union relatives from Kentucky—notably Colonel John Mason Brown, USA, who in 1863 was able to prevent Wickliffe Place from being taken over as a Federal military hospital. By December 1865, although it was against his economic interests, Preston—large slave owner though he had been—favored abolition "so as to leave no future and useless seeds of discord."[41]

After the Civil War, Preston complained to William Preston Johnston: "I have more land than money, and am generally hard up for the latter." But the Prestons lived high. Their dining room table in their home Preston Place sat twenty-four, and they had the only gold service in Lexington. Their dinners were so elaborate that a guest said one could become inebriated and return to sobriety three times in the course of a meal at their house. The bitterness of the war years eventually abated. In 1869, as noted in chapter 6, Preston's daughter Mary Owen married John Mason Brown, who had been a Union colonel and had become a successful lawyer. In 1890, one of Preston's youngest daughters married William F. Draper, a rich Massachusetts mill owner who had been a Union general, and her younger sister married Draper's younger brother.

Preston's own marriage deteriorated as Margaret grew inordinately heavy and as her belief grew that Preston had tried to cheat her of some of her land and might have also been unfaithful to her. The two spent much of his last years living apart. Preston stayed active in land dealing and business—including an unsuccessful attempt, with help from his lawyer son-in-law John Mason Brown, to preserve his interest in the twelve thousand square miles of north-central Texas he and other Louisvillians had been granted in 1841. After he was granted a full pardon in 1868, regaining full civil rights after swearing allegiance to the United States, Preston became active in Democratic politics, serving in the Kentucky General Assembly. He also was a favorite speaker on Confederate achievements.

After his cousin General John C. Breckinridge died in 1875, Preston's eulogy received from the Louisville *Courier-Journal* the unrestrained headline "The Greatest Living Kentuckian on the Greatest Dead Kentuckian: Magnificent Oration of General William Preston." Preston, as his ailments increased, wrote his nephew William Preston Johnston in December 1886: "My struggle with men is over; my contemplation of God and his mysteries begins in earnest." He died on September 21, 1887, aged 70, gout-ridden and in opium-numbed pain. His friend and fellow Confederate general from Kentucky, Basil Duke, said Preston was "more a representative of an order that had passed away than of the society which knew him in his later years." The obituary in the *Courier-Journal* described him as "The Last of the Cavaliers."[42]

8

A Killing in the Philippines

I n a folder on the floor of my cluttered office is a sheaf of papers four inches thick. It looks like—and is—a record of legal proceedings: the court-martial and sentencing of an army officer and his efforts to get his sentence commuted. The army officer was my great-uncle Preston Brown, son of Colonel John Mason Brown and grandson of General William Preston.

Three days before Christmas 1900, during the Philippine War (1899–1902), Preston Brown, 28 years old, a first lieutenant in the United States Army, shot and killed an unarmed Filipino captive. Brown was charged with murder, convicted by court-martial of manslaughter, and sentenced to dismissal from the Army and five years of hard labor in a federal penitentiary. President Theodore Roosevelt commuted the sentence to a loss of a few months' pay and a brief delay in promotion. Brown subsequently rose in the ranks, served with distinction in World War I, and retired in 1934 as a major general.

What happened in the Philippine matter? If Preston Brown was a killer, why was he pardoned? The incident raises timeless issues relating to counterinsurgent warfare, including the lack of clear rules as to the treatment of captives and the difficulty of distinguishing insurgents from indigenous civilians. Brown's case also illustrates how family connections may skillfully be used in seeking commutation of such a sentence. In addition, the commutation reflected policy and legal decisions made by Roosevelt and by Secretary of War Elihu Root about the way America would conduct war as an occupying power.

I remember my great-uncle clearly, although he died in 1948, when I was only seven. He was the closest thing I had to a viable grandfather, my father's father having died when my father was young and my mother's father being a heavy drinker. Every summer, when I was a small child, our family stayed at Uncle Preston's house on Martha's Vineyard. His only child, a son, had died in his twenties. Uncle Preston and his wife took my brother and me in as if we were their children. Uncle Preston had long been retired, but as he had been a major general, he was the ranking retired army officer (among many retired army officers) on Martha's Vineyard. To me, he was a kindly bald old man. In Martha's Vineyard, he wore immaculate white shirts, white trousers, and white bucks, and he would let me crawl up in his lap while he read me the newspaper.[1] One time when I was about six, sick in bed in my family's apartment in New York, Uncle Preston came to my room. As my father played a record of the great Metropolitan Opera baritone Lawrence Tibbett singing "The Battle Hymn of the Republic," Uncle Preston stood at attention at the foot of my bed, saluting, and had me join him in singing along and saluting. I remember only one other quasi-military act by Uncle Preston: when Japan surrendered in August 1945, he provided pans and kitchen spoons to my older brother and me (aged eight and four) so we could march up and down pounding the kitchenware in a small but noisy victory parade in the road that ran by his house in Martha's Vineyard. He was tough-minded. When I was about five I climbed up on a rock behind his house. The rock was perhaps four feet high. My great-aunt Mary, Uncle Preston's sister, cried out: "Do something, Preston! If that boy falls from the rock, he'll hurt himself!" Uncle Preston said: "Yes, Mary, he will."

As a boy, I had heard from my father that there had been a blot on Uncle Preston's record years before—something about shooting a native in the Philippines. The story wasn't clear. My father thought the Filipino had been carrying some U.S. Army supplies on his head while wading across a stream, had tried to run off with the goods, and Uncle Preston had shot him when he kept on running after Uncle Preston ordered him to halt. Some 50 years after Preston Brown's death, I retrieved from the National Archives a copy of the record of his court martial and of the petitions for clemency that followed. The story that emerges from the Archives bears little resemblance to what I had heard from my father. It is, instead, the Philippine War in miniature, a mirror of guerilla warfare, and a story of impulsive acts under fire, friendships, hatreds, lobbying, and influence.

Preston Brown's story can only be understood in the context of the Philippine War, a conflict into which the United States stumbled immediately after the Spanish-American War. The American navy had crushed the Spanish fleet in Manila Bay on May 1, 1898, only a few days after America declared war against Spain. In August 1898, the Americans had taken Manila. President William McKinley said later, "When the Philippines dropped into our laps I confess I did not know what to do with them." Indeed, as he put it, "I looked up their location on the globe. I could not have told you where those darned islands were within 2,000 miles!" But after praying on his knees to God for guidance, he decided to occupy the islands. To return them to Spain would be "cowardly and dishonorable." There was real risk of seizure by another European power such as Germany. McKinley did not believe Philippine independence was a viable option, because he thought the islands were "unfit for self government—and they would soon have anarchy and misrule over there worse than Spain's was." So, as McKinley saw it, "there was nothing left for us to do but to take them all, and to educate the Filipinos, and uplift and civilize and Christianize them, and by God's grace do the very best we could by them, as our fellow-men for whom Christ also died."[2] That was how McKinley, more than a year after deciding to take the Philippines, reconstructed his reasoning to the General Missionary Committee of the Methodist Episcopal Church (without focusing on the fact that most of the Filipinos were already Christian, albeit of the Catholic persuasion). But he had also reminded the delegates he sent to negotiate peace terms with Spain of "the commercial opportunity to which American statesmanship cannot be indifferent."[3] To attain these mixed objectives, McKinley decided upon "benevolent assimilation" of the Philippines.[4]

Before the Spanish-American War, Filipino insurgents led by Emilio Aguinaldo had been fighting for the island's independence from Spain. The insurgents did not intend to substitute one colonial power for another. In June 1898, not long after Dewey's victory at Manila Bay, Aguinaldo proclaimed that the Philippines were independent. Although Dewey had given some arms to Aguinaldo (presumably on the theory that the enemy of my enemy is my friend), McKinley ordered that the Filipino insurgents should have no part in the capture of Manila. After Manila was taken by the Americans, and after months of tension between American troops in the capital and insurgents in the suburbs, bloody fighting broke out between the two in February 1899—including street fighting, arson, and reported atrocities on both sides, among them shootings by American soldiers of Filipino prisoners.[5] So began what was to become a prolonged war that would cost 4,234 American deaths—more than ten times the 379 Americans killed in combat during all of the Spanish-American War.[6]

Fighting in the Philippines was tropical warfare, fought through mud, swamps, rice paddies, bamboo thickets, and cutting grasses, accompanied by dysentery, cholera, malaria, and other tropical diseases. Disease accounted for over 60 percent of the American deaths in the war. Most of the American soldiers had no clear idea of the American objective in the war. One trooper wrote home: "We feel that every man of ours that's lost is worth more than the whole damned island. . . . We don't know what we're fighting for hardly."[7]

In November 1899, Aguinaldo, having been beaten repeatedly by American troops in conventional engagements, disbanded his Army of Liberation and adopted instead a program of guerrilla warfare. The fighting shifted from battles to skirmishes and ambushes. American troops were split up into smaller forces and garrisons and dispersed throughout the archipelago. The guerrillas were mostly in the countryside, but their allies in the towns supplied food and shelter and hid weapons, out of sympathy with the insurgent cause or to avoid guerrilla reprisals. Guerrilla warfare made it even harder for the American soldiers to identify their enemies. As one captain wrote to his mother in January 1900, if the Americans go after insurgents "they scatter, hide their uniform and rifle, don [a] white suit they carry with them and meekly claim to be amigos (friends)."[8]

It didn't make matters easier that the Filipinos spoke languages other than English and did not look like most Americans. William Howard Taft, the 325-pound future president who was the first civilian U.S. commissioner of the Philippines (see figure 8.2), referred to the Filipinos as "our little brown brothers." The American soldiers sang "He may be a brother of Big Bill Taft, but he ain't no brother of mine" and tended to refer to the locals as "niggers" or "gugus" (derived from *gugo,* the name of a tree bark used as a shampoo by Filipino women). One soldier from Kansas wrote home that the Philippine Islands would not be pacified "until the niggers are killed off like the Indians."[9] American troops changed the chorus to the Civil War song "Tramp! Tramp! Tramp! The boys are marching," in ways that reflected the soldiers' views of the Filipinos:

> Damn, damn, damn the Filipinos!
> Cut-throat khakiac *ladrones*!
> Underneath the starry flag,
> Civilize them with a Krag,
> And return us to our own beloved homes.

The Krag was the Krag-Jorgenson rifle used by the U.S. troops at the time, *ladrones* is Spanish for thieves, and *khakiac* appears to be related to the Tagalog word *khaki*, meaning dull yellowish brown. The c in Tagalog is soft. Perhaps the American soldiers were singing, phonetically, about brown-assed thieves. There were atrocity stories, true or false, circulating about the Filipinos. At least some American soldiers believed that insurgents mutilated captives or that "some were buried and molasses applied to head so that ants would eat."[10]

By the fall of 1900, when Brown's regiment arrived on Luzon, the Philippines' largest island and Aguinaldo's base, guerrilla activity had increased sharply. Aguinaldo hoped that higher American casualties would cause Americans in the 1900 presidential election to vote for the anti-imperialist Democratic candidate William Jennings Bryan, not for re-election of the annexationist McKinley, but McKinley was overwhelmingly re-elected. The commanding general/military governor in the Philippines, General Arthur MacArthur—Civil War hero, winner of the Medal of Honor, father of World War II General Douglas MacArthur, and no better than his son would prove to be at maintaining good relations with his civilian commander in chief—announced new get-tough policies. MacArthur, who had been criticized for not being sufficiently aggressive against the insurgents, on December 19, 1900, notified his department commanders of a "new and more stringent policy" and stated: "whenever action is necessary the more drastic the application the better," although there should be no violations of the rules of war. One day later—two days before Preston Brown shot the Filipino—MacArthur issued a proclamation declaring that the guerillas were violating the rules of war by conducting hostilities without belonging to an organized, uniformed military force and so were subject to exemplary punishments. The proclamation was based on General Orders No. 100, a Civil War directive under which continued resistance to an occupying army through guerrilla fighting or assisting the enemy warranted immediate retaliation, including destruction of property and in some cases summary execution.[11]

The U.S. Army began a series of campaigns that, over the next two years, ended guerrilla resistance in most of the Philippines. The army's tactics were not gentle. Loyd Wheaton, commanding the Department of Northern Luzon, told a correspondent, "It's no use going with a sword in one hand, a pacifist pamphlet in the other and trailing the model of a schoolhouse after you. . . . You can't put down a rebellion by throwing confetti and sprinkling perfumery." Prisoners were detained until they talked. More and more often, prisoners were tortured during interrogation—notoriously, by the "water cure," in which, as one witness reported: "The victim is laid flat on his back and held down by his tormentors. Then a bamboo tube is thrust into his mouth and some dirty water, the filthier the better, is poured down his unwilling throat." Every few minutes a soldier would step on the victim's stomach to make him vomit the water, and the process would begin again.[12] Crops were burnt, municipal governments were purged, and populations were forcibly resettled away from guerilla areas under a policy of "reconcentration" not vastly different from the reconcentration policy that the Spanish had applied in Cuba and that had galvanized American public opinion against Spain. Insurgent leaders surrendered or were captured: Aguinaldo himself was captured in March 1901.

Apart from their military campaigns, Americans were fighting for the hearts and minds of the Filipinos. The commanding general of the American army in the Philippines was also military governor of the Philippines, and the Office of Military Governor (and, as the provinces were pacified, the civilian Philippine Commission) sought to reform municipal government; improve public health; build roads, bridges, and schools; teach English; and revise the criminal code and the tax codes. Americans also coupled their military campaigns with support for a new Filipino party, the *Partido Federal*, launched with the encouragement of William Howard Taft in December 1900. Led by prosperous *ilustrados* (European-educated elites) and former insurgents, the new party urged the end of the insurgency and the acceptance of American rule pending the setting up of a representative government. The new party flourished in part because Taft banned opposition parties and awarded to *Federalistas* all official jobs reserved for Filipinos.[13]

This was the unconventional war in which Preston Brown found himself in late 1900. He had longed from boyhood to be a soldier, but his father wanted him to be a lawyer and would not let him accept an appointment to West Point. So Brown went to Yale as an undergraduate and then took law courses at the University of Virginia. He practiced briefly at a Long Island firm, which sent him to California to work on a law encyclopedia. The work was stultifying. In 1894, two years after graduating from Yale, Brown, aged 22, joined the army at the Presidio in San Francisco as a private in an artillery regiment, where he was taught soldiering by an old-style first sergeant named Joseph Haifer. Brown was commissioned as an officer in March 1897, with his instructor First Sergeant Haifer standing proudly beside him.[14] He was then posted to Montana, before being sent to Cuba during the Spanish-American War. As a second lieutenant, he commanded a company during the Santiago campaign in July 1898 that led to Spain's capitulation in Cuba. Transferred back to the States, Brown was promoted to first lieutenant (see figure 8.1 for Brown as a lieutenant). His regiment was sent to the Philippines in the fall of 1900. By December, his company was posted in Binangonan, a town not far from Manila.[15]

What happened on December 22, 1900, when Brown killed a Filipino captive? The statements and testimony of the soldiers as to the killing of the Filipino diverge wildly, depending on whether the soldier was from Preston Brown's company, Company F, Second Infantry, or from Company G, Second Infantry, commanded by First Lieutenant Paul H. McCook.

Let's start with what is not in dispute about that day. Six men from Brown's company, led by Acting Corporal Charles D. Weidner, had gone out from Binangonan on what was described in the officers' formal reports as a scouting party. Brown and others later testified that the men had gone out to look for chickens for Christmas dinner. When Weidner's men reached a low-lying small island or bar in the Agoos (now more often spelled Agos) River, they came under fire from the far (north) bank of the river, where *insurrectos* were suspected of hanging out. The shooting was heard by the men at Binangonan. Captain Francis P. Fremont ordered the call to arms to be sounded.

Fig. 8.1. Preston Brown as a lieutenant. *Author's collection.*

Brown, with about 25 men from his company, ran to the scene of the firing. Weidner's scouting party, retreating from the south bank of the river, pointed out the island in the river where they had come under fire and the far bank where the fire had come from. Brown and his men forded the shallow water to the island. Ahead of them was the fast-flowing main channel of the river, which had been swollen by rains. Brown swam across, calling for volunteers who knew how to swim to follow him, and a number of his men followed him. Weidner managed to get close to the far bank but was swept downstream and drowned.

The American soldiers scrambled up the far bank, near where the firing had come from. As the *insurrectos* retreated toward Pamplona, the next barrio, an American private brought in a Filipino he had captured on the north bank, a man wearing only a breechcloth. The private told Brown that the Filipino had been on the river bank near where Weidner was swept away and could have saved him but did not. Brown asked the Filipino some questions about where the *insurrectos* were—in Spanish and, according to Brown, in Tagalog. The man indicated that he did not understand, and Brown hit him and knocked him down. Within a few minutes, Brown ordered the men to move toward Pamplona, and, under disputed circumstances, the Filipino began to move away from the soldiers. Brown turned and shot him in the back of the head with his Colt .45 pistol. No one had cried for the man to halt. The man fell forward, face down, and died immediately, and Brown led the soldiers on to Pamplona. The Americans burnt part of the village in retaliation for having been shot at by men believed to have come from there.

So much for the agreed upon events of the day.

Brown reported the killing of the Filipino orally to Captain Fremont, but Brown's written report of the skirmish made no separate mention of the shooting. According to the report, there were about 30 *insurrectos*, armed with Mausers, two Remingtons, and some Krag-Jorgensons. Brown concluded his report: "The firing was quite hot for a while. My casualties: none in action—one man drowned. Insurrectos: 18 killed and counted— their wounded not known." Nor was there any mention of the shooting of the captured native in the post-skirmish reports by Captain Fremont and by Lieutenant McCook.[16] The reports were likewise silent as to the burning of part of the village of Pamplona. The burning of villages that housed *insurrectos* was becoming increasingly frequent as the war against the guerillas turned harder, although these burnings were often not reported. One American colonel recognized that burning villages suspected of sheltering *insurrectos* "will cause innocent civilians to suffer—but the Almighty destroyed Sodom notwithstanding the fact that there were a few just people in that community."[17]

By early March 1901, Brown's and McCook's companies were transferred to Marinduque, a smaller island off the coast of Luzon. Marinduque had been the scene of one of the guerrillas' greatest successes: in September 1900, *insurrectos* had ambushed, defeated, and captured 51 American soldiers. The American response was to treat all males on the island as potential enemies, destroy crops, move civilians into occupied towns, and hold suspects as hostages until April 1901, when the island's guerrilla leader surrendered.[18]

In mid-March 1901, Lieutenant McCook for the first time raised a complaint about Brown's shooting of the captive, filing a written description of the incident, accompanied by seven affidavits, all dated March 10, 1901, from enlisted men in his company, Company G. The seven affidavits closely resemble McCook's description—not surprisingly, because McCook had asked the men for the affidavits, handed or read to them a copy of his own statement, and asked if that was how they remembered it, before telling them to make out their statements.[19]

Major Robert A. Brown (no kin to Preston Brown), inspector general in the Department of Southern Luzon, investigated the shooting. Preston Brown submitted statements by himself, Captain Fremont, an army doctor, and affidavits from 12 enlisted men of Company F. These affidavits, too, bear a strong family resemblance to each other, Brown having asked for them.[20]

The investigator, after examining the soldiers in person at Marinduque, reported to the adjutant general of the Department of Southern Luzon: "The scene which took place between Lieut. Brown and the native is described as very different between Lieut. McCook and the men of Company 'G,' 2d Infantry, from the description given by Lieut. Brown and the men of Company 'F,' 2d Infantry, and on the vital point of the killing of the native there is absolute contradiction between the two descriptions." The investigator concluded that a general court-martial was necessary to adjudicate the case, given the serious nature of the allegations and "the peculiar conditions surrounding the various incidents and persons involved."[21]

The general court-martial was held at army headquarters in Manila beginning on July 10, 1901. The court consisted of four lieutenant colonels, seven majors, and two captains, not including the captain acting as judge advocate. The court addressed the following charge and specification:

> Charge: Murder, in violation of the 58th Article of War. Specification: In that First Lieutenant Preston Brown, 2d Infantry, did willfully, feloniously and with malice aforethought, murder and kill by shooting with a pistol an unarmed, unresisting native Filipino, name unknown, a prisoner of war in his charge and as a result of said shooting, the native did then and there die.

Brown was represented by a second lieutenant, Blanton Winship, who went on to win a Silver Star and a Distinguished Service Cross in World War I and to become judge advocate general and then governor of Puerto Rico. The testimony at the court-martial was as contradictory as the accounts given to the investigator.

According to Lieutenant McCook and his men from Company G, the native was old or middle-aged (about 40 or 35; one soldier guessed 50).[22] Some (notably McCook) said the Filipino was blind or somehow disfigured in one eye. Some said the man had been squatting by the river bank with a fish net beside him.[23] The Company G soldiers said Brown had his pistol out throughout his questioning of the native and had struck the man with his pistol. Lieutenant McCook said the pistol blow caused a bloody gash on the native's face. Others described it as a slight scratch.[24] Brown spoke loudly to the native, cursed him, and told him to vamoose. After hearing from one of the soldiers that the native could have saved Weidner but didn't, Brown turned and shot the native, who was only a few paces away. Private John Walker, the lead prosecution witness, acknowledged that the Filipino "might have made one or two steps" before being shot.[25] The next prosecution witness said he was unable to say whether the native had been running toward the bushes when he was shot.[26] Lieutenant McCook alone testified that the native was "tottering."[27] Several of the Company G soldiers said they had heard Brown say, referring to the death of Weidner, words to the effect that "he wouldn't give Weidner for all the natives [or niggers, or gugus] there was in the Philippine Islands."[28]

According to Brown and the other witnesses from Company F, the native was vigorous, around 30 or 35 years old.[29] What did the man look like? As one Company F private put it: "I couldn't express his features. He looked like any other gugu around here."[30] Several of the men from Company F reported that the native not only made no attempt to save Weidner but, as Weidner clung to a bush on the north bank of the river, kicked him back into the river to his death.[31] One of those who testified to this effect was Private Henry Oiler, whom the investigator in his report described as "a man of very inferior intelligence" who "is very much mixed about the testimony he gives" and who had to be re-examined at the second day of the investigator's examination because he had been drinking the first day.[32] According to the Company F witnesses, Brown struck the native only with his fist. After Brown directed the men to advance towards Pamplona, there was an outcry behind Brown, who turned, saw the man running toward the bush, unholstered his pistol, and shot him at some distance—estimates ranged from around 15 to 30 feet. Several of the Company F witnesses testified that they would have shot the running Filipino themselves and were getting ready to do so, but Brown shot him first.[33] According to one Company F private, "it was a fine shot; several of the men said it was an awful fine shot."[34]

So what actually happened? A gratuitous, hotheaded killing of an aged, infirm, and uncomprehending local fisherman by an excited young officer who lost his head in the heat of the action and the emotion of having lost one of his men? Brown had seen his troops die in combat before; as he testified, "I commanded the color company of my regiment at Santiago, at San Juan Hill, and saw a good many men killed."[35] In the Philippines incident, however, Brown had led his men into swimming the fast-moving river and so may have felt more personal responsibility for his soldier's death. Or was the incident, as Brown and the men from his company described it, a justified shooting of an escaping prisoner who might have been an *insurrecto* or who might have informed the *insurrectos* how many American soldiers had crossed the river and where they were heading?

And why did McCook report the incident, when numerous questionable incidents were going unreported? As a leading historian of the Philippine

War put it, in considering possible violations of the laws of war in the Philippines, "most senior officers preferred a policy of 'don't ask, don't tell.'"[36] In this case, it is abundantly clear that McCook did not like Brown. At the court-martial, McCook said he had nothing against Brown, "except the uniform discourtesy with which he has usually treated me."[37] McCook had told the officer investigating the incident that Brown "had always treated him with lack of any consideration," often failing to return his salutes and several times speaking rudely of him in the presence of enlisted men and giving orders "in a way to junior officers, like as if they were enlisted men he was talking to."[38] Captain Fremont stated in his report to the investigator: "It was a matter of common noteriety that Lieut. McCook was bitterly inimical to Lieut. Brown and desirous of injuring him."[39] The investigator noted in his report that McCook's testimony "is weakened by the fact that there is a sort of fewd between Lieutenant McCook and Lieut. Brown dating back to service at Fort Thomas [Kentucky, where the division had been stationed before being shipped to the Philippines] in 1899 and 1900" and also said McCook was "peculiar and eccentric to the extent of being unreliable."[40]

According to Brown's sisters, McCook had resented some correction on his report made while Brown was acting adjutant at Fort Thomas.[41] An officer under whom Brown had served said that McCook brought charges against Brown in retaliation for Brown's having reprimanded McCook for having lost the rations of his company.[42] If Brown reproved McCook, it is likely he did so undiplomatically. According to Robert Lee Bullard, an officer who testified at Brown's court-martial about how customary it was to shoot escaping prisoners of war and who later worked closely with Brown in World War I, Brown was "no diplomat," was noted in the Army for his "facility of expression," "always picturesque and strikingly apt, often keenly witty or contemptuous at another's expense," and was "usually arbitrary, fierce and satirical in reproving and punishing."[43]

Major F. A. Smith, who commanded the American troops on Marinduque, told the investigator that McCook suffered from malaria and "when so suffering his mind does not seem to work." Smith also said McCook's men were undisciplined and that McCook "was very easy in his ways and matters of discipline" and "is not a good Company Commander." By contrast, Smith said, "Lieut. Brown is a good officer and a man who is absolutely truthful.

I would believe anything he told me. He has faults, impulsive, headstrong and inclined to be arbitrary and positive and is also inclined to neglect small details. He is however a good and competent officer."[44]

McCook also did not get on with Captain Fremont. Fremont used, as scouts against the Tagalog *insurrectos*, men from a native tribe, the Macabebes, who were traditional enemies of the Tagalogs. According to McCook, Fremont's Macabebe scouts were in the habit of urinating against the palm thatch wall of the church in Binangonan where McCook's men slept, and they continued to do so even after McCook complained about it four times to Captain Fremont. McCook, who kept a notebook of his grievances, also reported Captain Fremont for striking one of the privates in McCook's company.[45] The record of the court-martial did not bring out that Fremont was a relative of Preston Brown. Fremont's full name was Francis Preston Fremont. He and Brown both were descended from Colonel William Preston of Virginia, who was Brown's great-great-grandfather.[46] Despite this kinship, Fremont told the investigator that he was on none too good terms with Brown, who "was very much inclined to take things in his own hands."[47]

The animosity between McCook and Brown extended to the men of their companies. One of the Company F privates said he had "often heard men of Co. G 2d Inf. express their ill feeling towards Lt. Brown and say that they would get even with him some day if ever they had the chance."[48] The commanding officer on Marinduque told the investigator, "A very bitter feeling seemed to exist between the enlisted men of the two companies." It was also true that Brown had disciplined the lead prosecution witness, Private Walker, from McCook's company, for being drunk at retreat.[49]

The record creates an overwhelming sense of two groups of men, working in unpleasant circumstances, who disliked each other to the extent that each was willing to stretch the truth to get at the other. Did the native really kick Weidner back in the water, or was that a story made up after the fact by Company F privates trying to help Brown? Was the Filipino really, as McCook would have it, a tottering old man? Had Brown told the native to vamoose, as several of McCook's men testified, or was he a prisoner trying to run away into the bushes? Perhaps when Brown told the Filipino "*vamanos*" ("let's go") or "*vamos*" (we're going), McCook and his men (who may have spoken less Spanish than Brown, who was good with languages) took that to mean "vamoose"—to scram, to beat it, in American slang—rather than to come along with the American soldiers.

The court-martial ended on July 27, 1901. The court found Brown guilty, not of the original charge of murder with malice aforethought, but of manslaughter. The 29-year-old lieutenant was sentenced to dismissal from the army and to five years' hard labor. On August 31, Brigadier General James F. Wade, the commanding officer of the Department of Southern Luzon, approved the findings and sentence but provided Brown with a breathing space by adding: "The execution of the sentence is suspended and the proceedings are transmitted to the President for his action under the 111th Article of War. Clemency is recommended."[50] Article 111 empowered an officer who had authority to carry into execution a sentence of death or dismissal of an officer to "suspend the same until the pleasure of the President is known" and to send the record of the proceedings to the president.

Brown and his family and friends used this breathing space to the fullest. Brown, although young, was well connected. His father, John Mason Brown, who had died in 1890, had been a colonel in the United States Army during the Civil War, a prominent lawyer in Kentucky, and a factor in the Republican Party in Kentucky. He also knew many political leaders in Kentucky, Ohio, and national political life—including Theodore Roosevelt, who had become president on September 14, 1901, after McKinley's assassination. Preston Brown's uncle, Benjamin Gratz Brown, had been a U.S. senator from Missouri before becoming that state's governor. Preston Brown and his allies made the most of these connections.[51]

Within weeks of General Wade's order, an article summarizing the evidence at the court martial in a light favorable to Brown (the native was shot while "running for the bushes") appeared in the *Army and Navy Journal*. Friends and relatives of Brown caused the article to be sent to President Roosevelt and also to Adjutant General Henry C. Corbin, who had become the most influential officer in the army, given Roosevelt's scant respect for the army's commanding general, Lieutenant General Nelson A. Miles.[52]

Brown's uncle by marriage, Robert A. Thornton, a lawyer in Lexington, Kentucky, visited Washington to plead that no action be taken until the record had been thoroughly reviewed. Thornton, who was active in Republican politics in Kentucky, prepared the way for his visit by a barrage of letters of introduction to President Roosevelt and Secretary of War Elihu Root from, among others, John G. Carlisle (former speaker of the House, secretary of the treasury, and senator from Kentucky), William G. Draper (former U.S. ambassador to Italy and Preston Brown's uncle by marriage), and Colonel Reuben T. Durrett (whose help in early Kentucky history Roosevelt had acknowledged with thanks in his book *The Winning of the West*).[53] The letters went to the right people. Roosevelt, as president, would ultimately decide Brown's sentence. Root not only headed the War Department but was Roosevelt's most trusted adviser. That relationship of trust dated back to 1898, when Root, a leading New York City lawyer, helped Roosevelt become the Republican candidate for governor of New York despite a substantial legal question as to whether Roosevelt was in fact a New York resident and thus eligible to be governor of the state.[54]

Thornton's visit to Washington went well. Brown's sister Mary, in a letter asking former U.S. Attorney General Wayne MacVeagh to intercede with the War Department, reported that her uncle Thornton "has just returned from Washington and has the assurance of Mr. Roosevelt, who was a friend of my father's, that if the facts are as stated in the Army and Navy Journal, he [Brown] will not be 'subordinated for an instant' by the findings of the court."[55] Others wrote directly to Roosevelt and to Root. William J. Deboe, Republican senator from Kentucky, reminded Secretary Root that Brown's father "was a strong Union man." Brown's relative, former Congressman William Campbell Preston (that name again!) Breckinridge, writing to Roosevelt, sounded themes of history and valor that were likely to appeal to the president by telling him that young Brown "comes from a race of soldiers. There has been no war in America for 150 years in which his ancestors have not participated; and I appeal to you as a soldier, as a man of courage and spirit, as well as of kindness, to examine for yourself before this young soldier is disgraced by your approval of an adverse sentence." Sam J. Roberts, editor of the *Lexington Leader* and a political operative for the Republican party in Kentucky, reminded Roosevelt that Brown's father John Mason Brown had been "a matchless Republican leader" and that Brown's uncle Robert Thornton has "courageously supported the Republican cause in every campaign since 1896" and "has indeed been one of our strongest allies in the new political alignment in Kentucky." Roberts trusted that after reviewing the merits of the case, President Roosevelt "will extend such executive clemency as will soon restore Brown to his good standing in the Army."[56]

A personal vignette came from Captain George Gatley, under whom Brown had served as an enlisted man. Gatley wrote the Adjutant General's Office that he had "never known a man who gave finer promise as an officer." Gatley reported that when Brown joined his battery,

> There was about as tough a gang of blackguards in it as ever fell together to curse an organization. Brown was promptly promoted corporal, and this with the fact that he was a gentleman and the further fact that he did his duty regardlessly of whom he stepped on made him temporarily unpopular. One afternoon some ten or a dozen jumped him in the barracks, two with Krag bayonets and the rest with anything they could get hold of. He managed to gain the stove poker and a corner before anyone else and then proceeded to reduce chaos and mutiny to order in a manner that was highly approved by everybody, including the General Court Martial that tried these pirates who assaulted him. His testimony convicted them, too, for they threatened everything against any man of the battery who testified against them. They didn't "bluff" Brown an inch. While this is a little thing, it shows the stuff that is in him, and that stuff is *force*, the one most valuable quality of an officer, and one that no examination ever does or can reach.[57]

Weightiest of the letters was one to Root from William Howard Taft, the commissioner of the Philippines who was to succeed Theodore Roosevelt as president of the United States. Taft, who had been a judge on the United States Circuit Court in Cincinnati and who was to become chief justice of the United States, wrote Root that he "had read every word of the record and I am bound to say that sitting as a judge I could never have convicted [Brown]. The weight of the evidence was decidedly with him." Based on his review of the record, Taft said he ventured "to speak a word on behalf of a son of an old and cherished friend." He noted that "the court martial consisted of many officers who had seen no active service in these Islands and knew little of actual conditions." Although he had only met Brown

Fig. 8.2. William Howard Taft, commissioner of the Philippines, on a water buffalo.
U.S. Army Military History Institute.

once, Taft added a shrewd personal observation: "Brown talks too much and knows a good deal in a bumptious way and this characteristic may have injured him."[58] Taft had identified the bumptiousness that springs forth from a review of Brown's testimony and report of the incident (Brown running to lead the men to where the firing had been and Brown cross-ing the rushing river without first consulting Captain Fremont), Captain Fremont's comments as to Brown's tendency to take matters into his own hands, and Major Smith's comment that Brown, although a good and competent officer, is "impulsive, headstrong and inclined to be arbitrary and positive." The same bumptiousness leaps from the cable Brown had sent in late September to his uncle Thornton, a distinguished man almost 30 years his senior, when Brown was about to return to the States from Manila to fight his sentence. That cable reads in its entirety:

I sail Tuesday Palace Hotel San Francisco write demand immedi-ately no action War Dept before my arrival Important documents coming official record should reach Washington Oct eighth Vital importance no action War Dept Taft read record says wont stand he so writes Roosevelt Root acknowledge. Preston.[59]

As Bullard was to note in his biographical sketch, Brown throughout his career was marked by his "alertness, his cocksureness, abruptness and bluntness of speech and manner."[60]

Two Supreme Court justices wrote Root on Brown's behalf. Kentuckian John Marshall Harlan, a classmate of Brown's father at Yale, asked "that no action be taken in this case until I have had an opportunity to look into it for the purpose of ascertaining the facts as disclosed by the record."[61] Harlan is remembered now for his stinging dissent ("Our Constitution is color-blind") to the Supreme Court's 1896 decision in *Plessy v. Ferguson*, upholding "separate but equal" treatment of African Americans. The other Supreme Court justice (and Yale classmate of Brown's father) who wrote to Root was Henry B. Brown, author of the majority opinion in *Plessy v. Ferguson*, who told Root that Brown's father at the time of his death was a candidate for the Supreme Court. He referred Root to a case in which he (Justice Brown) had discharged, on preliminary examination, a charge against a soldier who had shot an escaping deserter.[62] The two justices, so opposed to each other in the *Plessy* case, were united in their efforts to help Preston Brown.

Similar letters were sent to Adjutant General Henry C. Corbin. Former Attorney General Wayne MacVeagh forwarded to Corbin a summary of the case from Brown's sister Mary. Corbin said he would forward the letter to the secretary of war and added: "I do not believe [Brown's] friends need have any grave concern as to the final outcome."[63] Major General Adna R. Chaffee, who in July 1901 became the commanding general of the U.S. Army in the Philippines, sent Corbin a succinct cable: "know him well excellent officer clemency CHAFFEE." Other letters to Corbin came from Brigadier General John C. Bates, who had commanded the Department of Southern Luzon until April 1901 and had seen Brown "under fire in front of Santiago in 1898"; retired Brigadier General William Montrose Graham, who, as commander of the artillery regiment in which Brown had enlisted, had seen Brown's "exemplary conduct, fine abilities and superior soldierly qualities"; and William Lindsay, a former senator from

Kentucky, who extolled the worth and prominence of Brown's father and his grandfather General William Preston.[64]

The heavy volleys of letters from persons in high places must have helped Brown's cause. So must the fact that Roosevelt had known and been helped by Preston Brown's father. In 1888, before Roosevelt turned 30, he began work on what he called his *magnum opus*—*The Winning of the West*, a red-blooded history of the westward expansion of Americans across the continent, starting with Daniel Boone's crossing of the Cumberland Gap. The theme was the winning of the American West as "the crowning and greatest achievement" of the spread of "the English-speaking peoples."[65] To write it, Roosevelt visited Kentucky and other states in the old West and also gathered source materials from private collectors—among them, Brown's father, Colonel John Mason Brown, who had a dinner at his house for Roosevelt during Roosevelt's 1888 visit to Louisville.[66] In his preface to *The Winning of the West*, Roosevelt, acknowledging his access to original material relating to Kentucky, wrote that he was "under great obligations to Col. John Mason Brown of Louisville . . . for assistance rendered me; particularly for having sent me six bound volumes of MSS., containing the correspondence of Spanish Minister Gardoquí, copied from the Spanish archives."[67] Those manuscripts helped Roosevelt's analysis of Spain's efforts to use its control of the Mississippi to pry Kentucky loose from the new United States after the Revolution.

Roosevelt liked and admired Brown's father. In December 1902, Roosevelt spoke at a banquet in honor of Justice Harlan, who, like Brown's father, had chosen to fight for the North in the Civil War, although Kentucky was a state with deeply divided loyalties. Roosevelt told the story of another Kentuckian whose mother, when he came home as a young man from a long trip early in the Civil War, showed him the sword his father had carried in the Mexican War and told him: "I hope you will draw it on the side that defends the flag for which your father fought, but, for one side or the other, draw it you must." Turning to Harlan, Roosevelt said he had heard this from the Kentuckian who had to make the choice—"a Kentuckian who was a staunch friend of yours and one of the greatest lawyers and most patriotic citizens whom this country had—John Mason Brown."[68]

Preston Brown's quest for clemency was also helped by the timing of developments in the Philippine War, which was becoming much rougher as Brown's sentence was being considered in Washington. General Chaffee and the army were implementing the get-tough policies General MacArthur had announced in December 1900. On Sunday, September 28, 1901, the day on which Major General Chaffee cabled Corbin recommending clemency for Brown, the bloodiest slaughter of Americans during the war took place at Balangiga on the island of Samar, southeast of Luzon. Guerrillas had infiltrated the town dressed as laborers or as women. Early in the morning, the town police chief cut down an American sentry with a bolo. Conch shells sounded, and bolomen poured out of the church and the surrounding jungles, slashing the surprised soldiers. The American captain, still in his pajamas, jumped from his second-story window into the plaza and was hacked to death. Forty-seven of his men were killed. Only 26 survived, all but four of them wounded. News of the killings produced an outcry for vengeance throughout the United States and led to a campaign in the Philippines over the next seven months marked by destruction of rice, carabao (domesticated water buffalo), and houses; the execution of civilians and prisoners; and the forcible concentration of the population into pacified towns—"the longest and most brutal pacification campaign in the Philippine War."[69]

For months, U.S. news about the Philippines focused on the "Balangiga Massacre" and the campaigns to take guerrilla strongholds. Not until April 1902 was there widespread disclosure of, and public revulsion against, American excesses in Samar and elsewhere in the Philippines. Brown had the good fortune to have his case reviewed before the worst of the news about American abuses became public.

In late October 1901, legal issues caused an alarming turn in Brown's case. Judge Advocate General George B. Davis, who had taught law and history at West Point and had written a treatise on the military law of the United States, pointed out to Root that under the 58th Article of War, the punishments for certain offenses triable by court-martial—including manslaughter—could never be less than those provided by the laws of the local jurisdiction in which they had been committed. Under Article 403 of the Philippine Penal Code, the minimum sentence for manslaughter was 12 years and a day of hard labor. Concluding that the sentence of five years' imprisonment imposed at Brown's court-martial was unauthorized, Davis recommended that the case be returned to the court-martial for revision of the sentence to conform with the Philippine minimum sentence.[70] On October 26, Root signed an endorsement to this effect.

Under this turn of events, unless Roosevelt granted clemency to Brown, his imprisonment would be not five years, but at least twelve years and a day of hard labor, because of the reference to local law in Article 58. That article had been adopted, as a later judge advocate general noted when Congress in 1919 totally revised the long-obsolete Articles of War, "at a time when the territorial jurisdiction of the United States did not extend beyond the geographical limits of what now constitutes the States of the Union and the District of Columbia."[71]

Within days, the concluding recommendation in Davis's memorandum to Root was changed dramatically. The final version of the memorandum noted that General Chaffee had informed Corbin that only six of the thirteen original members of the court-martial were available and that the judge advocate who had tried the case was no longer in the Philippines. Davis believed it improbable "that even a minority quorum of five members can be called together when the record reaches the Islands" and accordingly did "not feel justified in adhering to the recommendation that the proceedings be returned to the court for a revision of the sentence. Where such revision is impracticable, it has been the practice of this office to recommend that the illegal part of the sentence be disapproved, and it is recommended that that course be pursued in this case." In brief, Davis ended up disapproving the part of Brown's sentence imposing prison time for manslaughter.[72]

Davis then analyzed whether Brown had violated not the Philippine criminal laws relating to homicide, but the laws of war—a violation for which Brown could have been tried by a military commission. Davis noted that an engagement was in progress when the Filipino was shot, and Brown's

> excitement was great. Just as he was about to advance there was an outcry and commotion among the men who had crossed the stream with him, which caused him to turn in the direction of the prisoner who appeared to be in the act of escaping. Laboring under an excitement so intense, apparently, as to preclude an exercise of the reasoning faculty, he fired and the prisoner fell dead. . . . The

situation was a critical one for an officer of his age and experience. He had already delayed his advance somewhat, and he was on the enemy's side of a swollen stream with a small detachment of men and out of supporting distance of the main body of the command. . . . If a prisoner of war attempts to escape, the laws of war justify the use of such force as may be necessary to prevent it. In the condition of excitement in which the accused was at the moment, it is impossible to make nice distinctions as to the amount of force used, or as to the method of its employment.

Davis concluded: "While the circumstances which attended the taking of human life in this case are such as to diminish materially the criminal responsibility of the accused, [Brown] cannot, in my opinion, be entirely absolved from blame. . . . The Government has a right to expect from its commissioned officers such an exercise of self-control in action as will ensure the proper employment of its forces against the enemy, and secure a reasonable enforcement of the laws and usages of war during the actual pendency of hostilities." Davis recommended that "so much of the sentence as imposes confinement in the penitentiary be disapproved as illegal and inoperative; but that the sentence of dismissal be approved and commuted to a reduction of thirty files in lineal rank on the rank of first lieutenants of infantry and to a forfeiture of one-half of his monthly pay for a period of nine months."

Why the sudden change in the Judge Advocate General's recommendation? One suspects that Root (an outstanding lawyer) or Corbin looked at the earlier version and told Davis how the report should come out. Roosevelt's thumb may also have been on the scales. Both Root and Roosevelt must have realized that sentencing Brown to long imprisonment would likely have undercut the morale of army officers and troops charged with carrying out the army's pacification program in the Philippines.

Davis's revised memorandum to Root was routed first through the commanding general of the Army, Lieutenant General Nelson A. Miles. This was another threatening development for Brown. Even though Miles, two days after the American Navy's victory at Manila Bay, had recommended to the secretary of war that an expedition be sent "to occupy the Philippines," he had since become a vocal anti-imperialist. Moreover,

Roosevelt and Miles disliked each other profoundly. On the eve of the Spanish-American War, Roosevelt had found Miles's lack of planning "almost inconceivable" and had described Miles in his pocket diary as a "brave peacock." In addition, Miles apparently wanted to run against Roosevelt as the Democratic candidate for president in 1904, and he was suspected by Root and Roosevelt of attempting to further that effort by leaking to anti-imperialist Democratic senators embarrassing material about the conduct of the Philippine War from classified dispatches Miles had seen as commanding general.[73]

Miles wrote a blistering endorsement on Davis's recommendation in the Brown case. Evidently accepting without question the testimony of McCook and his company, Miles said the testimony left "no room for doubt" that the native was an "old, half-blind fisherman, and a non-combatant, who . . . had been told by Brown to go. Hence, the killing, on plea of the attempt of a prisoner to escape, is neither justified nor extenuated." Miles found the sentence "not too severe." If the law forbade the confinement imposed and the court could not be reconvened, Miles recommended approval of that portion of the sentence requiring that Brown be dismissed from the Army, saying that mitigation of the sentence "to the mere reduction of 30 files in lineal rank and forfeiture of one-half pay for nine months would seem to me to be a travesty of justice."[74]

On December 17, barely two weeks after writing this endorsement, Miles managed to irritate Root and Roosevelt further by publicly criticizing a naval court's investigation of a dispute between two senior Navy officers. Root told Miles, on behalf of the president, that a senior officer in one service had "no business" criticizing legal proceedings in another service. Miles went to the White House to tell Roosevelt that his comment had been merely personal. Roosevelt, in an open reception, shouted at Miles: "I will have no criticism of my Administration from you, or any other officer in the Army. Your conduct is worthy of censure, sir."[75]

On January 27, 1902, Root, by an endorsement that rejected Miles's views without mentioning them, approved Davis's recommendation, writing: "The weight of the evidence is that the defendant shot a prisoner of war while attempting to escape in the heat of action near the enemy who might well have been informed of the strength and movement of the detachment if the escape had been effected. I do not think the facts justify the treatment of the prisoner but, to a large extent, they excuse it. The recommendation of the Judge-Advocate General is approved."[76]

On the same day, President Roosevelt scribbled in pencil and then signed a typed commutation of Preston Brown's sentence:

> So much of the sentence in this case as imposed imprisonment is disapproved and so much of the sentence as imposed dismissal is confirmed and commuted to a reduction of thirty files in lineal rank on the list of first lieutenants of Infantry and a forfeiture of one-half of the officer's monthly pay for a period of nine months.

Roosevelt added an explanation that adapted Davis's recommendation, but he made it his own by putting it in the first person:

> While the circumstances attending the act, which took place during the progress of an engagement with the enemy, were such as to excuse the method to which the accused resorted in order to prevent an escape, and to diminish to that extent his criminal responsibility in the matter, they do not justify the lack of self-control which he displayed in the treatment of an unarmed native who had fallen into his hands as a prisoner of war. While I expect, and shall insist that all operations against the enemy shall be prosecuted with such vigor and determination as are demanded by the importance of the undertaking or the emergency of the case, I shall also expect from every officer of the Army such an exercise of forbearance and self-restraint in the conduct of hostilities as will be calculated to insure a reasonable and humane observance of the laws and usages of war.[77]

On its way back to the Adjutant General's Office, the commutation received three favorable endorsements. Major General Loyd Wheaton, commanding officer of the Department of North Philippines and a proponent of hard war in the Philippines, was "of the opinion that it will be for the interest of the service that the unexecuted portion of the sentence as mitigated in his case be remitted," as Brown's trial, conviction and sentence "had an injurious effect upon the troops serving in this Department." He noted that the court "was largely composed of officers of brief service in the Archipelago and that want of experience in dealing with the treachery of the natives possibly had an influence upon their action." General Chaffee wrote: "I know nothing of the evidence in this case, but I know Lieutenant Brown, 2d Infantry personally, and that his previous service as an officer has been extremely creditable to him." The final endorsement, by Judge Advocate General Davis, was not surprising, because Roosevelt's mitigation of Brown's sentence was precisely what Davis had recommended in the final version of his memorandum to Root. Davis concluded that "the clemency shown by the President in this case was all that was deserved in view of the facts disclosed by the record" and recommended that Brown be ordered to duty with his command without further delay.[78]

The final endorsement, on April 14, 1902, came just in time. By mid-April 1902, the press in the United States, probably aided by leaks from General Miles, was filled with news of American abuses in Samar and elsewhere. On April 11, Senator Lodge's committee on the Philippines published a report of brutalities by American soldiers in Tayabas Province, and of the common use by American soldiers and of many officers of the term "niggers" to refer to Filipinos. Witnesses at Senator Lodge's hearings on the Philippines repeatedly testified as to interrogation by "water cure." Lodge stated with regret that some American soldiers had tortured and killed Filipino guerrillas and said that no effort would be spared in bringing the guilty to judgment— but he also reported that some American prisoners of war had had their eyes slashed, their ears cut off, and their bowels cut out; others had been dismembered with axes, buried alive, or stoned to death. In private, Lodge reported that some captive Americans had been castrated and gagged with their own testicles. "Perhaps," as Lodge dryly told the Senate, "the action of the American soldier is not altogether without provocation." Also made public in mid-April was testimony by Major Littleton Waller, at his court-martial in Manila for executing 12 Filipino civilians in Samar without trial, that his superior officer Brigadier General Jacob H. Smith, the American commander in Samar, had ordered him to "kill and burn, the more you kill and burn the better you will please me" and had also ordered that "the interior of Samar must be made a howling wilderness."[79]

Brown was sent back to the Second Infantry. On July 2, 1902, he was promoted to captain. His military career was back on track. On July 14,

Root delivered to Roosevelt a transcript of General Smith's court-martial in Manila. The court found Smith guilty of excessive zeal and merely admonished him. President Roosevelt ordered Smith—whose offenses were far graver and more publicized than the allegations against Brown—dismissed from the Army.[80]

On the same day Brown was promoted to captain, but by proclamation postdated to July 4 because of the happy connotations of that date, President Roosevelt proclaimed that the Philippines had been pacified, turned the islands over to civil government, and issued a general amnesty to all political prisoners save the Moslem rebels in the south.[81] While campaigns against the southern rebels and against small bands of guerillas were to continue until 1913, the insurrection in the Philippines had been broken. The process was far from the "benevolent assimilation" McKinley had envisaged. More than four thousand American soldiers had died and perhaps sixteen thousand Filipino *insurrectos*. Estimates of Filipino civilian deaths from fighting and disease (in particular a cholera epidemic from 1902 to 1904) range from two hundred thousand to one million.[82]

9

An Award from General Pershing

Preston Brown remained in the U. S. Army. He rose rapidly through the ranks, distinguishing himself particularly in World War I, when he was promoted to brigadier general by General John Pershing. In due course he became a major general. His record bears out the confidence in him displayed by his superior officers and by President Roosevelt in commuting his sentence for the killing in the Philippines.

In January 1919, months after the end of World War I, the War Department notified Brown of the award to him, by President Wilson, of the Distinguished Service Medal. The typed one-page notice, on yellowing paper, on my office wall, contains this citation:

> Brigadier General Preston Brown, U.S. Army
>
> For exceptionally meritorious and distinguished services.
>
> As Chief of Staff of the Second Division he directed the details of the battles near Château-Thierry, Soissons and at the St. Mihiel salient with great credit. Later, in command of the Third Division in the Argonne-Meuse Offensive, at a most critical time, by his splendid judgment and energetic action the division was able to carry to a successful conclusion the operations at Clair Chêne and Hill 294.
>
> By Command of General Pershing[1]

The American battles in World War I are much less familiar to most of us than the major battles of World War II or, for that matter, battles like

Fig. 9.1. General Preston Brown. *Author's collection.*

Gettysburg and Antietam in the Civil War. Although World War I lasted more than four years (August 1914–November 1918), the United States was involved for less than two years, and Americans fought in the war for only 150 days. America, however, contributed directly to Germany's defeat—and the battles listed in Brown's citation, unfamiliar though they now may be, were key components in blocking (less than 50 miles from Paris) and then turning back the Germans' final massive 1918 offensive and in leading Germany to ask for an armistice. (See map 9.1 for American battles in World War I.) Moreover, the American experience in the war—short though it was as compared with the involvement of the British, French, Italians, Russians, Germans, and Austrians—trained the U.S. Army and officers like George C. Patton, Douglas MacArthur, and George C. Marshall for the challenges of World War II, which began for America little more than 20 years after the first world war ended.

World War I broke out in Europe with the brainless unstoppability of a doomsday machine. The powers of Europe had been polarized into competing alliances, with Germany and Austria-Hungary in an alliance of Central Powers and Britain, France, and Russia in a Triple Entente. Germany and Britain were engaged in an ever-escalating naval armaments race. The assassination in June 1914 of Archduke Franz Ferdinand of Austria in Sarajevo by a young Bosnian Serb led to an Austrian ultimatum to Serbia. When Serbia declined to comply with all of Austria's demands, Austria began to mobilize its armed forces. Russia in turn began to mobilize its army. Germany responded by starting to mobilize, which led France at the start of August 1914 to order mobilization, after which Germany declared war on Russia. It may well be that Austria-Hungary, a multiethnic agglomeration, was itching to attack Serbia before the archduke's assassination and that Germany was eager to take territory from Russia, which had shown its weakness in its war with Japan in 1905. Alternatively, it is possible that Russia and Germany were competing over which would have the greater influence over Asiatic Turkey.[2]

To many Americans, this multinational war sounded like a pan-European mess that was better to avoid than to step into. The sympathies of America's President Woodrow Wilson, a Democrat, were with France and Britain, not with the Central Powers, but he hoped his role would be that of peacemaker, not leader of a nation at war. On August 19, 1914, in a message to Congress, Wilson noted that the people of the United States are drawn "chiefly from the nations now at war" and declared that America "must be neutral in fact, as well as in name" if it, "as the one great nation at peace," is to be "ready to play a part of impartial mediation."[3] Career soldiers like Preston Brown, however, recognized the likelihood of war. As one junior American officer in World War I put it, officers knew that "war was inevitable—two big dogs on the same street will always fight" and that "the politicians had retired to a collective farm—an ostrich farm."[4]

Brown and officers like him sought to position themselves to play a part in the war they foresaw—knowing well that promotions come quickly in wartime and with painful slowness in peace. During the Spanish-American and Philippine Wars, Brown (despite the setback caused by his court-martial) had advanced in three years, between 1899 and 1902, from second lieutenant to captain—but he then stayed at that rank, once peace broke out, until 1916, when he was promoted to major while posted in the Philippines. In April 1914, months before the war broke out, Brown, then in the Staff Class at the Army Service Schools in Fort Leavenworth, Kansas, wrote to the adjutant general of the Army requesting that he "be detailed to serve with the German Army during the ensuing year." Presumably he wanted to see how a large modern army functioned and to learn about a major potential enemy of the United States. The acting commandant at the Army Service Schools wrote a cover letter to the adjutant general that contained a highly qualified endorsement of Brown's request: "Captain Brown reads, speaks and writes French well, but has a very limited knowledge of the German language. In my opinion Captain Brown is an excellent officer for detail with a French regiment, and if his deficiency in German is not an objection, favorable consideration of this application is urged."[5] Not surprisingly, Brown was not detailed to the German army.

In 1916, Wilson was elected to a second term as president in a close election, helped by the Democratic Party slogan "He kept us out of war." But America was looking less and less neutral. Relations with Germany had come close to breaking in May 1915, when a German submarine torpedoed the Cunard liner *Lusitania*, which was carrying from New York to Britain not only passengers but also war materiel, including forty-two hundred boxes of .303 caliber cartridges for British rifles. Of the 1,195 who died in the liner's sinking, 128 were Americans. In the face of American and international outrage, Germany announced restrictions on its torpedoing of ships from neutral nations. America continued, however, to supply large amounts of war materiel to Britain and France.

At the beginning of 1917, the American army numbered only about two hundred thousand soldiers, including the National Guard, with fewer than fifteen hundred machine guns among them. The Americans had no tanks. Even a year later, Dwight Eisenhower, then a young captain in charge of training more than ten thousand men in a new Tank Corps, had to do so without any tanks: he had to make do with machine guns mounted on flatbed trucks. The total number of American troops was a small fraction of the 2.5 million men the Central Powers had on their Western Front.[6] Germany saw the United States as a likely ally of France, Great Britain, and Russia but believed it would be able to defeat the Allies before America could build up its small army, that German submarines could block the transport of American troops to Europe ("I guarantee on my word as a naval officer that no American will set foot on the Continent!" Germany's chief of naval general staff told the kaiser), and that torpedoing merchant ships to cut off the supply of American munitions was key to the Allied defeat. At the beginning of February 1917, Germany announced it was resuming unrestricted submarine warfare. In late February, American feelings against Germany were further inflamed by publication of a telegram that had been deciphered by British Naval Intelligence, in which the German foreign secretary, Arthur Zimmerman, proposed a German alliance with Mexico, including the understanding that Mexico would recover the territory it had lost to the United States in the Mexican War.[7] On April 6, 1917, Congress, acting on Wilson's request, declared war on the German empire.

What followed was a race against time. Both sides of the fighting in Europe were exhausted. By the beginning of 1917, France and Germany had each suffered the deaths of close to a million soldiers, and British military dead were not far fewer. Roughly three times as many soldiers had been wounded. Russia had lost even more in dead and wounded than France, Britain, or Germany. The cost in blood, coupled with shortages of food, the Russian Revolution, and the Czar's abdication in March 1917, led the Russians to stop fighting. Even before Lenin's government in October

1917 declared a three-month armistice, which eventually led to lasting cessation of Russian fighting under a treaty dictated by the Germans, the Russian army had melted away. In Lenin's words, Russia's soldiers had "voted for peace with their feet." The end of Russian willingness to keep on fighting meant that Germany could shift to the Western Front fifty divisions—more than seven hundred thousand combat-hardened men—who had been fighting on the Eastern Front.[8]

The German commanders saw this as an opportunity to launch what they hoped would be one final, crushing offensive on the Western Front early in 1918, thrusting toward Paris. If successful, according to German Chief of Staff General Erich Ludendorff, the drive would "cut the bulk of the English Army from the French, and crowd it up with its back against the sea." The Germans had the resources for only one offensive. Ludendorff told a meeting of German general staff officers in November 1917: "Our general situation requires that we should strike at the earliest moment, if possible at the end of February or beginning of March, before the Americans can throw strong forces into the scale."[9]

The question was whether the American forces could tip the scale in time. The challenge for the United States was immense, given the small size and inadequate arms of its army when Congress declared war in April 1917. Before American soldiers could make a difference on the Western front, the United States had to draft, train, and transport many hundreds of thousands of troops to France and provide them with adequate weapons. None of this happened overnight—but, with supreme effort and with the French and the British supplying most of the needed artillery, tanks, and aircraft, it did eventually happen.

A week after America's declaration of war, Wilson established a Committee of Public Information, chaired by George Creel, to start whipping up American enthusiasm for the war. Propaganda stories of German atrocities were circulated. George M. Cohan's song "Over There," written days after war was declared, became a national favorite, with crowds roaring out "We'll be over, we're coming over, and we won't be back till it's over over there!" Eventually patriotic anti-German sentiment in the United States was to manifest itself by people killing dachshunds. One victim, a dog named Fritzi, was owned by the family of my mother, then a 10-year-old girl in Harrisburg, Pennsylvania. My mother's grandfather had come to America from Germany, and my mother had been raised in part by a German governess. The dog was poisoned to death, presumably by neighbors. Notwithstanding the poisoning, my mother's father, having fought for the U.S. Army in the Spanish-American War, fought with the Americans in France in World War I.[10]

On May 19, 1917, Congress passed the Selective Service Act. The first drawing of draft numbers was on July 20. In time, 24 million Americans were registered for the draft, and 2.4 million were inducted into service. On May 2, Major General John J. Pershing, whose largest prior command had been of fifteen thousand men in the Punitive Expedition into Mexico in 1916–1917 in response to Pancho Villa's raids into America, was informed that he was to command all of the American forces. By mid-June, Pershing was in Paris, being greeted ecstatically by the French. On July 4, in ceremonies at Lafayette's tomb, with American officers acknowledging the crucial role played by Lafayette and the French troops he commanded in the American Revolution, Colonel Charles E. Stanton, an officer on Pershing's staff, voiced America's determination to repay its debt to France with the phrase (often incorrectly attributed to Pershing), "Lafayette, we are here."[11]

The "we" at the time was tiny in number—but the Americans kept coming. Admiral Eduard von Capelle, Germany's secretary of state for the Navy, had assured a German parliamentary committee in January 1917 not to be concerned about American soldiers: "They will not even come, because our submarines will sink them. Thus America from a military point of view means nothing, and again nothing, and for a third time nothing." But use of convoys and destroyers protected the troop ships from submarine attack, and the Americans did come to France, with increasing speed. By mid-March 1918, barely a year after the American declaration of war, close to five hundred thousand U.S. troops were in France. That number grew to 1.3 million by August 1918.[12]

It was many months after Pershing's arrival in France, however, before American troops were numerous and trained enough to be able to fight against the Germans on the Western Front. The delay resulted in part from Pershing's refusal, consistent with his instructions from U.S. Secretary of War Newton D. Baker, to accede to repeated requests of French and British senior staff officers to use American troops not as a unified American command but instead as soldiers to be dispersed to fill gaps in depleted French and British units. Under Baker's instructions, Pershing was to cooperate with the other countries fighting Germany, "but in so doing the underlying view must be kept in view that the forces of the United States are a separate and distinct component of the combined forces, the identity of which must be preserved," though this "fundamental rule" was "subject to such minor exceptions in particular circumstances as your judgment may approve."[13]

In October 1917, American troops fired for the first time on German positions in France, near Nancy. On the early morning of November 3, on the heels of a shattering artillery barrage, a German patrol attacked an American platoon, killing three—the first Americans killed in the war. By March 1918, the total American Expeditionary Force numbered about half a million men. But although the AEF added strength to the Allies, the addition of troops transferred from the Eastern Front meant that the Germans had 3,575,000 officers and men, organized in 192 divisions, available on the Western Front. Sixty-nine divisions were available for Ludendorff's Operation Michael grand offensive, facing 33 British divisions. The German attack began on March 21, 1918, preceded by a barrage from 6,700 German guns.[14] On March 23, the Germans began to lob giant shells into Paris from a huge gun, 120 feet long with a range of 75 miles, which came to be known as Big Bertha. By April 5, the first of Ludendorff's 1918 offensives had advanced 40 miles. The farthest point reached in the German advance, near Montdidier, was only 45 miles from Paris.[15]

In late May, General Robert Lee Bullard, commanding the American 1st Division, sent a regiment to take the town of Cantigny. The Americans took the town and were able to hold it, despite German barrages and counter-attacks. Although not large, the operation had morale-building significance for the Americans and their allies, because it showed that American troops could advance against seasoned German forces. On May 27, a day before the American attack on Cantigny, Ludendorff launched another offensive, farther to the south—a drive toward Soissons, which was an important rail center, and the Marne River. Ludendorff originally intended the drive as a feint, intended to cause the French to move some of their forces south to protect Paris so the Germans could push harder in the north to split the British from the French forces—but the speed and extent of the German advance to the south led Ludendorff to change his plans, with the hope of driving south to the Marne and then marching west to Paris. By June 3, barely a week after the start of the new offensive, German troops had advanced 30 miles to the south and crossed the Marne east of Château-Thierry—56 miles from Paris. The Germans had taken sixty thousand French prisoners, six hundred and fifty artillery pieces, and two thousand machine guns.[16]

On May 30, General Henri-Philippe Pétain, the French commander in chief, called on Pershing for American troops to be sent to the Château-Thierry region, to join with the French in attempting to block the German drive. The only American divisions reasonably close were the 3rd Division, under General Joseph Dickman, and the 2nd Division, commanded by General Omar Bundy.[17] Preston Brown, who had arrived in France in August 1917 as a lieutenant colonel and who became a full colonel in February 1918, was Bundy's chief of staff. According to the military historian Brigadier General John S. D. Eisenhower, "Bundy was not a born warrior," but Brown, "sharp-witted and pugnacious . . , was a capable officer and Bundy often allowed him to carry the brunt of negotiations with the French—and anyone else."[18] It helped that Brown spoke French, as a fellow officer put it, "fluently at times, vehemently always when it fell to him to negotiate."[19] Occasionally Brown was so vocal in his criticism of the French (bumptiousness, again) that Pershing had to clamp down on him.[20] Colonel Rozet, on the staff of General Pétain, complained in May 1918 that Brown was disposed "to keep the French at arm's length and act with almost complete independence of them. However well instructed and capable Colonel Brown may be, he should not indulge the illusion that he cannot profit by the counsel and example of excellent French officers who have made war for nearly four years; he has never made war."[21]

Brown soon put to use both his knowledge of French and his military training. On June 1, Bundy and Brown arrived at the headquarters of General Jean Degoutte, commander of the French XXI Corps, not far from Château-Thierry. Degoutte explained that the Germans had taken Hill 204, only four miles away, which dominated the area, and were preparing to move west on the highway to Paris. Only two exhausted French divisions stood in their way. Degoutte planned to send the American units into battle one at a time, under French command. Brown, as spokesman for the

Americans, contended that piecemeal use of the Americans would be inef-
fective and that the right course was for the Americans to form a secondary
defensive line behind the French and hold that line as the French dropped
back through it. "Can the Americans really hold?" Degoutte asked. Brown
replied, with some hyperbole: "General, these are American regulars. In
a hundred and fifty years they have never been beaten. They will hold."[22]
They did.

On June 6, the left sector of the 2nd Division, led by the 4th Marine
Brigade, attacked Belleau Wood, a few miles northwest of Château-
Thierry. The Marines charged in rows, in the face of heavy machine gun
fire. On that single day, the 4th Brigade suffered 1,087 casualties, including
222 deaths. The Germans, after yielding some ground in heavy fighting,
determined to counterattack. As Max von Boehm, the German general
commanding Germany's Seventh Army, put it, "An American success
along our front, even if only temporary, may have the most unfavorable
influence on the attitude of the Entente and the duration of the war. In
the coming battles, therefore, it is not a question of the possession of this
or that village or woods, insignificant in itself; it is a question of whether
the Anglo-American claims that the American Army is the equal or even
the superior of the German Army is to be made good."[23] What followed
was a bloody struggle for Belleau Wood, with the Americans taking still
more horrendous casualties. In one of those fights, Marine First Sergeant
Daniel Joseph Daly, with the Sixth Marine Division, attacking Belleau
Wood from the south, is said to have urged his men forward in the face of
German machine gun fire by calling out "Come on, you sons of bitches,
do you want to live forever?" Daly, 5' 6", not much over 130 pounds, had
already won two Medals of Honor, one in the siege of Peking in 1900,
one in Haiti in 1915. For his actions at Belleau Wood, including taking
out a German machine gun nest by himself, he was recommended for a
third Medal of Honor and awarded the Distinguished Service Cross and
the Navy Cross.[24] Belleau Wood was not finally cleared of Germans until
June 26, and the operations of the 2nd Division around Château-Thierry
did not end until July 1, with the capture of the town of Vaux, just west of
Château-Thierry. In a single month, the 2nd Division had suffered 9,777
casualties, including 1,811 dead, out of what had been a total strength of
17,000. Many of the living casualties had been wounded in mustard gas

barrages, the mustard gas blistering their bodies and leaving them, as an American in an evacuation hospital reported, "nearly all blinded, many delirious, all crying, moaning, tossing about." Others were shell-shock cases, some of whom, as an American medical officer reported, "cursed and raved and had to be tied to their litters; some shook violently . . . some trembled and slunk away in apparent abject fear of every incoming shell, while others simply stood speechless, oblivious to all surroundings."[25] But the 2nd Division near Château-Thierry had proven the American willingness to fight. A German intelligence officer rated the division "very good," noting: "The spirit of the troops is high and they possess an innocent self confidence." According to Ludendorff, they were a "crack unit"; "Their nerves are still strong and they are well fed."[26] "They fight like devils," a German lieutenant wrote in his diary, after an American night attack that made for what the lieutenant called "the worst night in my life."[27]

The Germans did not continue down the main road toward Paris from Château-Thierry—in part because of fights like Belleau Wood and others in the region, but in large part because of logistical difficulties: the two roads and single railroad at the Germans' disposal were far from enough to move the supplies they needed to continue their drive. Ludendorff shifted his efforts to the northwest of Château-Thierry, starting an attack on July 8. The German army had already suffered half a million casualties. Food supplies were low, and German troops were being laid low by a flu epidemic that hit the Germans before it hit the Allies and by the end of the war was to cost the lives of 186,000 German troops.[28] Still, in mid-July, the Germans poured across the Marne and south in the valley of the Surmelin River, which was defended by the American 3rd Division—earning it the name "The Rock of the Marne" as it held its positions and destroyed the German attackers despite suffering terrible casualties. The German offensive failed. The ferocity of the American fighting left a deep mark on the German soldiers. One German officer, after describing the action as "the heaviest defeat of the war," wrote: "Never have I seen so many dead men, never such frightful battle scenes. . . . The American had nerve; we must give him credit for that; but he also displayed a savage roughness. 'The Americans kill everybody!' was the cry of terror of July 15th, which for a long time stuck in the bones of our men. . . . Of the troops led into action on July 15th, more than 60 per cent were left dead or wounded, lying on the field of battle."[29]

General Ferdinand Foch, the Supreme Commander of the Allied Forces, believed that the Germans had been sufficiently battered by this time that the Allies could take the offensive by reducing the salient that had been caused by the German drive south from the Aisne River to Château-Thierry and the Marne, focusing on the rail center at Soissons. Pershing had the same idea. The American Expeditionary Force's 2nd Division (under its new commander, Major General James G. Harbord, with Brown continuing as chief of staff) and 1st Division (under General Charles P. Summerall) played a central part in the attack, fighting under French command alongside the 1st Moroccan Colonial Division. Within days in mid-July, the three divisions had broken the German lines and taken the road between Soissons and Château-Thierry—but the 2nd Division had suffered forty-three hundred casualties and the 1st Division sixty-nine hundred. All told, three hundred thousand American troops took part in eliminating the Aisne-Marne salient, at a cost of fifty thousand casualties.[30] The Americans fought hard. The Jesuit priest Pierre Teilhard de Chardin, then a corporal and stretcher-bearer in the Moroccan division, wrote a friend a week after July 18 that the Americans are "first-rate troops, fighting with intense *individual* passion (concentrated on the enemy) and wonderful courage. The only complaint one would make about them is that they don't take sufficient care; they're too apt to get themselves killed."[31]

German Chancellor von Hertling later wrote that on July 15, the Germans expected to be in Paris by the end of July, but by July 18, "even the most optimistic among us understood that all was lost." According to Field Marshal von Hindenburg, "it was of the greatest and most fateful importance that we had lost the initiative to the enemy," and "the steady arrival of American reinforcements," though "not yet quite up to the level of modern requirements in a purely military sense," had to be "particularly valuable for the enemy. . . . How many hopes, cherished during the last few months, had probably collapsed at one blow!"[32]

At the end of the attacks, Pershing visited 2nd Division headquarters. Finding Harbord and Brown hardly able to "express their enthusiasm over the achievements of their division," Pershing happily congratulated them "on its splendid conduct," saying, "even though the 1st and 2nd Divisions should never fire another shot they had made themselves and their commanders immortal."[33] As then-colonel George C. Marshall wrote soon after the war,

> The entire aspect of the war had changed. The great counteroffensive on July 18th at Soissons had swung the tide of battle in favor of the Allies, and the profound depression which had been accumulating since March 21st was in a day dissipated and replaced by a wild enthusiasm throughout France and especially directed toward the American troops who had so unexpectedly assumed the leading role in the Marne operation. Only someone who has witnessed the despair and experienced the desperate resolution when defeat is anticipated can fully realize the reversal of feeling flowing from the sudden vision of a not too distant victory. The stock of confidence in America, which had been quoted far below par, was in a day sold at a premium.[34]

Preston Brown, for his part in the 2nd Division's successful operations at Soissons, was promoted to brigadier general in August 1918.[35]

The AEF now had 1.2 million men in France and was growing at two hundred fifty thousand per month—the only Allied force that was continuing to grow.[36] Momentum was with the Allies, but bitter fighting lay ahead. The next major American fight was the first large-scale offensive in the war that was undertaken primarily by an American army. The army was the newly formed 1st Army, commanded by Pershing himself. Its first mission was the reduction of the St. Mihiel salient. Between Verdun and Nancy, not far from the German border, the Germans in 1914 had driven a bulge (the French referred to it as "The Hernia") that guarded the German rail center at Metz and pointed south and west toward Paris. Foch gave the 1st Army (including Preston Brown's 2nd Division) the job of crushing the salient and then moving most of its troops 60 miles north to the Meuse-Argonne, north of Verdun, to take part in a massive effort by Belgian, British, French, and American troops to push the German line back from Verdun all the way north to the English Channel. In two days, between September 12 and September 14, after a massive artillery barrage by 3,010 guns (none American made), American troops, aided by 267 French tanks manned by Americans and French and by French aircraft flown by American airmen under Colonel Billy Mitchell, eliminated the salient, with the 2nd and 89th Divisions taking the town of Thiaucourt. The operation was much less bloody than anticipated, because Ludendorff had already ordered his forces to fall back to shorten the German lines, but the 1st Army nonetheless suffered 7,000 killed or wounded in the two-day fight. The speed of the Americans' taking of the salient, attributable in large part to Ludendorff's evacuation order, gave the Americans an unwarranted sense of confidence. Pershing told his intelligence officer that "the reason for the American triumph lay in the superior nature of the American character," because Americans—descended from bold immigrants—"had the willpower and spirit that Europeans lacked." As soon as the St. Mihiel salient fell, much of the 1st Army was moved north to the Meuse-Argonne region, a massive movement of troops and materiel carried out under what Pershing correctly described as "the able direction of Colonel George C. Marshall, Jr." The Meuse-Argonne was to prove a far more brutal fighting ground than the St. Mihiel salient.[37]

The area between the Meuse River on the east and the Argonne Forest on the west was controlled by German guns in the Argonne Forest and on the Heights of the Meuse, east of that river. On September 26, the Americans started their attack. On the first day, Lieutenant Colonel George S. Patton, Jr., in charge of the new American Tank Corps (made up entirely of French tanks), got his first taste of tank warfare. His tanks mired down and he made some Americans hiding in trenches dig a passage to free the tanks. "I think I killed one man here," Patton later recalled; "He would not work, so I hit him over the head with a shovel." Patton was wounded in the leg and put out of action on the first day, and within days most of the U.S. tank corps broke down or was knocked out of service by German gunfire. The American offensive came to a standstill, as ten German divisions were poured into the Meuse-Argonne Valley by September 30.[38] Because of American inexperience and the inability to shift enough troops and artillery from St. Mihiel to the Meuse-Argonne before the Germans could reinforce their troops there, a dangerous stalemate had developed.

The American troops kept driving forward, however, in the face of heavy machine gun and artillery fire. One young lieutenant who took charge of his company after his captain was killed advanced until a bursting shell reduced two of his runners to "a pile of horrible red guts and blood and meat" and tore out part of his shoulder blade and collar bone. The lieutenant was to remember the high explosives bursting overhead as "a great swishing stream, a smash-bang, and it seems to tear everything loose from you. The intensity of it simply enters your heart and brain, and tears every nerve to pieces." But the Americans on the east side of the Meuse-Argonne drive were able to get north of and behind the Germans in the Argonne Forest, forcing them to pull out. As part of that drive, Corporal Alvin C. York, a woodsman and hunter from Wolf Valley, Tennessee, took charge of a squad sent to reduce a machine gun nest after his sergeant was wounded, shot and killed at least twenty Germans, and, with the help of a German major the squad had taken prisoner, induced the gun crews of other German machine gun nests to surrender. York and what was left of his squad brought back to American lines 132 German prisoners. The number of surrendering Germans was clear evidence that German soldiers were recognizing their cause was becoming lost. By October 10, the Germans had left the Argonne Forest.[39]

The cost to the Americans of the Meuse-Argonne offensive was painfully high: 26,277 dead and 95,786 wounded.[40] But the German thrust had been stopped, and the German armies were beginning to be pushed back. As early as August 9, after 50,000 German troops surrendered in a single day in the face of a combined British-French attack near Cambrai, Ludendorff had told another officer "We cannot win this war any more, but we must not lose it." By late September, with the commencement of a giant drive by eight Allied armies that extended all the way from a thrust by Americans and French toward Sedan on the Meuse to attacks by Belgian and British armies in Flanders, Ludendorff and von Hindenburg both decided it was time to seek an armistice, with the hope of avoiding a shameful peace. By October 6, a new German chancellor sent a message to President Wilson requesting the immediate conclusion of an armistice. Jockeying began regarding the terms of the armistice while soldiers on both sides continued to die by the tens of thousands.[41]

On October 18, Pershing placed Preston Brown in command of the 3rd Division, which had been stalled in its efforts to drive north to the Kriemhilde portion of the Hindenburg Line. Brown pushed the division forward to the Hindenburg Line, with the notable captures of the Bois Clairs Chênes and Hill 294, although the effort took such a toll on the division that it was withdrawn for a much-needed rest on October 27. The division had taken Bois Clairs Chênes early on October 20, lost it in a counterattack, and later in the same day recaptured it.[42] By the end of October, American troops had broken through the Hindenburg line to the north of the Meuse-Argonne in bloody fighting that earned Douglas MacArthur a Distinguished Service Cross. Pershing urged his tired troops on, wiring all his corps and division commanders: "Now that Germany and the Central Powers are losing, they are begging for an armistice . . . [We] must strike harder than ever. Our strong blows are telling, and continued pressure by us has compelled the enemy to meet us, enabling our Allies to gain on other parts of the line. There can be no conclusion to this war until Germany is brought to her knees." The Americans kept driving north toward Sedan on the Meuse, the town where the Prussians had captured the French emperor Napoleon III in 1870. In their zeal, the Americans (encouraged by Pershing) managed to step on French toes by threatening to take Sedan before the French could take it and so avenge their 1870 humiliation there.[43]

The Allied commanders in chief formulated armistice terms that were intended to cripple Germany's ability to keep fighting. Under those terms, the Germans had to evacuate Belgium, France, and Alsace-Lorraine; surrender five thousand cannon, thirty thousand machine guns, five thousand locomotives, one hundred fifty thousand railway cars, and one hundred fifty submarines; evacuate the left bank of the Rhine; and permit Allied forces to occupy bridgeheads on the Rhine's right bank. On October 26, with strong encouragement from the kaiser , Ludendorff resigned. Germany was in turmoil. Bolshevik uprisings in parts of the German Navy in early November were suppressed with difficulty. On November 9, the German chancellor announced that the kaiser had abdicated. Early in the morning of November 11, Germany acceded to the Allied terms. The armistice went into effect at 11 AM on November 11, 1918—the eleventh hour of the eleventh day of the eleventh month. The war was over. The American Expeditionary Force was demobilized and sent back to the United States as promptly as possible, except for a number of divisions (including Preston Brown's 3rd Division) that were posted in the bridgeheads across the Rhine at least until the Treaty of Versailles was signed on June 28, 1919.[44]

In battle in the war, 53,500 Americans died. Another 63,000 died from diseases (primarily influenza) and other causes, and American troops

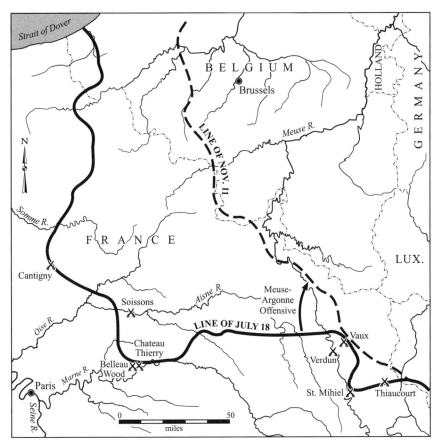

Map 9.1. American Battles in World War I; Allied Advances, July 18–November 11, 1918

suffered 204,000 nonfatal wounds. Many of those wounds had lifelong effects: I remember one of my high school teachers in the 1950s who coughed repeatedly from lung damage inflicted by a German gas attack in 1918. But the U.S. casualties during America's brief involvement in the war were far fewer than those suffered by countries that had been in the war since 1914. Some 900,000 British were killed, more than 1.3 million French, nearly 3 million Germans and Austrians, and 1.7 million Russians.[45]

Preston Brown continued as a career officer. He was assistant chief of staff at the AEF's Advanced General Headquarters at Trier, Germany, after the Armistice. From 1919 to 1921, he was acting commandant of the Army War College. In December 1925, he became a major general.

Retired Sergeant Joseph Haifer, who years before had taught Brown soldiering when Brown was a private and who had been at Brown's side in 1897 when Brown was commissioned as a second lieutenant, stood beside Brown as he took the oath as a major general. Brown served as deputy chief of staff of the Army (1930), commanding general of the Panama Canal Department (1930-1933), and commanding general of the Second Army (1933-1934) before he retired in November 1934 (see figure 9.1 for Brown as general).[46]

The engagements listed in Brown's Distinguished Service Medal citation, which took place between June and October 1918, were key actions in America's involvement in the First World War. In each engagement, Brown drove himself and his troops forward under fire with the aggressiveness—bumptiousness—that proved essential and that had been foreshadowed by Brown's willingness to take action as a young first lieutenant in the Philippines. Thanks in part to that aggressive drive, more American troops died in battle and of battle wounds in the 2nd Division, for which Brown was for many months the key officer, than in any other division in the AEF—and the 2nd Division earned more decorations for valor than any other AEF division.[47]

What was Brown like? My father told military historian Edward M. Coffman, who was writing a book about the American involvement in World War I, that Preston Brown was "one of the wittiest and most colorful of men, a thunderer when it came to demanding discipline of his officers but kind and tender beneath all the bluster. . . . He was greatly loved and greatly hated, and I discovered . . . that those who hated him were usually lax soldiers, and those who loved him were usually good ones. General Bradley was among the latter."[48] My brother, decades ago, met a man who had served with Brown and referred to him as "the meanest son of a bitch ever to have been in the United States Army." That was far from my brother's or my own impression of the general. Years after World War I, my father ran across a man who had been a private in the 2nd Division and who had only good things to say about Preston Brown. The man had come to France in spring or early summer 1917, almost a year before the Americans began fighting, and went AWOL because there was nothing much going on. He came back to the division when he heard it was soon to go into battle. Preston Brown told him he could have him shot for desertion, but because he came back when the fighting was about to start, Brown was sending him to the front.

Some years after World War I, Robert Lee Bullard included a profile of Brown in his book *Fighting Generals: Illustrated Biographical Sketches of Seven Major Generals in World War I.* Bullard had known Brown in the Philippines and, as a captain in 1901, had testified at Brown's court-martial as to the practice of shooting escaping prisoners. As a major general in World War I, Bullard commanded III Corps, which included Brown's divisions, before becoming commander of the American 2nd Army as the war drew to a close. In 1933, Bullard wrote to Blanton Winship, who as a captain had defended Brown in the 1901 court-martial and who by this time had become judge advocate general, to ask if he could take a look at the record of Brown's court martial, because he was working on a brief biography of Brown—whom he remembered as a "striking and outstanding soldier."[49]

In his book, Bullard remembered seeing Brown as a defendant in the court-martial in Manila—"built like a greyhound; his eyes were keen, his jaw and lips tightly closed. When he spoke, his words were quick and decided. These were all outward signs of a man of strong feelings and sudden impulses, of a man forceful and determined in his actions." Bullard noted that Brown's speech could be "rough and contemptuous, as when after the battle of Soissons, dissatisfied with the conduct of some of the officers of his division, he exclaimed to the provost marshal: 'Take them to the rear and put them in the dog pound.'" According to Bullard, Brown's "manner left none who were associated with him indifferent to him. Because of his force and drive, superiors generally admired him and let him have his way. But on account of a habit that he had of making sudden, fierce, and unusual demands and exactions upon them, his subordinates, especially the officers, stood in 'holy terror' of him." After describing the magnitude of Brown's achievements in World War I, Bullard ended his sketch of Brown:

> As a fighting soldier he had always been confident of himself; at times he was an autocrat. In crises he did not fail to act whether he had authority or not, and he used his power with an energy and determination that won the admiration even of his strongest critics.[50]

10

The Czar of Halfaday Creek and Hitler's Toilet Bowl

The final relics are a Western novel (see figure 10.1) and a piece of toilet bowl (see figure 10.5). To me, they stand for the Allied invasion in Normandy and the liberation of Nazi Europe (see map 10.1).

The Western novel is a hardcover book called *The Czar of Halfaday Creek*. It's a cheerful tale about people with lives to leave behind who go to live in a frontier mining community in the Yukon at the time of the Klondike Gold Rush. The edition I had was published in 1942. The book's browning and brittle paper reflects its wartime manufacture. My father gave it to me more than forty years ago. In 1992, I gave the book to the Eisenhower Presidential Library and Museum in Abilene, Kansas, because it was the book Eisenhower was reading in early June 1944, when the Normandy invasion was postponed for a day and before Eisenhower heard the first reports of how the invasion was going.

Dad was on the staff of Rear Admiral Alan G. Kirk, who commanded the Western Naval Task Force at Normandy. Dad had been on the admiral's staff when the Americans landed at Scoglitti, Sicily, in July 1943. In civilian life, Dad was a drama critic and lecturer. When he joined the Navy in 1943, at the age of 43—Dad was born in 1900, so it always was easy to figure his age—he claimed to be the oldest lieutenant j.g. in the United States Navy.

Admiral Kirk figured out a good use for Dad's civilian training: Dad served as a public relations officer; he was used as a way of keeping the

Fig. 10.1. Spine and cover of *The Czar of Halfaday Creek,* the western novel General Eisenhower was reading while D-Day was delayed because of bad weather. *Courtesy of Dwight D. Eisenhower Presidential Library and Museum, Abilene, Kansas. Gift of the author.*

sailors posted on what Kirk described as "the yarn of our daily lives and the news of great events." When the admiral was at sea, Dad would broadcast every day over the ship's public address system to the ship's crew, including the seven of every eight men who served below decks and could not see what was going on. Those broadcasts became the raw material for two books he wrote, *To All Hands* (on the Sicilian landing) and *Many a*

Watchful Night (on the Normandy invasion). Those books, wonderfully illustrated by Navy combat artists and photographers, tell me—as they told the many thousands who read them during the war—what it was like to be there.[1]

Dad was a small cog in the immense machine that became the Allied invasion of France. He was part of the flood of American resources that poured across the Atlantic into England—what Dad described as "a man-made Mississippi of strength and arms, of steel and gasoline, of concrete and woolens, of foodstuffs and homesickness." He was at United States Naval Command in London during the planning of the invasion—one of the Americans who, as he put it, "must have appeared as inexhaustible to Londoners as England's supply of Brussels sprouts did to Americans."[2]

Dad lived through the nighttime bombings of London. The raids involved fewer German planes than earlier in the war but were still deadly. He ran preparatory errands. He bought books about Normandy but—because there was reputed to be a German spy in the bookstore—also bought books on Calais and other possible invasion sites. Unbeknownst to Dad, the Allies had mounted a major effort to mislead the Germans into thinking that the long-awaited invasion effort would be directed at Calais, which was a major port and closer both to England and to Germany than was Normandy.

Dad also bought books on French art and history (I still have a small book on the Bayeux Tapestry that Dad bought as part of this effort). Tourist books and pictures of Normandy served an important intelligence-gathering function. A picture of a farmer's heavily laden hay wagon on an identifiable Normandy beach, for example, was graphic proof of the beach's ability to bear a calculable amount of weight at a particular point in the tide cycle. If a full hay wagon didn't sink down into the shingle, maybe a tank wouldn't, either.

Dad saw the signs of the coming of the long-awaited invasion—not just the immense build-up of soldiers but also the increasing number of conferences Admiral Kirk had with assorted "gold braid"—Generals Eisenhower, Bradley, and Montgomery; Admirals Stark, Hall, Wilkes, and Brereton—and their staffs. He saw the long hours of planning at the Naval Command, including the efforts of the photo interpreters and the shoreline map artists and the preparations by the force medical officer and his staff for the handling of the invasion's casualties. He saw the plans and maps of Admiral Kirk's command being shipped to the south of England for transfer to the admiral's flagship, the heavy cruiser *Augusta*. And, as May 1944 turned into June, King George VI himself came on board *Augusta* to inspect the American naval forces. The correspondents who were to cover the invasion were briefed on the plans and put aboard sealed ships. As a final talisman, Lieutenant General Omar N. Bradley, commander of the First Army and Eisenhower's second in command of the American Army, boarded *Augusta* with his staff.[3]

The invasion of France was scheduled to take place on Monday, June 5, 1944, when the tides were favorable. Daylight would be breaking at the time the incoming tides (bearing with them the invaders' demolition engineers) would reach the deadly obstacles Rommel's army had set up to hold and impale invading landing craft. Dad had heard the scuttlebutt. By June 3, his ship the *Augusta*—like all the thousands of ships taking part, ships assembling from all over England and from the Irish Sea—was sealed: you could get on, but you couldn't get off. How could the Germans not know what was coming, and where? The scale of the operation was immense: more than six thousand ships, eleven thousand planes, and two hundred thousand troops. Even if German intelligence was totally deficient, or misled by our planted leads that the invasion was aimed at Calais rather than the open beaches of Normandy, the carpeting of the sea with ships would tell any passing German plane what was afoot.

But the weather got worse and worse between Friday, June 2, and Sunday, June 4. If the decision to attack on Normandy's open beaches rather than at the port of Calais meant that the invaders would not have to contend with the immense fortifications and massed German armies at Calais, it also meant that the invaders were at the mercy of the waves as they tried to cross the Channel with ships of all kinds—not only trim destroyers but also landing craft and the cumbersome concrete shells that were towed to form the artificial harbors of Project Mulberry. Once the ships made it across, the invaders would be at the mercy of the surf as they tried to land on the well-defended beaches. Moreover, if the cloud cover was low, the Allies would not have the benefit of their air superiority over the Germans.

So General Eisenhower (see figure 10.2), as supreme commander of the Allied Expeditionary Force, faced a horrendous decision on Sunday, June

4. Do we launch the invasion in stormy weather—weather that could prove a more powerful enemy than the Germans? After all, storms had sunk far more Spanish ships in the Armada than Drake and his fellow English captains. Or do we defer a day, at the risk of a total loss of surprise and the chance that the weather will be no better the next day? Eisenhower also knew that if the invasion were deferred beyond June 6, the tides would not be favorable again until June 19–20—a postponement of two weeks that would surely carry with it the risk of demoralizing the invading forces and giving the Germans time to bring up crack troops to reinforce those manning the Normandy beaches. As it turned out, a vicious summer storm hit the Channel on June 18; the invasion would have had to be postponed another two weeks until the next favorable set of tides, and the delay would likely have meant that the invading forces would have been fighting in France, not in Germany, during the winter of 1944–1945.

On Friday, June 2, 1944, Eisenhower arrived at Southwick House, a Georgian country mansion outside of Portsmouth which served as headquarters for the Allied naval forces. He stayed in what he called "my circus wagon"—a trailer parked not far from the main building. Despite the deteriorating weather, Eisenhower on June 2 and 3 started into motion the units that would take the longest to reach Normandy—the midget submarines and the ships starting from the most distant points, Belfast and Clyde and Scapa Flow. There were numerous briefings by the meteorologists. At one briefing on Saturday, June 3, the sideline gossip included a definition of a meteorologist: an expert who can look into a girl's eyes and tell whether.[4]

Here's how Eisenhower described the situation in his diary for Saturday, June 3—writing for history, speaking of himself occasionally in a magisterial third person:

> The weather in this country is practically unpredictable. For some days our experts have been meeting almost hourly, and I have been holding commander-in-chief meetings once or twice daily to consider the reports and tentative predictions. While at this moment, the morning of June 3, it appears that the weather will not be so bad as to preclude landings and will possibly even permit reasonably effective gunfire support from the navy, the picture from the air viewpoint is not so good.

Fig. 10.2. Photograph of General Dwight D. Eisenhower, inscribed to the author and his brother. *Photograph by Bachrach. Author's collection.*

Probably no one who does not have the specific and direct respon-sibility of making the final decision as to what to do can under-stand the intensity of these burdens. The supreme commander, much more than any of his subordinates, is kept informed of the political issues involved, particularly the anticipated effect of delay upon the Russians. He, likewise, is in close touch with all the advice from his military subordinates and must face the issue even when technical advice as to weather is not unanimous from the several experts. Success or failure might easily hinge upon the effectiveness, for example, of airborne operations. If the weather is suitable for everything else, but unsuitable for airborne operations, the question becomes whether to risk the airborne movement anyway or to defer the whole affair in hopes of getting weather that is a little better.

My tentative thought is that the desirability for getting started on the next favorable tide is so great and the uncertainty of the weather is such that we could never anticipate really perfect weather coincident with proper tidal conditions, that we must go unless there is a real and very serious deterioration in the weather. . . .

Because the enemy in great strength is occupying a country that is interlaced with a fine communications system, our attack can be looked upon as reasonable only if our tremendous air force is able to attack his concentrations against us and to help destroy the effectiveness of any of his counterattacks. Weather again comes into this problem.[5]

The weather got worse, not better. The cloud layer became too low for the planes. Eisenhower polled his subordinates. The air commanders, Tedder and Leigh-Mallory, favored postponement; General Montgomery favored going ahead; the Navy commanders said the Navy could do its part, but the accuracy of naval bombardment would be badly reduced and the landing craft would be hard to control. Admiral Ramsay also warned Eisenhower that although a postponement of 24 hours was operationally possible, the invasion couldn't be postponed for another 24 hours after an initial postponement because the fleet would have to refuel, an operation that would force a postponement until the next favorable tide, which was not until June 19.

At 6 AM on Sunday, June 4, Eisenhower decided to postpone D-Day by 24 hours. The advance ships turned back to England in the foul weather.

The waiting on that windy, rainy day was not made easier by the behavior of Winston Churchill and Charles de Gaulle. Only days before, Churchill had announced that as head of the government, he intended to be part of the invading forces and to be there at the beaches. Churchill, who had shot Fuzzy-Wuzzies with a Mauser pistol at the Battle of Omdurman in 1898; Churchill, who had escaped from enemy captivity by crawling out a bathroom window in 1899, during the Boer War—Churchill, now 70 years old and gout-ridden, wanted to be in at the fighting, at the start of the decisive battle for Europe. Eisenhower did not need to add this to the problems of the invasion. He told Churchill that he, Eisenhower, was in command of the operation, and that Churchill couldn't be part of the invasion; Eisenhower wasn't going to risk losing him. Churchill said that although Eisenhower had operational command, he was not responsible administratively for the makeup of the ship's crews, and therefore "I can sign on as a member of the crew of one of His Majesty's ships, and there's nothing you can do about it." Eisenhower had his chief of staff tell the king of England about the problem. The king told Churchill that if Churchill went as head of the government, the king would feel obligated to go as well, as head of state. Churchill knew that the king couldn't be allowed to go, which meant that he, Churchill, couldn't be allowed to go either. Churchill, feeling that he had been outmaneuvered, and convinced that Eisenhower was behind it, was distinctly "peevish" when he visited Eisenhower's headquarters on June 2 and 3 after the king had prevented Churchill's boat ride in the invasion.[6]

Both Churchill and Eisenhower also had a number of run-ins in the days before D-Day with General de Gaulle. The British and the Americans wanted de Gaulle to deliver a broadcast to the people of France on D-Day urging the French people to obey instructions from SHAEF (Supreme Headquarters, Allied Expeditionary Force), but de Gaulle had his own ideas on what to say about who was running the liberated parts of France. It had been arranged that de Gaulle would meet with Eisenhower and Churchill in Portsmouth on Sunday, June 4, to work this out.

Once the decision to postpone the invasion had been made, there was nothing more for General Eisenhower to do but wait to see if the weather cleared up enough to permit the launching of the invasion. Eisenhower, we are told by his naval aide Harry C. Butcher, went to his sleeping caravan and stayed in bed late, reading a Western novel.[7]

That novel, *The Czar of Halfaday Creek*, by James B. Hendryx, was the book my father gave me and that I in turn gave to the Eisenhower Library. Dad, as a public relations officer for Admiral Kirk, was a friend of Eisenhower's aide Butcher, a former CBS radio executive who handled press relations for Eisenhower. After Dad returned to London from Normandy, Butcher gave Dad the actual book Eisenhower had been reading on D-Day and the day before.

The book is pleasant and non-taxing. The time is 1898 or 1899, during the Klondike Gold Rush. Cushing's Fort on Halfaday Creek is a community of outlaws conveniently located one mile away from the Alaskan border in the Yukon Territory. When Canadian police come looking, a wanted miscreant can go into Alaska, or into Canada if the searchers are American police. The center of the community is a saloon and trading post presided over by Cushing and Black John Smith, who keep order by convening miners' courts and hanging anyone convicted of specified crimes or the more inclusive offense of "skullduggery." New arrivals draw aliases, for use during their stay in the area, from the "name can" at the end of the bar—a molasses can in which Cushing and Smith have put slips of paper with names copied from a history book, but with first and last names mixed up. We read of the doings, for example, of George Cornwallis, Benedict Hale, Nathan Arnold, Eli Fulton, and Robert Whitney.

It is a moral tale. Black John Smith retrieves gold dust and money and bonds that have been stolen from the innocent. We do not see anyone die. The dialogue is cheerful:

> "Let's see, yer name is—er—?"
>
> "Smith," replied Black John. "It's a name that, once you get the hang of it, is fairly easy to remember."

Or Smith, again, to a malefactor:

"Yer guilty of the crime of extortion by means of kidnappin', of the larceny of fifty thousand dollars, of double-crossin' yer pardner, to say nothin' of such minor infringements as lyin' an' not brushin' yer teeth. We've hung dozens of men for less."[8]

This is the sort of thing Eisenhower was reading as Sunday, June 4, unfolded. He also met with de Gaulle, who objected to Eisenhower's proposed D-Day message because it did not mention de Gaulle or the role of the Provisional Government of France, over which he presided. The three leaders argued so heatedly that they went outside, which gave the tall de Gaulle room to wave his long arms. Eisenhower refused to share his temporary authority over the battle zone with de Gaulle; de Gaulle refused to deliver any speech unless this was done. Not until 24 hours later did de Gaulle agree to tape a broadcast.[9]

The rain kept pouring down throughout June 4. At 9:30 PM, the senior meteorologist, Group Captain J. M. Stagg, reported to Eisenhower and the other senior commanders in the mess room at Southwick House his prediction that the rain would stop before daybreak and there would be 36 hours of more or less clear weather. The planes should be able to operate on the night of June 5–6, although hampered by scattered clouds.

Once again, the air commanders favored postponement, and General Montgomery favored going ahead. Eisenhower paced up and down the mess room as the wind and the rain rattled the French doors. At 9:45 PM, Eisenhower announced his decision: "I am quite positive that the order must be given." By 11 PM, the fleet had been ordered to resume sailing: D-Day would be June 6, 1944.

There was still a final chance to abort the invasion early in the morning of Monday, June 5. At a meeting at Southwick House at 4:15 AM, although the wind was still blowing the rain in horizontal sheets, Stagg repeated his prediction that the storm would break before dawn. He added, however, that good weather was only likely through June 6 and that June 7 could be rough again. Montgomery wanted to go; Ramsay thought the risk worth taking; the air commanders were reluctant. More pacing by Eisenhower. "OK, we'll go," Eisenhower said. His subordinates cheered. Eisenhower had breakfast and went down to Portsmouth to watch the ships leaving harbor. After lunch he scrawled out a press release he hoped he did not have to use.

"Our landings have failed," it began, "and I have withdrawn the troops. . . . The troops, the air and the Navy did all that bravery and devotion to duty could do. If any blame or fault attaches to the attempt it is mine alone."[10]

None of the details of these high-level decisions was known to my father at the time. He and his fellows on *Augusta* only thought, based on all the clues, that the invasion was going to leave England on Sunday. But let my father describe it:

> [On Sunday,] the church services were held in the hot confines of the forward Mess Hall. Captains, messboys, petty officers, yeomen, gunners, marines, cooks, junior officers, and soldiers—we had all come unordered to this service which we suspected of being the last one—well, the last one before the Invasion. We had all come, or almost all, including the fellows who seem incapable of avoiding in every service a certain blunt, four-letter word which serves as a whole dictionary, since they are given to using it as a noun, adjective, or verb, and using it abusively as if it had no association with pleasure. . . .
>
> The hymns were properly amphibious—"For Those in Peril on the Sea," "Onward Christian Soldiers," and "O God, Our Help in Ages Past." They were those sturdy standbys, in which, comfortably familiar as they are, men keep rediscovering new meanings when danger rewrites them.

The leaflet for the services also quoted from the 121st Psalm—"The Lord shall preserve thy going out and thy coming in, from this time forth, and even forever." The leaflet, under the heading "Our Purpose," also quoted from the Atlantic Charter, the predecessor of the charter of the United Nations: "To destroy Nazi tyranny and establish a peace which will afford to all nations the means of dwelling in safety within their own boundaries, and which will afford insurance that all the men in all the lands may live out their lives in freedom from fear and want."[11]

For the men on *Augusta*, those words had a special association, because the Atlantic Charter had been written on board their ship. President Roosevelt had steamed north on *Augusta* to meet Prime Minister Churchill off of Newfoundland to hammer out the charter in August 1941. The president had slept and worked in what, four years later, was Admiral Kirk's cabin; the two leaders had conferred under an awning stretched across the big guns of *Augusta's* forward turret.

It was late afternoon that Sunday before Dad learned that the invasion had been postponed for a day. As Dad wrote: "Dinner advertised the fact that it had been scheduled for this Sunday. Dinner consisted of mounds of turkey and ice cream and all those . . . trimmings with which the Navy, in Sing Sing's most benevolent manner, prepares the stomach for the end."

By early afternoon on Monday, June 5, the men on *Augusta* knew that the higher-ups had decided that the invasion was on. They heard the rumble of the anchor being hoisted at 2:30 that afternoon. Dad wrote his script for the night's broadcast, shared in what he called the second of their Last Suppers, and climbed up to the pilot house to the fore of the admiral's bridge to the broadcast station.

"Are you going to give us the hot dope tonight?" asked a gunner.

"Are you going to spill the beans tonight, Mr. Brown?" asked the chief on the signal bridge.

Like most of the ship's crew, these were men probably less than half Dad's age.

And Dad, over the ship's public address system, told them about the invasion they would be taking part in:

> May I have your attention? Your undivided attention?
>
> I could not have more serious things to say to you on matters more demanding of your most earnest listening.
>
> It is here. It has come. It has come at last.
>
> After all these months of rigorous training, after all these weary months of waiting, after all the tedium of inaction, after all these preliminary exercises and maneuvers, after the long exhausting vigils of planning, after the last-minute threats of bad weather, and yesterday's postponement, the Invasion has begun. We are on the move and so is history. . . .
>
> The whole wide waiting world hangs upon what will be the outcome of these next few days and nights—the whole wide waiting world and history. The future of the world—its hopes, its decencies, its dreams of freedom, of peace and of order—all these

depend, no less than the future of our country, upon what these days and nights bring forth. For this is one of those moments when history holds its breath. . . .

First of all, our objective.

We are headed for France, as you have guessed. To be specific, we are headed for the beaches in the Bay of the Seine, immediately to the east of the Cherbourg peninsula.

We are the Western or American Task Force. To the east of us in the same area will be the Eastern or British Task Force.

Dad outlined for the listening sailors and soldiers the commanding officers in the two task forces and the mission of those task forces.

Our job is to land our men before the Germans can mass theirs. Our assets in the initial attack are our air supremacy and the strength and accuracy of our naval guns.

The naval forces with which we sail represent the greatest ever assembled in history. Counting all American and British craft with us, we will have some 2400 craft in the Western Task Force alone, of which about 1300 are ships of, or above, the size of LCTs.

To be more specific, when we confront those German-held beaches tomorrow, our Western Task Force will have with it three American battleships—the *Arkansas*, the *Texas*, and the *Nevada*; three American cruisers—the *Tuscaloosa*, the *Quincy*, and the *Augusta*; thirty-two destroyers; eighteen patrol craft; two French cruisers; one . . . British monitor; and five British cruisers.

After his address, sailors came up to Dad in the Pilot House: "The *Nevada*? Sunk at Pearl Harbor and now here. Kee-rist, that's sumpin!"

Dad went on to describe the other forces in the invasion: the waves of airborne troops to come over at about midnight that night "in such numbers that their passing will take three hours"; the more than six thousand planes expected to be in the air over Normandy the following day; the two Corps of the First Army, commanded by Lieutenant General Bradley, that the Navy was to land. He also reviewed the German forces:

the capital ships, the E-boats and U-boats, the mines, the Luftwaffe, and the long-range coastal batteries.

By this time, the grayness of the day was darkening into night. *Augusta* had joined up with other Allied ships and was heading into the Channel. Dad, the drama student, the drama critic, closed his broadcast:

> In these hours of testing, which will, which must, lead to triumph,
> may I remind you of three lines from Shakespeare:
> > "Therefore, my lords, omit no happy hour
> > Which may give furth'rance to our expedition
> > For we have now no thought but France."
> Good luck![12]

The call to General Quarters on *Augusta* came at 10:30 that night. By 4:15 AM on Tuesday, June 6, land was sighted. Within two minutes, a group of destroyers steamed for the beaches. At 5:50 AM, the great naval guns opened up; the battleships were ablaze with their own fire. The sound was deafening, even through cotton-stuffed ears. By 6:45 AM, the first landing ships had hit the beaches.

Dad could only imagine the horror of the beach. "Seen through binoculars on the large ships, the shore is an anthill in turmoil. The death cries do not reach us. The falling bodies we do not see. The first desperate dash through the water is beyond our vision. The first contacts with the barriers and obstacles we can only guess at. The first, and all-important, hand-to-hand test of arms we do not share. We do not even hear the sulphurous stammering of the machine guns."[13]

Dad was at least able to see something of the fighting. For Eisenhower in his trailer in Portsmouth, there were only scattered reports throughout the day—less information than expected, because of a tremendous flood of communications into SHAEF and the breakdown of a decoding machine. The first report Eisenhower received, at around 7 AM on June 6, was from Butcher, who had heard from Air Marshall Leigh-Mallory that most of the air transports and gliders had gotten through and that there had been very little flak and no fighter opposition. Enemy air was active around Le Havre, near Calais, where the Germans expected the main attack to take place. When Butcher was delivering this report, Admiral Ramsay called

Eisenhower to say that the winds had not abated, but sun breaking over Normandy gave fair visibility for naval gunfire support, and there had been little naval opposition to the invading fleet. Butcher said he found Eisenhower propped up in bed reading a Western with a full ashtray at his bedside. Eisenhower's orderly similarly reported that when he poked his head into Eisenhower's trailer at about 7:15 on the morning of June 6, he found him awake reading a Western novel, his ashtray—empty four hours earlier—filled with cigarette butts.[14]

I like to think that Eisenhower was trying to distract himself by finishing *Czar of Halfaday Creek*. As noted earlier, the prose isn't memorable, but it's lively. Here's another sample, forty pages from the end of the book:

> The one-armed man entered and approached the bar as Old Cush slid a glass toward him. "There's a woman," he announced, "comin' up the crick."
>
> "A woman!" exclaimed Cush, "Dead er alive?"
>
> "A dead woman," grinned Black Jack, "might be comin' down a crick, Cush, but not up one."[15]

Once Butcher made his report, Eisenhower was up. He spent most of the day in the trailer, drinking endless cups of coffee, waiting for the reports to come in—of the relatively smooth landings on the British and Canadian sectors, of the taking of Utah Beach by the Americans, of the desperate struggle by the Americans to fight up the bluffs and take the guns that killed so many of them on Omaha Beach.

By midnight on D-Day, 175,000 Allied troops had landed—but at a cost of 4,900 casualties on D-Day alone, and many thousands more dead and wounded in the bitter fighting for Normandy in the weeks that followed. The full cost of that day and its successors begins to come home to you only when you stand, as my father and I did in 1954, ten years after D-Day, in the middle of the vast American cemetery near Normandy's Omaha Beach where 9,400 troops are buried, and see the white crosses and Stars of David radiate diagonally in all directions, as far as you can see. But the Normandy beaches were in Allied hands by nightfall on June 6, 1944.

D-Day was horrible—but it could have been much worse. Field Marshall Erwin Rommel, Germany's great commander in North Africa, the commander in chief of the German army group in Calais, Normandy, and Brittany, the great fortifier of the beaches—was not in Normandy on June 5 and 6. Tuesday, June 6, was his wife's fiftieth birthday, and for the first time in weeks Rommel had taken a break from the front to go home. The vile weather in the Channel that caused the Allies to postpone the invasion for a day had led German meteorologists to conclude that the invasion wouldn't happen for many days.[16]

Rommel had told his aide "we'll have only one time to stop the enemy and that's while he's in the water. . . . The first 24 hours of the invasion will be decisive . . . for the Allies, as well as Germany, it will be the longest day." But Rommel, the master of the lightning counterattack, was at his home in Herrlingen in Germany, across the Black Forest from Strasbourg, when D-Day came. Not until 10:15 in the morning of D-Day did he hear of the invasion. And—in part because no one dared to wake Hitler from his sleep in his mountain headquarters in Berchtesgaden—it was not until 3:40 PM that Hitler released Germany's two reserve Panzer divisions for a counterattack.

Augusta herself was unscathed. No German bomb or shell came close to her. The foul weather that delayed the crossing had also shielded the invasion fleet from detection by the German air force before D-Day. There were German raids at night after D-Day. The sky over *Augusta* would light up with tracer bullets, the risk as much from falling ack-ack fragments as from German bombs. During one such raid, a mess boy taking a pee in a head on an upper deck on *Augusta* found that a falling piece of flak had severed his penis; what he was holding in his hand was no longer connected to his body. He was rushed to the operating table and his penis was reattached. Admiral Kirk asked to be kept posted on the man's progress. The admiral, who was something of a ladies' man, was interested to hear that the end of the man's penis had been sown back on at an angle. "The ladies will like that," Admiral Kirk told my father. But the flak fragment had also cut into the femoral artery. The mess boy bled to death.

On D plus 2 and each of the next two days, Dad and some other correspondents went ashore with General Bradley to hear and see the land side of the invasion.

Sounds: the occasional *crump* of an incoming enemy shell; the more distant sound of gunfire and exploding mines inland; the bustle and traffic of the beaches—"the backfires of huge trucks, the shout of voices, the scrape of feet, the grinding of brakes, the giant grunts and groans of bulldozers breaking their way through the landscape, and the scrunching wheels of DUKW's as they grabbed onto the gravel near the shore to lift them from the water."

Sights: Debris— from the destroyed German barriers, debris lapping the coast line at the water's edge. "Broached landing craft or the skeletons of wrecked vessels sprawled against the shore. An LST, scorched as if forgotten in an oven, was near us, with its cargo of tanks burned paintless and blistered, with the brown blankets of its men charred into little chips the size of cornflakes. Its sole survivor was a pair of freshly polished tan shoes, belonging to an officer. They were untouched, placed neatly side by side, waiting patiently to be used. Heaps of discarded life belts, no longer needed by GI's headed inland."

Other sights included freight being unloaded, stacks of crates and boxes, roads being built, trucks groaning up the hills and heading inland. As Dad put it, the beaches were a "freight yard on the sand"—the caption for one of the Navy pictures in his book. The picture (see figure 10.3) shows stacks of crates on the gravel, with helmeted soldiers standing near. Only after the book was published did Dad realize that one of the soldiers was apparently urinating on the crates as the picture was taken. The soldier stares at the camera with a look that says, "Why in hell are you taking a picture of a man taking a leak?"

General Bradley hitchhiked around the beach to see what was going on. He told Dad and the other correspondents he was going to hitchhike, and he did exactly that, jerking his thumb at the line of jeeps and trucks. A driver would see the three stars on the helmet, or recognize the face, and screech to a halt. A private would offer the general his place; Bradley would decline, stand on the running board, and go to the next outpost. He hitchhiked in this fashion across the beaches, heading back each evening on a landing craft to *Augusta* before, on D plus four, his own headquarters was set up ashore.[17] The troops took heart seeing Bradley on their beaches. As Eisenhower said of a visit of generals and admirals a few days later, "The soldier has a sense of gratification whenever he sees very high rank in his particular vicinity, possibly on the theory that the area is a safe one or the rank wouldn't be there."[18]

Fig. 10.3. "Freight Yard on the Sand." A Normandy beach soon after the landing. US Navy photo.

Dad did his own reconnoitering and reported what he saw to the crew of *Augusta*. He saw huge German gun emplacements that had been silenced by Navy guns, ruined farmhouses, gliders that had landed safely, and those that hadn't. Near a front headquarters, he saw the disemboweled body of a young American. The body had been kept there as a warning to others not to walk across fields that had not yet been cleared of mines. He saw a French boy of about eight respond to the greetings of American troops by raising his right hand in Hitlerian fashion—and then spreading the small fingers in that hand to form Churchill's V for victory. He saw three American platoons kill a German sniper. He saw long lines of German prisoners, not looking much like a master race, much sorrier looking than the prisoners he had seen in North Africa and Sicily. He saw the gore of field hospitals and many dead—Germans and Americans. As he recorded it:

> One meadow, high on a hilltop overlooking the sea darkened by
> Allied ships, had been turned into a cemetery in which prisoners

dug the graves. Some four hundred Americans, soldiers and sailors, and about two hundred Germans were awaiting burial.

The smell of death was heavily upon this meadow. The smell haunted our nostrils. It was sickly sweet, and over-sweetly sick, as if a gardenia had been dipped in vomit.[19]

The sight was one Dad never forgot.

Few now remember Ernie Pyle, the greatest of the American war correspondents in World War II. During that war, Pyle was so well-known that at a bar in London, when Dad was talking to Ernest Hemingway, who was also covering the war, a young American soldier came up to Hemingway and said: "Don't I know you? Aren't you Ernie Pyle?" And Hemingway said. "I'm afraid not, son. I'm only Ernie Hemorrhoid, the poor man's Pyle." Pyle was at Normandy, landing on Omaha Beach the day after D-Day, seeing lying on the beach, "expended, sufficient men and mechanism for a small war," seeing among the litter on the beach "a tennis racket that some soldier had brought along . . . clamped in its rack, not a string broken"— and realizing that behind the dead and living Allied invaders, "men and equipment were flowing from England in such a gigantic stream that it made the waste on the beachhead seem like nothing at all, really nothing at all." Pyle covered the war from December 1940, when he came to London during the Battle of Britain, until he was killed by a Japanese sniper's bullet on Ie Shima, a tiny island west of Okinawa, on April 18, 1945, twenty days before the Germans surrendered. On his body was a draft of a column he was writing for release when the war ended in Europe. In the column Pyle urged readers not to forget the dead:

There are many of the living who have burned into their brains forever the unnatural sight of cold dead men scattered over the hillsides and in the ditches along the high rows of hedge throughout the world.

Dead men by mass production—in one country after another— month after month and year after year. Dead men in winter and dead men in summer.

Dead men in such familiar promiscuity that they become monotonous.

Dead men in such monstrous infinity that you almost come to hate them.

These are the things that you at home need not even try to understand. To you at home they are columns of figures, or he is a near one who went away and just didn't come back. You didn't see him lying so grotesque and pasty beside the gravel road in France.

We saw him, saw him by the multiple thousands. That's the difference.[20]

Dad—like so many who had been at Normandy—did see those dead men.

Once General Bradley had moved his headquarters ashore, Dad no longer had a reason for coming to the Normandy beaches. Dad went back to the *Augusta*. He took with him one of the bits of debris he had found floating at the water's edge, among the wrecked landing craft, on one of the American beaches at Normandy—a wooden Madonna, worm-eaten and paintless, about a foot tall, that now stands on a bookshelf in my house. Dad had no idea how the Madonna came to be washing up on the beach at Normandy.

The Western novel and the wooden Madonna are relics to remind me of the beginning of the Allied drive across northern France towards Germany. The other, less seemly relic—the fragment of toilet bowl—speaks to me of the completeness of the collapse of the Third Reich. Soon after the Allied occupation of Germany, my godfather, Donald M. Oenslager, picked it up from the floor of Hitler's bathroom in the Berghof, Hitler's house in his mountain headquarters in Berchtesgaden, in southern Bavaria.

Oenslager—to me, "Uncle Donny"—was one of my parents' oldest friends. He had grown up with my mother in Harrisburg, Pennsylvania; he had roomed with my father at college and had introduced him to my mother when she was a young drama student in New York and Dad was teaching a course at drama school. During the war, Oenslager, an outstanding stage designer in civilian life, put his talents to use as a camouflage designer for the Army, in which he served as a major.

Oenslager had his first contact with the Axis before he joined the Army. He and his wife were giving a dinner party at their penthouse apartment on Fifth Avenue between 63rd and 64th Streets, overlooking Central Park and much of Manhattan, when the doorbell rang and the

FBI appeared to arrest the Oenslagers' butler and his wife the maid, a German couple who, it turned out, had been studying ship movements in the harbor through powerful binoculars and transmitting the information back to Germany by a short-wave radio tucked into a chest of drawers in the maid's bedroom. Oenslager's wife pointed out to the FBI that the elevator was the only way out of the apartment, which was on a very high floor. She asked if the FBI could wait in the hallway by the elevator until the couple had done the dishes from the dinner party. The FBI kindly waited before arresting the spies.

Most of Oenslager's service was in the Pacific, camouflaging air fields and gun emplacements. While stationed on one island recently liberated from the Japanese, Oenslager was responsible for the capture of a Japanese soldier who had remained behind in underground tunnels. One hot evening, Oenslager and other troops were sitting on the rocks in a natural amphitheater, watching a Betty Grable movie being projected on a sheet. He turned to his neighbor and said: "Say, didn't that rock in front of us just move?" "Hell it did," the neighboring soldier said. "Hell it didn't," said Oenslager. To settle the question, the two men turned the rock over, and found a Japanese soldier in his singlet, who had also been watching the Betty Grable movie.

After his Pacific tour, Oenslager joined Army intelligence in Europe. He was in Germany soon after that country's surrender early in the morning on Monday, May 7, 1945. After the German representatives signed the surrender document, Eisenhower went to bed with another Western novel, this one entitled *Cartridge Carnival.* [21]

Almost a year passed between the Normandy landings and Germany's surrender. In the east, the massive Soviet build-up steadily pushed the German armies back until, in the spring of 1945, more than 2.5 million Russian soldiers were converging on Berlin. In the west, Allied armies liberated Paris, pushed painfully up Italy, opened another front by landing in the south of France, and drove east towards Germany.

On December 15, 1944, Eisenhower heard that he was to be promoted to five-star general, along with Marshall and MacArthur. The next day, Germany began its last large counteroffensive, the bloody Battle of the Bulge in the Ardennes forest, which until well into January 1945 stopped the Allies' eastward drive.[22] The German thrust worked for the first few days, when foul weather denied the Americans the benefits of their air superiority. General George Patton asked the chaplain of the Third Army to pray for clear weather for killing Germans. The conversation went along the following lines:

> CHAPLAIN: May I say, General, that it usually isn't a customary thing among men of my profession to pray for clear weather to kill fellow men.
>
> PATTON: Chaplain, are you teaching me theology or are you the Chaplain of the Third Army? I want a prayer.
>
> CHAPLAIN: Yes, sir.

The chaplain fashioned a prayer that was somewhat more theologically correct than what Patton wanted: "Grant us fair weather for battle. Graciously hearken to us as soldiers who call upon Thee that, armed with Thy power, we may advance from victory to victory, and crush the oppression and wickedness of our enemies, and establish Thy justice among men and nations."

The weather cleared, enabling the Allied bombing and strafing to resume. Patton gave the chaplain a medal.[23] And the Bulge was straightened out, at a cost to the Germans of more than a hundred thousand casualties, six hundred tanks, and most of their remaining aircraft. The cost to the Allies was nearly as high—seventy-seven thousand men killed, wounded, captured or missing and more than seven hundred tanks and tank destroyers lost.[24]

The Allies pressed east into Germany. On March 3, Churchill came to inspect the progress of the British troops. Driving into Germany from the Netherlands, he stopped the car on the German side, at the dragon's teeth anti-tank defense the Germans had built as part of their West Wall. He was joined by Generals Montgomery, Brooke, and Simpson. "Gentlemen," he said, "I'd like you to join me. Let us all urinate on the great West Wall of Germany." The press photographers raised their cameras. Churchill wagged a finger at them, and said: "This is one of those operations connected with this great war which must not be reproduced graphically."[25]

Later in March, the Allied forces crossed the Rhine. The first across were American troops, who, on March 7, managed to get across at Remagen, on

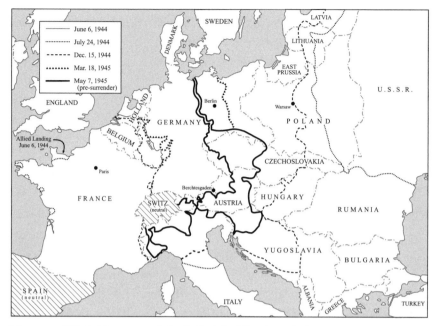

Map 10.1. Allied Advances and the Fall of the Third Reich, June 6, 1944–May 7, 1945.

a railroad bridge the Germans had badly damaged but not destroyed. On the night of March 22–23, further south, a division of Patton's Third Army made it across in small boats. To note the crossing, on March 23, General Patton walked across a pontoon bridge his engineers had built, stopped in the middle, and pissed into the Rhine. "I've waited a long time to do that," he said as he buttoned up. "I didn't even piss this morning when I got up, so that I would have a really full load."[26] By late March, Allied armies had crossed the Rhine in at least seven places. Churchill, near the site of one airborne attack across the Rhine, told Eisenhower with delight: "My dear General, the German is whipped. We've got him. He's all through."[27]

A main worry of the Allies was that Hitler and the Nazi high command would leave Berlin before it fell and would establish a new headquarters in and around the mountain village of Berchtesgaden, Hitler's headquarters on the Obersalzberg in the Bavarian Alps. There in the mountain fast-nesses—according to a neo-Wagnerian myth nourished by Josef Goebbels, Hitler's supreme propagandist—the last and best of the Nazis would build a "National Redoubt" and fight on forever, commanded by Hitler himself.

According to a March 1945 report on the National Redoubt from SHAEF intelligence: "Here, defended by nature and by the most efficient secret weapons yet invented, the powers that have hitherto guided Germany will survive to reorganize her resurrection; here armaments will be manufactured in bombproof factories, food and equipment will be stored in vast underground caverns and a specially selected corps of young men will be trained in guerilla warfare, so that a whole underground army can be fitted and directed to liberate Germany from the occupying forces."[28]

Hitler had spent much of his rise to power on the Obersalzberg, ever since the early 1920s, when some of his rich supporters enabled him to stay at the Platterhof inn on the mountain. With their help, he bought a neighboring chalet, the Villa Wacherfeld, and rebuilt and renamed it the Berghof. Near it he wrote most of *Mein Kampf*. He had spent summers there with his beautiful blonde niece, Geli Raubal, who killed herself (or—as some rumors had it—was murdered because the relationship was an embarrassment to the Nazi cause) in Hitler's Munich apartment in 1931. At the Berghof, he decided to breach the Versailles Treaty and to decree universal military service and the build-up of a peacetime army of 36 divisions; there he waited out the reaction of France and Britain to the invasion of the Sudetenland; from there he instructed von Ribbentrop in the negotiation of the non-aggression pact with Russia; and there he decided on the invasion of Poland that started the Second World War. He spent much of the war at the Berghof—including a routine day on June 5, 1944, when he and the German High Command had been completely unaware of the impending D-Day invasion, and the next day, when Hitler, convinced that the Normandy action was a diversion from a main attack at Calais, initially prevented reinforcements from being sent to Normandy until they were too late to push back the Allied invasion, and then issued an order, based on pure wishful thinking, "to have the enemy in the bridgehead annihilated by the evening of June 6" and to have the beachhead "cleaned up by not later than tonight." It was also at the Berghof that he rejected the advice of von Runstedt and Rommel to try to end the war while Germany was intact and parts of the German army were still functioning. Germany would win the war, Hitler told them, because it had "miracle weapons."[29]

Toward the end of the war, the British worked on a plan, code-named Operation Foxley, to assassinate Hitler at Berchtesgaden or on Hitler's personal train, the Führerzug. The British Public Record Office in 1998 made publicly available its file on the plan, stamped "Top Secret." The plan's stated object was: "The elimination of HITLER and any high-ranking Nazis or members of the Führer's entourage who may be present at the attempt." The plan includes maps of the Berchtesgaden from aerial photographs and discusses the topography ("very heavily wooded and, being also extremely hilly . . . a difficult area to guard"), the houses, and the security personnel. There are extraneous intelligence details ("The coiffeur in charge of the barbershop under the hospital [the Platterhof hotel had been converted into a hospital for wounded members of the Wehrmacht] speaks fluent Italian (and German with a Bavarian accent); the waitresses in the Bergschenke wear blue Dirndl dresses"). There are sketches of the uniforms of the different security units, to facilitate disguise and infiltration of the area. A photograph of the Berghof locates Hitler's bedroom on the first floor of the Berghof. The report describes Hitler's appearance ("Apart from the Iron Cross Hitler wears no military decorations") and daily routines (he is a "late riser," never getting up before 0900 or 1000 hrs"; he "always walks alone to the MOOSLANER KOPF"; if he sees the SS guard following him he shouts, "If you are frightened, go and guard yourself.") The easiest way to know that Hitler is at Berchtesgaden is "the big swastika flag which is flown on such occasions from the flagpole at the car park in front of the BERGHOF."

The plan recommended an attempt by two snipers, disguised in Gebirgajäger uniform, while Hitler was on his daily walk to the Mooslaner Kopf teahouse. Recommended weapons and equipment: "Mauser sniper's rifle, telescopic sight (carried in pocket), explosive bullets in magazine, wirecutters (for making holes in wire fence), H. E. grenades carried in haversack for close protection and assistance in making get-away."

An alternative suggestion was to attack Hitler's train, either with conventional weapons or by "doctoring" the train's water supply. An appendix to the report recommends "I" [whatever that poison may be] as "the most suitable medium" for clandestine means because it is tasteless and odorless, its delayed action "affords the best chance of the intended victim (Hitler) taking the necessary lethal quantity before any member of his entourage or of the train staff who has likewise taken beverages containing "I" [falls] ill," and "there is no antidote."[30]

The Foxley plan was vigorously debated within Britain's high command. It was not pursued, one gathers, not because of ethical squeamishness, but because several senior officers argued that Hitler's life would contribute more to an Allied victory than Hitler's death, thanks to his inept muddling in military affairs. That ineptitude, as we have seen, was exemplified by Hitler's refusal at the time of the Normandy invasion to permit reserves to move into Normandy until it was too late to overcome the Allied invaders. A similar ineptitude had led Hitler in 1942 to order the splitting of the German forces attacking Stalingrad and Rostov.

As the Allied forces rolled into Germany from east and west, the highest Nazi leaders urged Hitler to leave the bunker in Berlin for Berchtesgaden while there was still an open road. Hitler declined and sent his designated successor Reichsmarschall Hermann Göring instead. From Berchtesgaden, Göring, having heard of an apparent nervous collapse by Hitler, sent him a message asking if he wished Göring to assume complete control of the Reich—adding that he would do so if he did not hear from Hitler by 10 o'clock that night. Hitler wired back that Göring's message represented high treason against the Reich and that Göring would be executed unless he resigned all offices immediately.[31]

On April 25, 1945, SS officers tried to persuade Göring to sign a document resigning his positions because of ill health. He refused until the SS men pulled their guns. As Göring signed the resignation, the drone of approaching planes drove everyone into the bomb shelter. Two large waves of Allied bombers dumped high explosives on Berchtesgaden and the rest of the Obersalzberg. The Führer's home, the Berghof, took a direct hit that blew away one side of the building (see figure 10.4). Göring's house was destroyed. The SS barracks and the cottage where Hitler had written much of *Mein Kampf* were in flames. As Eisenhower put it, "That stronghold and symbol of Nazi arrogance was thoroughly pounded with high explosives. The bombing took place when we still thought the Nazis might attempt to establish themselves in their National Redoubt with Berchtesgaden as the capital. The photo reconnaissance units brought back pictures that showed our bombers had reduced the place to a shambles; from them we derived a gleeful and understandable satisfaction." Five days after the Berchtesgaden bombardment, as Soviet troops approached his bunker in Berlin, Hitler put a pistol in his mouth and killed himself.[32] A week later,

General Alfred Jodl, chief of staff of the German Army, signed Germany's unconditional surrender, which Eisenhower announced to the Combined Chiefs in a brief cable: "The mission of this Allied force was fulfilled at 0241 local time, May 7, 1945."[33]

My godfather Oenslager was not alone in taking a souvenir, a trophy, from the ruins of the buildings at Berchtesgaden. Major Dick Winters of the 101st Airborne Division, who had fought the Germans in Normandy and the Battle of the Bulge, soon after his division secured Berchtesgaden in early May 1945, went into the Berchtesgaden Hof with an American lieutenant and found a waiter gathering a very large set of silverware in a velvet-lined case. Seeing the American officers, the waiter took off, leaving the silver behind. Major Winters and the lieutenant decided to split the set and dined with that silverware in their homes for the rest of their lives. Winters, having taken his share of the silver, posted a double guard on the building to prevent further looting—and went on to discover in Göring's officers' club an immense trove of wine and liquor, which he and his men consumed. Eisenhower's aide Captain Harry Butcher—the man who gave my father the Western novel Eisenhower read as he waited for D-Day—on June 9, 1945, climbed up the Eagle's Nest, which by that time was policed by the 101st Airborne Division. The paratrooper on guard complained to Butcher that the troops who had come there earlier had collected so many souvenirs that troops had to be stationed to prevent further pilfering.

Butcher looked at Hitler's oval-shaped dining room in the Eagle's Nest and through the large windows with their splendid views of the snow-capped Bavarian Alps. He then went partway down the mountain to Hitler's chalet, which was badly burned but still standing, and collected a few pieces of marble from Hitler's fireplace. In Hitler's kitchen, three large brass cooking pots on the stove still contained decaying food—French-fried potatoes, carrots, and what looked like soup. As Butcher put it, it appeared that "the kitchen help had quickly abandoned their post when the bombers came."[34]

The Allies later dismantled the shattered remains of the Obersalzberg complex, hoping to avoid the creation of a shrine to Hitler. In November 1998, the State of Bavaria announced it had sold the 262-acre site to an investor planning to turn it into a tourist attraction. There now is a restaurant at what was Hitler's Eagle's Nest.

Fig. 10.4. The Berghof, Hitler's mountain retreat, after the Allied bombing on April 25, 1945. *Courtesy of Geoff Walden. Collection of George R. Walden.*

Uncle Donny Oenslager and his wife never had any children. They would have been wonderful parents—caring, teaching, loving, generous. Almost every time I visited their apartment—the same penthouse on Fifth Avenue that the FBI raided to arrest their butler and maid—he gave me a present. One day, a few years after World War II had ended, Uncle Donny pulled from his pocket a handkerchief which he unwrapped to reveal the piece of toilet bowl, which he gave to me portentously, as if bestowing an important relic.

I looked at it in some surprise, because it looked like a piece of toilet bowl.

"*This*, Mer," Uncle Donny said, "*this* is a piece of Hitler's toilet bowl!"

Uncle Donny said he had picked it up from the floor of Hitler's own bathroom, next to his bedroom in his house at Berchtesgaden. The toilet bowl, like the windows and most of the breakable things, had been shattered by the Allied bombing. He told me that U.S. troops were guarding the house when he visited, to prevent trophy taking.[35]

"So how'd you get it?" I asked.

"I told the soldier who was standing guard 'Gee, what an incredible view!', and I pointed out to the mountains and the valley. When he looked

Fig. 10.5. Piece of Hitler's toilet bowl, taken from the Berghof in May, 1945. *Author's collection.*

out the window, I picked this up and pocketed it. And I want you to have it."

I keep it now in a file cabinet, along with the shavings from John Brown's scaffold. It isn't a very clean piece of toilet bowl. Now that we are able to clone sheep from a single cell, I wonder whether it might be possible to clone Hitler from a cell in the grey-brown smear on the porcelain. I asked my son, who is far more technologically advanced than I am, whether he thought the cloning could be done—not that I was advocating that it should be done, mind you.

He gave the question some thought. "I don't think you could clone Hitler from it," he said. "You might be able to clone what he had for lunch."

AFTERWORD

The Shaping of America

Axehead, compass, rifle, letter from George Washington, sword, scaffold shavings, diaries, pistol, court-martial transcript, Western novel, piece of toilet bowl: this appears to be a motley assortment of artifacts, covering more than 300 years, from the early 1600s to 1945. Yet these widely differing objects call to mind nothing less than the birth, growth, and shaping of what is now America. In these centuries, Indian power is broken; a new nation is born and its union strengthened; slavery is ended; and the new country grows hugely in area, population, wealth, and strength.

At the time of the Pequot War in 1637, Indian tribes controlled all of what became the United States except for Spanish and French holdings and disparate British colonies with fewer than thirty thousand settlers among them, clustered along the Atlantic coast and substantially outnumbered by nearby Indian tribes. The killing and relocation of the Pequots in 1637–1638 foreshadowed the killing and moving of other Indian tribes that went on until the end of the nineteenth century—a process marked by fighting and by the taking of land and exemplified by the rifle and the compass. We see that process in the opening of Kentucky by men like William Preston and John Floyd in the 1770s and early 1780s; in the Seminole Wars and the forced relocation of the Creeks, Seminoles, and other eastern tribes in the first half of the nineteenth century; and in the confining of Indians to reservations, recorded in the diaries of John Mason Brown's trips to Indian country in 1861 and 1862.

The British colonies, in 1775–1783, rebelled against Britain and united to form a new country. Aided by George Washington's stature and leadership, the new country moved from a weak confederacy to a stronger federal government. The issue of slavery, which had festered for decades, became explosive in part because of the efforts of abolitionists such as John Brown and, in 1861, broke up the national union until the bloodshed of the Civil War ended slavery and reunited the country.

The United States grew not only by taking Indian lands but by purchases from France, Spain, and Russia; treaties with England; the annexation of Texas and Hawaii; and war with Mexico. In 1640, although Britain's claims to land in its colonies in what is now the United States up to the Appalachian Mountains may have approached a hundred and fifty thousand square miles, British colonists had settled fewer than seventy-five thousand square miles. By 1945, the United States, including the territories of Alaska and Hawaii, exceeded 3.6 million square miles—nearly 50 times the size of the land settled by British colonists in 1637. The country also soared in population: by 1945, more than 139 million people lived in America—more than forty-six hundred times the number of British colonists in 1640. The country's economy and military strength had also shot up. The United States, which had played only a supporting role in the First World War, was the decisive power in the Second World War, aided by a gross domestic product that was more than four times the size of the gross domestic product of any other country.[1]

Many of the different objects we have looked at in this book are weapons. Others—for example, the diaries from 1861 and 1862, the transcript from the Philippine War, the fragment of Hitler's toilet bowl—relate to wars. Each of these varied artifacts, with the possible exception of the stone adze head, originally belonged to or related to someone who was engaged in war. This recurring emphasis on war fairly reflects the history of the United States. Frequent use of military force underlay America's birth, growth, and transformation. Table A.1 shows a listing of American wars against foreign nations and the principal armed conflicts with Indian tribes from 1637 through 1945.

The table shows that American military forces were engaged in fighting in 149 of the 309 years—48 percent of the years—in the period 1637–1945. Engagements with Indians occurred in 136 of the 254 years, or 53 percent of the years, from 1637 to 1891 (which marked the end of the major Indian conflicts).

Table A.1 Wars and American Military Engagements, 1637–1945[2]

1637–38	Pequot War
1640–43	Kieft's War
1675–76	King Philip's War
1689–97	The Second Indian War (King William's War)
1701–11	Queen Anne's War (in Europe, War of the Spanish Succession)
1744–48	King George's War (part of War of Austrian Succession)
1755–63	French and Indian War (in Europe, the Seven Years' War)
1759–61	Cherokee War
1763–64	Pontiac's War
1774	Lord Dunmore's War
1775–83	Revolutionary War
1776–94	Chickamauga Cherokee Wars
1790–94	Wars with Indians in Ohio Valley
1801–05	First Barbary War
1812–15	War of 1812
1813–14	U.S. takes parts of Florida
1815	Second Barbary War
1816–18	First Seminole War
1822–25	U.S. Navy fights pirates in Cuba
1823	Arikara War
1827	Fever River (Winnebago) War
1832	Black Hawk War
1835–42	Second Seminole War
1836–38	Forcible removal of Cherokees (Trail of Tears)
1846–48	Mexican War
1847–55	Cayuse War
1849–66	Navajo Wars
1849–86	Apache Wars
1854–56	First Sioux War
1855–58	Third Seminole War
1858	Spokane–Coeur d'Alène–Paloos War
1861–65	Civil War
1862	Santee Sioux War
1863–64	Colorado War
1865	Powder River War
1867–75	Comanche Wars
1872–73	Modoc War
1876–77	Black Hills War
1877	Nez Perce War
1878	Bannock War
1878–79	Cheyenne War
1879–80	Ute War
1890–91	Ghost Dance War; Killings at Wounded Knee
1898–99	Spanish-American War
1900–02	Philippine War
1916–17	Pursuit of Pancho Villa in Mexico
1917–18	U.S. involvement in World War I
1918–20	American troops in Vladivostok and Archangel, Russia
1941–45	U.S. involvement in World War II

If willingness to fight drove much of America's growth and change in the more than three centuries we have considered, other attributes also underlay that extraordinary transformation. Not least among these were the urge to explore, the quest for land or other paths to financial betterment, intellectual curiosity, ingenuity, perseverance, and abundant courage.

NOTES

Prologue

1. Russ Banham, author of *The Ford Century*, quoted in Zaslow, 2003. According to Zaslow, Ford described the history in books as "mostly bunk," but said "history you can see is of great value."

1. Axe Head, Adze Head

1. Russell, *Indian New England Before the Mayflower*, 66 (17C shows grooved axes from the Connecticut River Valley of Massachusetts; the axe heads in figure 1.1 closely resemble the author's axe head), 67 (17D shows an adze blade from the same region that is like the author's adze head), 167 (picture of three tools—two very like the author's adze head—possibly used to remove bark from trees, from Fowler, "Procurement and Use of Bark," 18), and 180 (picture of three ball-headed clubs, one of which, #3, from Portsmouth, R.I., closely resembles the author's axe head, from Fowler, "Tomahawks of Central New England," 34); Dr. Kevin A. McBride, interview by Meredith Mason Brown, July 7, 2011.
2. Cave, *Pequot War*, 40–43.
3. Cave, *Pequot War*, 50.
4. Cave, *Pequot War*, 43; Hauptmand and Wherry, *Pequots*, 46.
5. Cave, *Pequot War*, 58.
6. Grandjean, "New World Tempests: Environment, Scarcity, and the Coming of the Pequot War."
7. Cave, *Pequot War*, 128–29.
8. Cave, *Pequot War*, 135–36.
9. To the best of the author's knowledge, Captain John Mason is not related to the author.
10. Underhill, *Newes from America*, 81.
11. Underhill, *Newes from America*, 84.
12. Saltonstall, *New and Further Narrative*, 90–91.
13. Church, *History of King Philip's War*, quoted in Lepore, *The Name of War: King Philip's War*, 125–26.
14. An archaeological survey in 1987 found, on top of Pequot Hill, ceramic and other evidence of a late 16th- or early 17th-century Indian settlement believed to be the fort site destroyed in 1637. McBride, "The Historical Archaeology of the Mashantucket Pequots," in Hauptman and Wherry, *The Pequots in Southern New England*, 98–99. For the 2010 discoveries, see Veninger and Pasteryak, "Battlefields of the Pequot War." In 2011, McBride-led archaeologists uncovered more artifacts from the site, including brass arrowheads and musket balls. Mancini, "McBride Lectures on Pequot War Findings."

15. De Forest, *Indians of Connecticut*, 445.

16. Hauptman and Wherry, *The Pequots in Southern New England*, 213.

17. "Foxwoods Debt Talks Are Test of Tribal Bets," *Wall Street Journal*, July 2, 2011; "Tribe Celebrates $3 Billion Milestone," *Mystic River Press*, May 20, 2010; "Proposed Foxwoods Deal Is Gamble for Creditors," *Wall Street Journal*, Aug. 15, 2011, C1.

2. A Compass, a Rifle, and the Opening of the West

1. Who was the unnamed "Genl"? It is possible that Gen. William Preston (the grandson of Col. William Preston, who would have surveyed his property in Montgomery County) gave the compass (with the note on the bottom) to former Union brevet general William F. Draper, who after the Civil War married one of Gen. Preston's daughters. Such a gift would have helped bind the families together. Gen. Draper was an ancestor and the namesake of William F. Draper, who gave the author the compass. See Sehlinger, *Kentucky's Last Cavalier*, 199–200.

2. My father inherited the rifle from his uncle General Preston Brown (see chapters 8 and 9), who noted on a label attached to the rifle that it had belonged to his great-aunt Susan Hepburn. Susan Preston Hepburn (1819–1897) was a granddaughter of Col. William Preston. Her sister Letitia Preston Floyd married John Floyd (1783–1837), the son of the John Floyd who owned the rifle. Dorman, *Prestons*, 60, 68–70. See Johnston, *Memorial History of Louisville*, 1:50 ("Humble made a rifle for Colonel John Floyd which yet exists as the property of Mrs. Colonel John Mason Brown"), 271 (Michael Humble opened his gunsmith shop in Louisville in 1782). But see Hankla, "Across the Woods with Kentucky's 'Humble' Gunsmiths," 2 (Michael Humble established a gunshop in what is now Louisville as early as 1777), 4 (Michael Humble was one of the settlers of Harrodstown in 1774). Theodore Roosevelt, whom Col. John Mason Brown had to dinner in Louisville in 1888 (see chapter 8, note 66 and accompanying text) when Roosevelt was researching the frontier history of Kentucky for his *The Winning of the West*, noted that he had seen, in the possession of Col. Reuben Durrett, one of Boone's rifles, which he described as "perfectly plain," and also "one of Floyd's rifles," which was "much more highly finished, and with some ornamentation." Roosevelt, *Winning of the West*, vol. 1, 149n28. I suspect Roosevelt saw Floyd's ornamented rifle at Col. Brown's house.

3. For Patton's career, see Johnson, *James Patton*. For Patton's possible tobacco smuggling, see Glanville and Mays, "The Mysterious Origins of James Patton, Part I," 57–58.

4. Glanville and Mays, "The Mysterious Origins of James Patton, Part I," 48–49 (Beverley offers Patton one quarter of the 30,000-acre grant, if Patton will endeavor to procure families to settle it); Johnson, *James Patton*, 9–13, 18–20; Johnson, *William Preston*, 3–6; Dorman, *Prestons*, 1–5.

5. Draper, *Life of Daniel Boone*, 47; Johnson, *James Patton*, 67, 77n3 (citing letter from John Madison to James Patton, June 4, 1753, State Historical Society of Wisconsin, Draper Manuscript Collection, 1QQ75).

6. Johnson, *James Patton*, 67–69; Bailey, *The Ohio Company*, 24. Patton had initially petitioned the Virginia government in 1743 for "200,000 acres of land on three branches of the Mississippia and the Waters thereof, on which I proposed to settle one family for each 1,000 acres." The Virginia council awarded Patton 100,000 acres in April 1745. Patton to John Blair, January 1753, State Historical Society of Wisconsin, Draper Manuscript Collection, 1QQ75.

7. Johnson, *James Patton*, 94–95.

8. Johnson, *James Patton*, 137–150.

9. Johnson, *William Preston*, 13–14.

10. Johnson, *James Patton*, 108, 183, 185; Mitchell, *Commercialism and Frontier*, 82; Sehlinger, *Kentucky's Last Cavalier*, 2.

11. Ellis, *His Excellency*, 5.

12. White, *The Middle Ground*, 40–41 (25%–90%); Miller and Pencak, *Pennsylvania*, 35 (95%).

13. Bureau of the Census, *Historical Statistics*, 2, 1168 (estimated population of American colonies was 1,170,760 in 1750 and 1,593, 624 in 1760); Calloway, *Scratch of a Pen*, 24, 113 (total French population in North America in 1763 was about 80,000, with the majority settled in the St. Lawrence Valley).

14. Wallace, *Conrad Weiser*, 530.

15. Ellis, *His Excellency*, 21; Ward, *Breaking the Backcountry*, 7, 42–43.

16. Ellis, *His Excellency*, 22.

17. Johnson, *William Preston*, 18–19; *James Patton*, 194–195.

18. Johnson, *William Preston*, 19, based on the 1843 account of Preston's daughter Letitia Floyd.

19. A relative of Patton gave the date of the attack as July 8—the day before Braddock's defeat. Letitia Floyd to Benjamin Rush Floyd, Feb. 22, 1843, quoted in Johnson, *James Patton*, 204. Other accounts, closer in time to the event, gave the date of the attack as July 30 or July 31. Johnson, *James Patton*, 207n16. For arguments as to the inaccuracy of the July 8 date, see Osborn, "William Preston of Virginia," 396–97.

20. For Patton's inept preliminaries at Logstown, see Thomas Cresap to Conrad Weiser, Feb. 20, 1752, quoted in Johnson, *James Patton*, 127; see also McConnell, *A Country Between*, 94.

21. Johnson, *James Patton*, 203, 207n12 (bounties for scalps of George Croghan and James Lowry).

22. Letitia Floyd to Benjamin Rush Floyd, Feb. 22, 1843; Johnson, *James Patton*, 207n21.

23. The ranger company included a surgeon, Dr. Thomas Loyd, who wrote to a friend in England, "We followed them 200 miles but to know [sic] purpose." Johnson, *William Preston*, 19.

24. Johnson, *William Preston*, 38.

25. Ward, *Breaking the Backcountry*, 104–106; Kincaid, *The Wilderness Road*, 62; Preston's journal of the expedition, State Historical Society of Wisconsin, Draper Manuscript Collection, 1QQ96–123; Johnson, *William Preston*, 35–43.

26. Johnson, *William Preston*, 55–59; Washington to John Robinson, Nov. 9, 1756, Abbot and Twohig, eds., *Papers of George Washington*, vol. 4, 16–17; Ward, *Breaking the Backcountry*, 57 and, for the effectiveness of raids in Virginia and Pennsylvania, 60–73.

27. Dorman, *Prestons*, 14–17, 19; Johnson, *William Preston*, 66, 107.

28. Thwaites and Kellogg, *Documentary History*, xv.

29. Rev. John Brown to Col. William Preston, May 28, 1774, State Historical Society of Wisconsin, Draper Manuscript Collection, 3QQ29, reprinted in Thwaites and Kellogg, *Documentary History*, 26. John Brown is an ancestor of the author.

30. Dorman, *Prestons*, 16–17, 14n14; Johnson, *William Preston*, 75–77, 108.

31. As early as 1759, Preston bought sixteen slaves in Maryland from a slave trader, paying 750 pounds cash for them. Johnson, *William Preston*, 65. Preston would have been

familiar with the trade in indentured servants, because James Patton was engaged in it. Preston had set up stills and started selling whiskey at Greenfield in the 1760s, and in 1779, he promised to send funds to his nephew John Brown, then at college, assuring the young man, "I have a good prospect at present of making pretty largely out of my Distillery and other means this spring." Johnson, *William Preston*, 84, 213.

32. Dorman, *Prestons*, 13n2.

33. Each chain measured 4 perches, or 22 yards, divided into 100 equal links. Ten square chains equaled one acre. That meant a surveyor could compute the area of a parcel of land in square chains and then divide by 10 to come up with the area in acres. See Linklater, *Measuring America*, 15–18, for a description of chains and their use.

34. Linklater, *Measuring America*, 45.

35. Ellis, *His Excellency*, 10, 35.

36. Washington to George Mercer, November 7, 1771, quoted in Ellis, *His Excellency*, 57.

37. Linklater, *Measuring America*, 45.

38. Linklater, *Measuring America*, 33, 38.

39. Tapp, "Colonel John Floyd," 2; Draper, *Life of Daniel Boone*, 559, 563; Johnson, *William Preston*, 100.

40. For an overview of the Fincastle surveyors, see Hammon, "The Fincastle Surveyors at the Falls of the Ohio" and "The Fincastle Surveyors in the Bluegrass."

41. See letter of Alexander Spottswood Dandridge to Col. William Preston, May 15, 1774, State Historical Society of Wisconsin, Draper Manuscript Collection, 3QQ26 ("According to your instructions Mr Floyd Surveyed for Colo. Washington 2000 Acres of Land and Sent a platt of the Same in a letter to you") and letter of Col. William Preston to Col. George Washington, Fincastle, May 27, 1774, State Historical Society of Wisconsin, Draper Manuscript Collection, 15S79 ("Agreeable to my promise, I directed Mr. Floyd, an assistant to survey your land on Cole river [Coal River, which flows into the Kanawha a few miles below Charleston], which he did."), in Thwaites and Kellogg, *Documentary History*, 22–24. Fitzpatrick's *Writings of George Washington* includes a letter from Washington to Preston, March 27, 1775, regarding Washington's receipt of the survey at the mouth of Coal River and payment for it (£3.6.8 for Preston, £2.10.0 for Capt. Floyd), and asking Preston for advice as to "a good piece of Land (not claimd by any)" in Fincastle County on which to locate a warrant for 3,000 acres.

42. Washington to William Crawford, in Consul W. Butterfield, ed., *The Washington-Crawford Letters, 1767–1781* (Cincinnati, 1877) 3, quoted in Calloway, *The Scratch of a Pen*, 99.

43. See note 41.

44. Sehlinger, *Kentucky's Last Cavalier*, 4.

45. Hammon, "Fincastle Surveyors at the Falls," 19, 23.

46. Hammon, "Fincastle Surveyors at the Falls," 25.

47. Hammon, "Fincastle Surveyors in the Bluegrass," 277–294.

48. Hammon, "Fincastle Surveyors in the Bluegrass," 283–86.

49. Journal of Thomas Hanson, State Historical Society of Wisconsin, Draper Manuscript Collection, 14J58–84, entry for July 1, 1774, in Thwaites and Kellogg, *Documentary History*, 129.

50. Abraham Hite to Col. William Preston, Hampshire, June 3, 1774, State Historical Society of Wisconsin, Draper Manuscript Collection, 3QQ35, in Thwaites and Kellogg, *Documentary History*, 31–32.

51. See Lord Dunmore's circular letter to the county lieutenants, State Historical Society of Wisconsin, Draper Manuscript Collection, 3QQ39, Williamsburg, June 10, 1774, in Thwaites and Kellogg, *Documentary History*, 33; for "destroy their Towns," Dunmore to Col. Andrew Lewis, Thwaites and Kellogg, *Documentary History*, 86.

52. Rasmussen, "Anarchy and Enterprise on the Imperial Frontier," 22 and n51.

53. Hammon, "Captain Harrod's Company," 227–28.

54. Draper, *Life of Daniel Boone*, 306–307, quoting letters of June 26 and July 13 to William Preston, State Historical Society of Wisconsin, Draper Manuscript Collection, 3QQ46 and 3QQ64. The letters are also printed in Thwaites and Kellogg, *Documentary History*, 49–51 and 88–91. The "best Hands" description is from the earlier letter.

55. Deposition of Daniel Boone in *Boofman Heirs v. James Hickman*, Circuit Court Records, Fayette County, Fayette County Complete Book A, 604–42, quoted in Hammon and Taylor, *Virginia's Western War*, xxix.

56. Brown, *Frontiersman*, 64–65.

57. Draper, *Life of Daniel Boone*, 321; Thwaites and Kellogg, *Documentary History*, 253–97, 368–95.

58. For the founding of St. Asaph's and Boonesborough and the plans of Henderson and the Transylvania Company, see Brown, *Frontiersman*, 68–90.

59. Floyd to Preston, July 21, 1776, State Historical Society of Wisconsin, Draper Manuscript Collection, 33S296–97, in Rothert, *John Floyd*, 171–73.

60. Floyd to Preston, Bear Grass, Nov. 26, 1779, State Historical Society of Wisconsin, Draper Manuscript Collection, 17CC167–69, in Hammon and Harris, "Letters of Col. John Floyd," 209–11.

61. Lord Germain to Sir Guy Carleton, White Hall, March 26, 1777, sent to Lt. Gov. Hamilton from Quebec, May 21, 1777, in Butterfield, *History of the Girtys*, 342–44.

62. Calloway, *The American Revolution in Indian Country*, 191–96.

63. "Tired of the confinement of the fort": Statement of Nathan Reid, no date, State Historical Society of Wisconsin, Draper Manuscript Collection, 31C2, 24–25.

64. Hammon, *My Father Daniel Boone*, 38, 49.

65. Statement of Nathan Reid, no date, State Historical Society of Wisconsin, Draper Manuscript Collection, 31C2[26].

66. Statement of Isaiah Boone, no date, State Historical Society of Wisconsin, Draper Manuscript Collection, 31C2[40].

67. Floyd to Preston, July 21, 1776, State Historical Society of Wisconsin, Draper Manuscript Collection, 33S300–305, in Rothert, "John Floyd—Pioneer and Hero," 171–73.

68. Statement of Nathan Reid, no date, State Historical Society of Wisconsin, Draper Manuscript Collection, 31C2[26].

69. Statement of Nathan Reid, no date, State Historical Society of Wisconsin, Draper Manuscript Collection, 31C2[25–26].

70. Hammon, *My Father Daniel Boone*, 50.

71. Draper interview with Jacob Boone, 1890, State Historical Society of Wisconsin, Draper Manuscript Collection, 14C84.

72. John Dabney Shane interview with Josiah Collins, 1840s, State Historical Society of Wisconsin, Draper Manuscript Collection, 12CC75.

73. Hammon, *My Father Daniel Boone*, 50.

74. Floyd to Preston, July 21, 1776, State Historical Society of Wisconsin, Draper Manuscript Collection, 33S300–303.

75. Floyd to Preston, July 21, 1776, State Historical Society of Wisconsin, Draper Manuscript Collection, 33S300–303.

76. Samuel H. Dixon to Draper, Feb. 3, 1852, State Historical Society of Wisconsin, Draper Manuscript Collection, 24C30, 5.

77. Elizabeth L. Coshow to Draper, May 2, 1885, State Historical Society of Wisconsin, Draper Manuscript Collection, 21C28–29. The story of the capture and the rescue of the girls has been told many times. Draper gathered some 40 accounts of it—most of them furnished decades after the event. See Draper, *Life of Daniel Boone*, 429–30n35 for Draper's sources for his version. Not surprisingly, the stories conflict in many details. For excellent efforts to thread the stories into a coherent narrative, see Faragher, *Daniel Boone*, 131–39; Draper, *Life of Daniel Boone*, 411–421, 428–30, 432–33; Bakeless, *Daniel Boone*, 124–39. See also Brown, *Frontiersman*, 104–114. Boone himself was succinct in what he told Filson about the capture and rescue of the girls: "On the fourteenth day of July, 1776, two of Col. Calaway's daughters, and one of mine, were taken prisoner near the fort. I immediately pursued the Indians, with only eight men, and on the sixteenth overtook them, killed two of the party, and recovered the girls." *Filson Club History Quarterly*, 60.

78. Ranck, *Boonesborough*, 54; Rice, *Frontier Kentucky*, 84.

79. John Floyd to William Preston, Dec. 16, 1779, State Historical Society of Wisconsin, Draper Manuscript Collection, 33SS308–12, in Hammon and Harris, "Letters of Floyd," 215–17.

80. Floyd to Preston, Bear Grass, Nov. 26, 1779, State Historical Society of Wisconsin, Draper Manuscript Collection, 17CC186–87, in Hammon and Harris, "Letters of Floyd," 217–18.

81. Floyd to Preston, May 5, 1780, State Historical Society of Wisconsin, Draper Manuscript Collection, 17CC125.

82. Hammon and Harris, "Letters of John Floyd," 228.

83. "A Narrative of the Incidents Attending the Capture, Detention and Ransom of Charles Johnston," in Drimmer, *Captured by the Indians*, 197.

84. Floyd to Preston, March 28, 1783, State Historical Society of Wisconsin, Draper Manuscript Collection, 17CC144–48, in Hammon and Harris, "Letters of Floyd," 234–36.

85. Letitia Floyd to Benjamin Rush Floyd, Feb. 22, 1843.

86. Osborn, "William Preston—Revolutionary," 7–20.

87. Dorman, *Prestons*, 18; Johnson, *William Preston*, 196.

88. Johnson, *William Preston*, 207–211.

89. Johnson, *William Preston*, 234; Dorman, *Prestons*, 19.

90. Preston to Jefferson, April 13, 1781, in Dorman, *Prestons*, 19, Johnson, *William Preston*, 292, and Cullen et al., *Papers of Thomas Jefferson*, 7: 436–38.

91. E.g., Floyd to Preston, April 26, 1781, State Historical Society of Wisconsin, Draper Manuscript Collection, 17CC135–37; September 30, 1781, 17CC138–39; Oct. 19, 1782, 17CC143–44; March 28, 1783, 17CC144–48; in Hammon and Harris, "Letters of John Floyd," 225–36.

92. Johnson, *William Preston*, 305–08; Dorman, *Prestons*, 21.

93. Johnson, *William Preston*, 310; Dorman, *Prestons*, 64, 69–70, 290. See also chapter 5 for more about John Buchanan Floyd.

94. Draper, *Life of Daniel Boone*, 403 (may have been 200 whites in Kentucky at the beginning of 1776); *Filson Club History Quarterly*, 28–29 (estimates population of Kentucky

in 1783 at 30,000); Bureau of the Census, *Historical Statistics*, Part 2, Chapter Z, 1168 (estimates population of Kentucky in 1780 at 45,000, including 7,200 African Americans). In 1774, the only station in Kentucky was Harrodsburg, which had been started in March 1774 but was abandoned because of Indian attacks from July 1774 to March 1775.

3. Y^r Most Ob^t Servt, G. Washington

1. George Washington to James Mercer, Mount Vernon, March 15, 1787, in the possession of the author. A transcription of the letter is in Fitzpatrick, *Writings of Washington*, vol. 29, 179–181. Washington had used the same argument (that he could not go to the Constitutional Convention in May 1787 without giving offense to the Cincinnati) in letters to James Madison in November and December 1786. Ellis, *His Excellency*, 173, 303n47.

2. Ferling, *Ascent of George Washington*, 242–44 (leave-taking at Fraunces Tavern, resignation of commission at Annapolis), 246–58 (Washington at Mt. Vernon); Chernow, *Washington* 141–42 (Mt. Vernon's businesses and fishery); Washington to Clement Biddle, Mount Vernon, March 14, 1787, in Fitzpatrick, *Writings of Washington*, vol. 29, 178–79 (consignment of herring).

3. Ferling, *Ascent of Washington*, 228–35, 257–58; Ellis, *His Excellency*, 142–44 (speech to his officers at Newburgh), 158–60 (Washington and the Cincinnati); Chernow, *Washington*, 433–36 (Newburgh), 444, 497–500 (the Cincinnati), 520–24 (Washington's reluctance to attend the Constitutional Convention, partly because of having declined the Cincinnati invitation); Weigley, *History of the U.S. Army*, 77–78; David Humphreys to George Washington, Sept. 24, 1786, George Washington Papers at the Library of Congress, 1741–1799, Series 4, General Correspondence. The Society of the Cincinnati still exists, with its membership based on primogeniture. The author, being a second son of a descendant of a Continental Army officer, is not eligible for membership—but the author's son (after filing an application to the remarkably named Committee on Pretensions) is a member, being the firstborn male descendant of an ancestor of my wife who was a captain in the Continental Army.

4. Rakove, *Annotated U.S. Constitution*, 25–26 (summary of the Articles of Confederation).

5. Ellis, *His Excellency*, 127, 168–71; Fitzpatrick, *Writings of Washington*, vol. 26, 276–77 (Washington to Hamilton, March 31, 1783), 484–89 (Washington, *Circular to the States*, June 8, 1783); Ferling, *Ascent of Washington*, 243, 259; Chernow, *Washington*, 514 (Washington to James McHenry, Aug. 22, 1785).

6. Ellis, *His Excellency*, 171–77; Ferling, *Ascent of George Washington*, 267, 283; Chernow, *Washington*, 522–24 and 845nn19–22 (letters from and to Knox and to Randolph).

7. Chernow, *Washington*, 534 (Washington to Hamilton, July 10, 1787). For Washington's diary entry for Sept. 17, 1787, see Jackson and Twohig, *Papers of George Washington*. Washington to Lafayette, Feb. 7, 1788, is cited in Chernow, *Washington*, 538.

8. Ferling, *Ascent of George Washington*, 271–74 (Washington's role in ratification, his election as president), 278–346 (his two terms as president); Rakove, *Annotated U.S. Constitution*, 50–57 (ratification of the Constitution); Ellis, *His Excellency*, 68–70 (Washington's stature and presence), 77 ("His Excellency"), 180–87 (ratification and Washington's election), 195–230 (Washington as president); Chernow, *Washington*, 770–71 (summarizing Washington's achievements as president).

9. Morris to Washington, October 30, 1787, Chernow, *Washington*, 542.
10. McCullough, *John Adams*, 417, 418 (Adams on Madison; Adams as "His Rotundity"); Chernow, *Washington*, 516 (appearance of Madison); U.S. Constitution, Art. II, Sec. 1, and Rakove, *Annotated U.S. Constitution* 180 (qualifications for election as president, Hamilton's eligibility); Ellis, *His Excellency*, 215–16 (Jefferson's views of Hamilton and vice versa); Chernow, *Alexander Hamilton*, 511, 521–22 (Adams on Hamilton); Bailyn, *To Begin the World Anew*, 102 (Hamilton wrote 52 of the 85 *Federalist* papers).

4. Daguerreotype and Sword

1. Richard B. Screven to Secretary of War John C. Calhoun, Coosawatchie, S.C. (Jan. 25, 1823), National Archives, file from U.S. Military Academy Cadet Application Papers, 1805–1866, File 115–1825, file for Richard Screven, RG 94, record of Adjutant General's Office.
2. Richard B. Screven to Secretary of War John C. Calhoun, Coosawatchie, S.C. (May 23, 1825), National Archives, 115/25; *Register of the Officers and Cadets of the U.S. Military Academy, June, 1829*, 6–7 (listing members of the graduating class, their rank in the class, and their age at time of admission); Weigley, *History of the U.S. Army*, 105–08 (founding of West Point; varying ages of the cadets); Albert Church, *Personal Reminiscences of the Military Academy*, 78 (Church died two days after reading this paper); Robbins, *Last in Their Class*, 15–18.
3. Weigley, *History of the U.S. Army*, 556 (size of army in 1829), 110 (brevet system). For Screven's promotions and transfers, see Cullum, *Biographical Register*, 359–60; Cullum and Heitman, *Historical Register*; 870–871, and letter from Major General Edward F. Witsell to Philip T. Meredith, Jan. 16, 1948 (in the possession of the author). See also the information on Screven's life and career in Ellis, *Norwich University*, vol. 2, 213. From 1823 to 1825, Screven was a cadet at The American Literary, Scientific, and Military Academy, which later was chartered as Norwich University.
4. Hurd, *History of Essex County*, vol. 1, 297.
5. Mahon, *Second Seminole War*, 2–7; Knetsch, *Fear and Anxiety*, 1–10 (importance of grazing and cattle to immigration of Seminoles).
6. Remini, *Andrew Jackson and His Indian Wars*, 130–66.
7. Mahon, *Second Seminole War*, 22–50.
8. Mahon, *Second Seminole War*, 96–112; Robbins, *Last in Their Class*, 36–39; Knetsch, *Fear and Anxiety*, 91–92.
9. Mahon, *Second Seminole War*, 115–6 (population), 120–23 (U.S. and Seminole shoulder arms, estimated number of Seminoles and Seminole warriors), 129–30 (terrain and climate), 133 (fever), 62 (speech by Tuckhose Emathla, known to whites as John Hicks: "Here our navel strings were first cut"); Knetsch, *Fear and Anxiety*, 59 (Gen. Jesup on the American ignorance of Florida's interior); Weigley, *History of the U.S. Army*, 161–162 (effective strength of army in 1835, number of regulars in Florida), 566 (strength of army in 1834–1842).
10. Mahon, *Second Seminole War*, 144–57.
11. Weigley, *History of the U.S. Army*, 556 (size of army in 1829 and in 1837); Mahon, *Second Seminole War*, 138, 164 (Congress allots $500,000 in January and another $1,500,000 in April 1836 for fighting in Florida), 175 (incidence of fever at Fort Drane), 188 (pay of a private, diary of Henry Hollingsworth on life of a private, officer resignations); Winders, *Mr. Polk's Army*, 122 (pay of infantry officers in 1841).

12. Mahon, *Second Seminole War*, 200–205 (the detention camp and the freeing of the detainees by Osceola and Sam Jones), 213–17 (the taking of several chiefs, including Osceola, and their followers).

13. Mahon, *Second Seminole War*, 219–30, 240; Howe, *What Hath God Wrought*, 744 (kin of Taylor).

14. Mahon, *Second Seminole War*, 218 (death of Osceola), 240 (Jesup's command), 245–55 (Taylor's command).

15. Mahon, *Second Seminole War*, 244 (cost of war through May 1838), 267 (increase in army and creation of Eighth Infantry), 255–61 (Macomb's declaration of peace and its disintegration), 274–87 (Armistead's command and his shipment west of Indians); Knetsch, *Fear and Anxiety*, 192–93 (role of Eighth Infantry in Trail of Tears); Weigley, *History of the U.S. Army*, 162 (increase in army, creation of Eighth Infantry); Perdue and Green, *The Cherokee Nation and the Trail of Tears*, 123–40; Ehle, *Trail of Tears*, 322–61; Wilkins, *Cherokee Tragedy*, 316–28; Howe, *What Hath God Wrought*, 416 (Trail of Tears).

16. Sprague, *Florida War*, 362 (destruction of Sam Jones' town), 365 (rattlesnakes), 368 (Screven too sick to proceed), 376 (end of Big Cypress campaign).

17. Mahon, *Second Seminole War*, 294–318 (Worth's command in Florida and his declaration of the war's end); "Aiken Suggests U.S. Say It Has Won the War," *New York Times*, Oct. 20, 1966.

18. Sprague, *Origin*, 500–501 (capture and shipment of Octiarche and his band); Mahon, *Second Seminole War*, 321 (number of Indians shipped west), 322 (future leaders in the Mexican War and the Civil War), 325 (number of regulars killed), and 326 (monetary cost of the war).

19. Borneman, *Polk*, 125–45; Howe, *What Hath God Wrought*, 702 (Polk's slaveholdings), 708 (Polk on the objectives in administration, including the acquisition of California); Merry, *A Country of Vast Designs*, 187 (border of Texas).

20. Weigley, *History of the U.S. Army*, 173 (forces with Taylor), 567 (size of active U.S. army in 1845 and 1848); Howe, *What Hath God Wrought*, 746 (U.S. and Mexican populations); Borneman, *Polk*, 200 (Hitchcock's diary).

21. Grant, *Memoirs and Selected Letters*, vol. 1, 65–67; Winders, *Mr. Polk's Army*, 89–100 (American artillery and shoulder arms during the war); Eisenhower, *So Far from God*, 65 (ambush of Thornton), 80 (wounding and death of Page); Ferrell, *Monterrey Is Ours*, 68–69 (the charge at Palo Alto).

22. Grant, *Memoirs and Selected Letters*, vol. 1, 65–69; Eisenhower, *So Far from God*, 76–85; Borneman, *Polk*, 211–214.

23. Borneman, *Polk*, 202–209; Eisenhower, *So Far from God*, 87–92; Merry, *A Country of Vast Designs*, 245–51; Polk, "A Special Message."

24. Grant, *Memoirs and Selected Letters*, vol. 1, 83; Eisenhower, *So Far from God*, 93–97; Winders, *Mr. Polk's Army*, 36–48, 75–76 (Polk's appointments of volunteer generals).

25. Eisenhower, *So Far from God*, 120–50; Ferrell, *Monterrey Is Ours!*, 131 (death of Captain McKavett); Grant, *Memoirs and Selected Letters*, vol. 1, 78, 81 (Grant's ride under fire); 919 (letter dated Oct. 3, 1846 to Julia Dent). In Screven's commission, as was typical in many documents of the time, the city we now spell "Monterrey" was spelled "Monterey."

26. Grant, *Memoirs and Selected Letters*, vol. 1, 83; Eisenhower, *So Far from God*, 149, 160–65, 170–72; Borneman, *Polk*, 258.

27. Borneman, *Polk*, 192–93, 197–99, 229–30, 245, 248; Eisenhower, *So Far from God*, 57–60, 114–116, 152–54 (by January 1847, Santa Anna's forces at San Luis Potosí exceeded 20,000), 175–76; Merry, *A Country of Vast Designs*, 310 (Santa Anna, regarding his return to Mexico).

28. Eisenhower, *So Far from God*, 178–79; Block, "Journal of Henry Clay, Jr."; Howe, *What Hath God Wrought*, 775–78 (battle of Buena Vista).

29. Eisenhower, *So Far from God*, 255, 257–65; Howe, *What Hath God Wrought*, 780–81; Ferrell, *Monterrey Is Ours!*, 190–95.

30. Eisenhower, *So Far from God*, 271–83, 294–95; Grant to Julia Dent, April 24, 1847, Grant, *Memoirs and Selected Letters*, vol. 1, 921; Howe, *What Hath God Wrought*, 780–83.

31. Eisenhower, *So Far from God*, 295–308.

32. Eisenhower, *So Far from God*, 316–36.

33. Eisenhower, *So Far from God*, 337–42.

34. Eisenhower, *So Far from God*, 359–68; Borneman, *Polk*, 301–15, 331. The Gadsden Purchase treaty was signed in 1853 and ratified in 1854.

35. Eisenhower, *So Far from God*, 369–70 (cost in dollars and in dead and wounded); Winders, *Mr. Polk's Army*, 139–40, 145, 239n2 (1,548 deaths due to battle and 10,970 deaths due to illness, mortality rate); Weigley, *History of the U.S. Army*, 184–86; Grant, *Memoirs and Selected Letters*, vol. 1, 129.

36. Grant, *Memoirs and Selected Letters*, vol. 1, 41.

37. Deposition of Louisa H. P. Screven before Gwinn Harris, JP, Dec. 28, 1853, National Archives, "Old War" Widow, File No. 3608. Screven's fifth child, Julia, born in 1843, married twice, the second time to a man named T. J. Meredith. The author is a descendant of that marriage. After the Civil War, Louisa Screven applied for reinstatement on the pension list. The file does not indicate whether the application was granted.

5. Shavings from a Scaffold

1. Oates, *To Purge This Land*, 43.

2. Oates, *To Purge This Land*, 22.

3. Letter to his father after his first wife's death, Oates, *To Purge This Land*, 25.

4. Sanborn, *Life and Letters of John Brown*, 58–59.

5. Oates, *To Purge This Land*, 49; Horwitz, *Midnight Rising*, 27.

6. Villard, *John Brown*, 4.

7. Oates, *To Purge This Land*, 41–2.

8. F. Douglass, *Life and Times of Frederick Douglass* (1892), vol. 2, 337–42, quoted in DuBois, *John Brown*, 46–49.

9. Horwitz, *Midnight Rising*, 50.

10. Oates, *To Purge This Land*, 130.

11. DuBois, *John Brown*, 77; for a similar account by Brown's son Jason, see Horwitz, *Midnight Rising*, 53. For accounts of the killings on the Pottawatomie, see, e.g., Oates, *To Purge This Land*, 133–37; Carton, *Patriotic Treason*, 187–93.

12. Oates, *To Purge This Land*, 54.

13. Horwitz, *Midnight Rising*, 59.

14. Oates, *To Purge This Land*, 222–23.

15. Sanborn, *Life and Letters of John Brown*, 444–45.

16. DuBois, *John Brown*, 128.

17. Villard, *John Brown*, 334.
18. Reynolds, *John Brown*, 271, 278, 292.
19. Villard, *John Brown*, 410–12, 638nn65,66. Floyd was a son of John Floyd, son of the surveyor John Floyd, and of Col. William Preston's daughter Letitia (Preston) Floyd. Dorman, *Prestons*, 22, 68, 289–91. For Preston and Floyd the surveyor, see chapter 2. For Secretary Floyd's transfer of small arms to Southern arsenals, see Reynolds, *John Brown*, 436; Grant, *Memoirs and Selected Letters*, vol. 1, 150.
20. Douglass, *Life and Times*, 388–91.
21. The letter, dated August 18, 1859, was from Owen Brown. Dreer Papers, Historical Society of Pennsylvania; Villard, *John Brown*, 416; Sanborn, *Life and Letters of John Brown*, 541.
22. DuBois, *John Brown*, 153.
23. Horwitz, *Midnight Rising*, 129.
24. Oates, *To Purge This Land*, 294.
25. Oates, *To Purge This Land*, 299, citing the statement of John T. Allstadt in Villard, *John Brown*, 401. But cf. Horwitz, *Midnight Rising*, 171 (Oliver was dead by this time; his brother Watson was begging to be put out of his misery; Brown told him "to endure a little longer and he might die as befitted a man").
26. DuBois, *John Brown*, 168.
27. Oates, *To Purge This Land*, 299–301; DuBois, *John Brown*, 168–69; Villard, *John Brown*, 452–54; Horwitz, *Midnight Rising*, 177–80.
28. Oates, *To Purge This Land*, 302.
29. Horwitz, *Midnight Rising*, 185.
30. The interview was published in the *New York Herald* and in the *Baltimore American* on Oct. 21, 1859. Villard, *John Brown*, 458–61; Sanborn, *Life and Letters of John Brown*, 562–569.
31. Oates, *To Purge This Land*, 308.
32. Horwitz, *Midnight Rising*, 193.
33. *Richmond Enquirer*, Oct. 25, 1859, in Villard, *John Brown*, 476.
34. Oates, *To Purge This Land*, 318–19; Reynolds, *John Brown*, 364–69; Horwitz, *Midnight Rising*, 214–15.
35. Brown to Thomas B. Musgrave, Nov. 17, 1859, Gilder Lehrman Collection, GLC07638.01, New York Historical Society.
36. Oates, *To Purge This Land*, 327; Reynolds, *John Brown*, 354; Horwitz, *Midnight Rising*, 211–13. Brown's speech appeared on Nov. 3, 1859, in two slightly different versions in the *New York Herald* and the *Baltimore American* and was printed and widely circulated as a broadside. One example is in the Gilder Lehrman Collection, GLC05508.051, New York Historical Society. Brown referred to Matthew 7:12 (do unto others what you would have them do unto you) and Hebrews 13:3 (remember them that are in bonds).
37. Oates, *To Purge This Land*, 335, 336.
38. Oates, *To Purge This Land*, 348.
39. Villard, *John Brown*, 554–55; Oates, *To Purge This Land*, 351; Reynolds, *John Brown*, 395.
40. Horwitz, *Midnight Rising*, 254–55.
41. Oates, *To Purge This Land*, 352; Sutler, "The Hanging of John Brown," 143–154. John Taylor Lewis Preston (1811–1890) was a relative of the author, both being descendants

of William Preston (1729–1783). See Dorman, *Prestons*, 71–72, 306–307. For J. T.L. Preston's account of the execution of John Brown, Dec. 2, 1859, see Allan, *Life and Letters of Margaret Junkin Preston*, 111–117.

42. Villard, *John Brown*, 562.

43. Horwitz, *Midnight Rising*, 262.

6. Diaries from Indian Country, Civil War Back Home

1. Freehling, *The South vs. the South*, 52.

2. Both journals are at The Filson Historical Society, Louisville, Ky. The 1861 journal was published in *Filson Club History Quarterly* 24 (April 1950): 103–36; entries after July 10, 1861, were published in 24 (July 1950): 246–75. The 1862 journal has not been published, except for excerpts included in Holmberg, "John Mason Brown's 1862 Journal of His Second Trip to the Rocky Mountains," 2–5. Also at The Filson Historical Society is William Struck's fine transcription of the 1862 journal. Diary entries in this chapter are identified by date of entry, without further citation. If the entry is on a particular date in 1861 or 1862, that means it will be found in the diary for that year (and, if in 1861, in the diary as published in the *Filson Club History Quarterly*), in the entry for that date. Much of Brown's correspondence as a Union officer was acquired in 2010 by the Filson Historical Society, and is now in their collections. It has not been previously published. The author has used Brown's spelling for the excerpts from Brown's diaries and for Brown's correspondence.

3. Dorman, *Prestons*, 40–43 (John Brown, 1757–1837), 151–52 (Mason Brown, 1799–1867), 153–54 (John Mason Brown, 1837–1890).

4. The 1859 trip of *Chippewa* and another American Fur Company steamboat, *Spread Eagle*, is described in Larsen and Cottrell, *Steamboats West*. See also Lass, *Navigating the Missouri*, 188–92.

5. For biographical sketches of John Mason Brown, see Preston Brown (son of John Mason Brown), "John Mason Brown, 1837–1890"; Davie, "Reminiscences"; and Depew, *My Memories of Eighty Years*, 4–6. For Pierre Chouteau, Jr., and Company and its interest in the American Fur Company, see Larsen and Cottrell, *Steamboats West*, 14–15, 29, and 150; and Sunder, *Fur Trade*. For Father De Smet, see Carriker, *Father Peter John De Smet*, and Terrell, *Black Robe: The Life of Pierre-Jean De Smet*.

6. Preston Brown, "Brown," 127; Davie, "Reminiscences," 132.

7. Harrison, *Civil War in Kentucky*, 8–9 (Kentucky's neutrality), 24–32 (driving Confederates out of Kentucky); McKnight, *Contested Borderland*, 25 and 240n60 (Gov. Beriah McGoffin's May 1, 1861 declaration on not sending troops to subdue Southern states).

8. Lass, *Navigating the Missouri*, 181–83.

9. For estimates of Indian deaths in the 1837 smallpox epidemic, see Lass, *Navigating the Missouri*, 102.

10. For reminiscences about Hugh Monroe, see Schutz, *Rising Wolf*.

11. John Mason Brown, "Traditions of the Blackfeet," 164.

12. For years in which the Company had the annuity contracts, see Sunder, *Fur Trade*, 28 (1830s), 112 (1849), 144 (1852 and all but four succeeding years through 1864), 197 (1857 and 1858), 221 (1861), 224 and 244 (1862).

13. 1861: May 8 (12 or 15 tons of annuities taken on board); May 12 (Omaha: freight for Pawnees); May 31 (Yankton, Nebraska: Yankton band of Sioux); June 5 (Ft.

Pierre: Yanktonais Sioux); June 12 (Ree village); June 14 (Ft. Berthold: Gros Ventres, Mandans); June 25 (Ft. Union: Assinaboines). 1862: May 18 (Omaha: Pawnees); May 22 (near Yankton—annuity distribution, tribe not named; presumably Yanktonais); May 28 (Ft. Pierre: "Annuities for the Minne Kanjous, Unk-Pa-Pas, Yanktonaise and Blackfoot Sioux tribes"; the Sioux insisted also on receiving all the Arikara annuities).

14. Larsen and Cottrell, *Steamboats West*, 178n56.

15. Davie, "Reminiscences," 131.

16. Carley, *Dakota War of 1862*, 1.

17. See Anderson, "Myrick's Insult," 198–206. Anderson says that the Dakota leader Little Crow, in a letter to Henry Sibley, commander of the Minnesota militia, dictated during the fighting, said that Myrick told the Dakota they could "eat grass or their own dung." "Myrick's Insult," 205. Another account has Myrick, in a meeting with the Indians in June 1862, saying "I will not let you have a thing. You and your wives and children may starve, or eat grass, or your own filth." Hubbard and Holcombe, *Minnesota in Three Centuries*, vol. 3, 286. For the hanging at Mankato, see Carley, *Dakota War of 1862*, 70–75.

18. Sunder, *Fur Trade*, 209, 230.

19. In the summer of 1862, Brown's friend Andrew Dawson, agent at Fort Benton, received a package of sand from a man (probably Jean L'Heureux, who lived among the Indians at Chief Mountain, pretending to be a priest) who said it was gold-bearing sand from a gulch up north—giving no details. The sand, washed at the fort, was rich in gold. A prospecting party of eleven men from Fort Benton, including Matt Carroll, worked the creeks from the Marias River to somewhere south of Edmonton, finding color but not enough to pay. Overholser, *Fort Benton*, 356; English and Bélanger, *Dictionary of Canadian Biography Online*, entry for Jean L'Heureux. This prospecting party sounds similar to Brown's smaller party, which included Matt Carroll (entry of July 10), crossed the Marias River (July 16), and found gold in a creek near the Bow River in what is now Alberta (July 29) before turning back to Fort Benton.

20. Lass, *Navigating the Missouri*, 210–11, 225, 230; Overholser, *Fort Benton*, 41–42 (gold brought down in 1862), 145–52 (estimate of total gold shipped from Fort Benton, 1862–69), and 165 (gold strike in July 1862); Malone, Roeder, and Lang, *Montana*, 64–71 (mining and population growth), 184–92 (silver), and 201–11 (copper). For overviews of western gold rushes, see Greever, *The Bonanza West*, and Paul, *Mining Frontiers of the Far West*.

21. Larsen and Cottrell, *Steamboats West*, 16 (draft of *Spread Eagle* and *Chippewa*), 34 (nearly 40 steamboats were lost in the Missouri River before 1900—most of them to snags); Lass, *Navigating the Missouri*, 21–21 (snags), 150 (boats in the 1848 fleet lasted on average 5.7 years), 155 (419 of 736 steamers destroyed through 1848 were sunk by snags or other obstructions).

22. Sunder, *Fur Trade*, 228.

23. See Harrison, *Civil War in Kentucky*, 11–17; Grant, *Memoirs and Selected Letters*, vol. 1, 174–75 (capture of Paducah); Freehling, *The South vs. the South*, 52–53 (Kentucky's legislature votes for neutrality), 66, 68 (Polk takes Columbus, Grant takes Paducah, Confederacy makes Bowling Green its western headquarters).

24. See Harrison, *Civil War in Kentucky*, 18–35, and chapter 7, below (Shiloh).

25. President Theodore Roosevelt told a similar story about Brown's choice. See chapter 8, note 68 and accompanying text.

26. Peterson, *Freedom and Franchise*, 62–68 (the duel in 1856 and the organization of the Republican party in Missouri); Dorman, *Prestons*, 101–102 (Breckinridge), 291 (Floyd), 156–57 (Orlando Brown, Jr.); Speed, *Union Regiments of Kentucky*, 504–12 (22nd Kentucky Infantry); Orlando Brown to Orlando Brown, Jr., Dec. 20, 1865, Orlando Brown Papers, Filson Historical Society, Louisville, A/.B879/25 (son as first young man in Frankfort to take up arms for the Union); Freehling, *The South vs. the South*, 54 (percentage of Kentucky white males of military age joining either, or neither, side's army), 57 (examples of close kin in Kentucky fighting on opposite sides). According to Speed, *Union Regiments*, 504, 508, Orlando Brown, Jr., joined the 22nd infantry as an adjutant in December 1861 and subsequently became lieutenant colonel of the 14th Kentucky Infantry. For Preston and Johnston, see chapter 7.

27. File B2488-US-1864, National Archives (in that file, date of Brown's commission as major [Oct. 27, 1862] is noted both on p. 360 of the Field and Staff Muster-Out Roll of the 10th Regiment, Kentucky, Cavalry, and on a notation by the Record and Pension Office, War Department, dated May 9, 1899, Book Mark B 2488-VS-1864, Compiled Military Service Records, John Mason Brown, RG 94, Records of Adjutant General's Office); Harrison, *Civil War in Kentucky*, 50–55 (Perryville and pursuit of Bragg), 63–64 (blocking Marshall's drive); Speed, *Union Regiments of Kentucky*, 216–18 (10th Kentucky Cavalry); McKnight, *Contested Borderland*, 47–48, 54–56, 99–100, 108–09 (Marshall).

28. Col. C. J. Walker, Sharpsburg, Ky. to Capt. W. L. M. Burger, Lexington, April 3, 1863, transmitting Brown's resignation from 10th Kentucky Cavalry, files of J. M. Brown, Major, 10th Ky. Cav., National Archives, RG 94; Major John Mason Brown to Maj. Gen. Burnside, Cincinnati, Ohio, Aug. 3, 1863, S.O. 292, B.295 (D.O) 1863, National Archives, RG 94 (requesting to be detached to raise a regiment); Speed, *Union Regiments of Kentucky*, 624–27 (45th Kentucky Mounted Infantry).

29. Brown to W. P. Anderson, Jan. 10, 1864, enclosing affidavit from a Union chaplain, Rev. Elisha Thacker, who, among other things, saw the major burst into a house, demand food of a woman, and "while she was in the act of stooping over the oven at the fire, he placed his hands on her hinder parts"; he later came back in the house "with his pants open in front with his finger in the opening saying 'My prick is loose, by God!',", before the chaplain was able to get him to leave (the author gratefully acknowledges his receipt of copies of the letter from Brown to W.P. Anderson and of the enclosed affidavit from Ronald Szudy of Parma, Ohio, whose ancestor served with Brown); W. P. Anderson to Brig. Gen. E. E. Potter, chief of staff, Knoxville, Feb. 6, 1864, in United States War Department, *The War of the Rebellion*, series 1, vol. 33, pt. 2, p. 338 (efforts against the Confederate guerrillas). Union sympathizer Frances Peter, of Lexington, noted in her diary for Feb. 1, 1864, that Brown had sent to Lexington four or five guerillas who had been captured at Mt. Sterling by men of the 45th while the guerillas were "in the act of putting a rope round the neck of a Union man for the purpose of hanging him." Her entry for Feb. 25, 1864, notes that Brown, then in Lexington, had been assigned to Owen County, Lebanon and Bardstown "for the suppression of guerrillas." Peter, *Diary*, 189.

30. McKnight, *Contested Borderland*, 198.

31. Copies of Brown's report, dated June 29, 1864, to Captain J. S. Butler, acting assistant adjutant general, on the pursuit of Morgan in June 1864 are in the John Mason Brown Papers, Filson Historical Society. See also Harrison, *Civil War in Kentucky*, 71–74 (Morgan's 1864 raid).

32. Speed, *Union Regiments of Kentucky*, 624–27 (45th Kentucky Mounted Infantry).

33. Capt. Stagg to Col. John Mason Brown, letters of Nov. 4 and Nov. 5, 1864, John Mason Brown Papers, Filson Historical Society (relating to having soldiers vote); Thomas M. Vincent, assistant adjutant general, to the governor of Kentucky (Dec. 27, 1864), United States War Department, *The War of the Rebellion*, series 3, vol. 4, 1019 (War Department's denial of Brown's request to form a regiment as part of the First Army Corps); Dorman, *Prestons*, 153 (date on which Brown was mustered out).

34. Preston Brown, "John Mason Brown," 129–33, and Davie, "Reminiscences," 130–32 (Brown's life after the Civil War); Harrison, *Civil War in Kentucky*, 93–106 (Kentucky politics at the end of the war); chapter 7, below (Gen. Preston); Depew, *My Memories of Eighty Years*, 6, and Justice Henry B. Brown to Elihu Root (Oct. 28, 1901; in Preston Brown File, 400729/C, Adjutant General's Office, RG 94, National Archives, Washington, D.C.) (Brown under consideration for appointment to Supreme Court when he died). Brown's historical writings include *An Oration at the Centennial Commemoration of the Battle of the Blue Licks* (Frankfort, Ky: Martin, Johnston & Barrett, 1882) and *The Political Beginnings of Kentucky* (Louisville: The Filson Club, 1889). He also wrote, in addition to the article on traditions of the Blackfeet (see note 8), "Songs of the Slave," *Lippincott's Magazine*, 2 (December, 1868), 617–23.

7. Travels of an English Pistol

1. The pistol depicted in figure 7.1, while not Preston's, is, to the best of the author's recollection, the same model as Preston's pistol.

2. For the career of Col. William Preston (1729–1783), see chapter 2.

3. Sehlinger, *Kentucky's Last Cavalier*, 10.

4. Dorman, *Prestons*, 57–60, 241; Sehlinger, *Kentucky's Last Cavalier*, 6–11.

5. Sehlinger, *Kentucky's Last Cavalier*, 19–35; Dorman, *Prestons*, 85–87.

6. Sehlinger, *Kentucky's Last Cavalier*, 35.

7. Sehlinger, *Kentucky's Last Cavalier*, 33–35.

8. Sehlinger, *Kentucky's Last Cavalier*, 8, 13–16, 28, 43.

9. Roland, *Albert Sidney Johnston*, 59–61 (Johnston's duel); Sehlinger, *Kentucky's Last Cavalier*, 24, 30.

10. Sehlinger, *Kentucky's Last Cavalier*, 16, 23, 63, 68. For examples of Southern mothers' emphasis to their sons on the importance of maintaining the family honor, see Wyatt-Brown, *Southern Honor*, 132, 134.

11. Sehlinger, *Kentucky's Last Cavalier*, 42, 36.

12. Sehlinger, *Kentucky's Last Cavalier*, 53–63, 212 (interest in Texas lands). For the background of the Mexican War, see chapter 4, above.

13. Sehlinger, *Kentucky's Last Cavalier*, 71–83. See chapter 5, above, for a discussion of the fighting in Kansas and of John Brown's role in that fighting.

14. Sehlinger, *Kentucky's Last Cavalier*, 86.

15. Richardson, *Cassius Marcellus Clay*, 68–70.

16. Sehlinger, *Kentucky's Last Cavalier*, 84–90.

17. Sehlinger, *Kentucky's Last Cavalier*, 94–97.

18. Sehlinger, *Kentucky's Last Cavalier*, 98–100.

19. Sehlinger, *Kentucky's Last Cavalier*, 100–08.

20. Sehlinger, *Kentucky's Last Cavalier*, 110–28.

21. Sehlinger, *Kentucky's Last Cavalier*, 109 (photograph of Queen Isabella from William Preston's album); Mosgrove, *Kentucky Cavaliers*, 46 ("notably handsome"); de Polnay,

A *Queen of Spain*, 20 (Isabella's birth), 97, 101 (Don Francisco's sexuality), 119–20 (Isabella's wedding night), 180 (birth of Pilar); Boetzkes, *The Little Queen*, 88–89 (Beramendi's impressions of the queen), 111–117 (Sickles and Isabella).

22. Sehlinger, *Kentucky's Last Cavalier*, 129–33.

23. Lincoln to Orville H. Browning, Sept. 22, 1861, Basler, *Works of Lincoln*, vol. 4, 532. Lincoln's purported statement that he'd like to have God on his side, but he must have Kentucky, is often quoted—never, to the best of my knowledge, with a demonstrable citation to Lincoln. The attribution to Lincoln is likely to be a misattribution from the abolitionist Moncure D. Conway, who wrote in an 1862 book "that the worthy President would *like to* have God on his side; he *must* have Kentucky." Conway, *The Golden Hour*, 119.

24. A Northern composer set to music the hasty retreat of Floyd and his fellow general Pillow, with the climactic line "Floyd steals his Pillow and skedaddles from Fort Donelson." "Floyd's Retreat from Fort Donelson, with a running description of the battle, by Skeddaddles" (St. Louis: J. L. Peters & Bro.). A copy is in the Filson Historical Society, Louisville.

25. Harrison, *The Civil War in Kentucky*, 28–32; McDonough, *Shiloh*, 6–7, 10 (map); Grant, *Memoirs and Selected Letters*, vol. 1, 222.

26. McDonough, *Shiloh*, 30–36.

27. Woodworth, *The Shiloh Campaign*, 18–19.

28. Sword, *Shiloh: Bloody April*, 460–62 (numbers on both sides); Grant, *Memoirs and Selected Letters*, vol. 1, 223, 1005 (letter to his father, Pittsburg Landing, April 26, 1862).

29. For the importance of Shiloh in the Old Testament, see, e.g., Joshua 18:1 (tabernacle set up at Shiloh); Judges 18:31 (the house of God was in Shiloh); 1 Samuel 1 (Hannah prays in Shiloh for a child, and brings the child Samuel to the house of the Lord in Shiloh), 3:21 (the Lord reveals himself to Samuel in Shiloh by the word of the Lord), 4:4 (ark of the covenant brought out from Shiloh). "Shiloh" may sound somewhat like "shalom" (peace), but the exegetes differ on its etymology. Rashi reads Shiloh in Genesis 49:10 to refer to the Messiah, but literally to mean "a gift to him."

30. Sehlinger, *Kentucky's Last Cavalier*, 136–37; Sehlinger, " 'At the Moment of Victory'"; Woodworth, *Shiloh Campaign*, 24–25 (Johnston's death), 55–76 (Hornets' Nest; argues it was not the most vicious or important engagement at Shiloh); McDonough, *Shiloh*, 92 (Sherman's surprise at the Confederate attack), 125–50 (the carnage at mid-day, the Hornets' Nest), 152–53 (Johnston's charge and death); Sword, *Shiloh: Bloody April*, 443–46 (Johnston's death; believes Johnston's wound was probably from a stray ball fired by a Confederate during the charge); Roland, *Albert Sidney Johnston*, 336, 338–39.

31. Sehlinger, "'At the Moment of Victory,'" 333; McDonough, *Shiloh*, 173–79 (gunboat fire more alarming than damaging, arrival of Buell's men); 181 (Beauregard's victory telegram); Woodworth, *Shiloh Campaign*, 102–105 (gunboats' fire), 110–20 (Beauregard's telegram and his order to withdraw).

32. Woodworth, *Shiloh Campaign*, 105–107 (effect of gunboats' fire), 131–33 (the chaotic retreat); McDonough, *Shiloh*, 180–96; Grant, *Memoirs and Selected Letters*, vol. 1, 235–36, 1002.

33. Grant, *Memoirs and Selected Letters*, vol. 1, 238–39; McDonough, *Shiloh*, 5 (Sherman's letter to his wife); Sword, *Shiloh: Bloody April*, 460–461 (deaths and casualties on each

side); Horwitz, *Confederates in the Attic*, 165 (casualties greater than combined casualties in prior wars).

34. Catton, *This Hallowed Ground*, 120; McDonough, *Shiloh*, 225 (Cable); Grant, *Memoirs and Selected Letters*, vol. 1, 246.

35. For some of the pros and cons of the "lost opportunity" argument, see Woodworth, *Shiloh Campaign*, 117–20; W. P. Johnston, *Life of Albert Sidney Johnston*, 627–39; McDonough, *Shiloh*, 153–55, 168–82; Roland, *Albert Sidney Johnston*, 339–50, 347 (Davis's estimation of Johnston); Sehlinger, *Kentucky's Last Cavalier*, 137–38; Grant, *Memoirs and Selected Letters*, vol. 1, 242–44; Watkins, *Company Aytch*, 27.

36. Sehlinger, *Kentucky's Last Cavalier*, 138–41; Freehling, *The South vs. the South*, 59 (Bragg's proclamation and installation of a secessionist as governor); Watkins, *Company Aytch*, 43.

37. Sehlinger, *Kentucky's Last Cavalier*, 141; Watkins, *Company Aytch*, 44; Harrison, *Civil War in Kentucky*, 50–56. See chapter 6 for raids by John Hunt Morgan into Kentucky.

38. Sehlinger, *Kentucky's Last Cavalier*, 143–46, 154 (letter to William Preston Johnston about Stones River as "a Banquet of Ghouls"); William Preston, Report, Jan. 12, 1863, United States War Department, *War of the Rebellion*, series 1, vol. 20, part 1, 818.

39. Sehlinger, *Kentucky's Last Cavalier*, 148–56; S. B. Buckner to W. S. Cooper, Oct. 1, 1863, Compiled Service Records of Confederate Generals and Staff Officers, microcopy 331, RG 94, National Archives, Washington, D.C. (recommending Preston's appointment as major general). See also Woodworth, *The Chickamauga Campaign*.

40. Sehlinger, *Kentucky's Last Cavalier*, 167–89.

41. Sehlinger, *Kentucky's Last Cavalier*, 162–64, 190–92.

42. Sehlinger, *Kentucky's Last Cavalier*, 196–200, 207–22.

8. A Killing in the Philippines

1. In 1947, a year before Preston Brown died, my father described him as "always as neat as if he were about to hold an inspection or to be inspected." John Mason Brown, *Seeing More Things*, 12.

2. Musikant, *Empire by Default*, 591; Leech, *Days of McKinley*, 345.

3. Karnow, *In Our Image*, 127.

4. Karnow, *In Our Image*, 134.

5. Linn, *Philippine War*, 64, 124–25.

6. Boot, *Savage Wars of Peace*, 125.

7. Linn, *Philippine War*, 117.

8. Linn, *Philippine War*, 190.

9. Karnow, *In Our Image*, 174 (first quote), 130–31 (second quote), 154 (third quote).

10. Questionnaire of Sergeant Robert Lichtig, 30th Infantry, in Linn, *Philippine War*, 195 (fourth quote). In June 1900, a U.S. infantry patrol in Leyte reporting finding the remains of an American soldier who had been buried alive with a trail of sugar leading to his propped-open mouth: "a trail of sugar laid to it through the forest. . . . Millions of ants had done the rest." Karnow, *In Our Image*, 178.

11. Linn, *Philippine War*, 9, 213–14.

12. Linn, *Philippine War*, 223 (first quote), 256 (second quote); Karnow, *In Our Image*, 179 (third quote, summarizing testimony of former Sergeant Charles S. Riley describing a water cure).

13. Karnow, *In Our Image*, 176.

14. Bullard, *Fighting Generals*, 184 ("I taught him everything," 1st Sgt. Haifer told Gen. Bullard).

15. Mary Mason Brown to Wayne MacVeagh, Oct. 17, 1902 (copy), attachment to MacVeagh to Adjutant General Henry C. Corbin, Preston Brown File, file 400729/C, Adjutant General's Office, RG 94, National Archives, Washington, D.C. (hereafter Brown AGO file); Verhoeff, "Major General Preston Brown," 248–51.

16. Testimony of Lt. Paul H. McCook, transcript of court-martial of Lt. Preston Brown (hereafter "transcript"), Brown AGO file, 89.

17. Linn, *Philippine War*, 220 (increased frequency of burning villages); Karnow, *In Our Image*, 179 (quoting Col. Arthur Lockwood).

18. Linn, *Philippine War*, 278–79; Birtle, "The U.S. Army's Pacification of Marinduque," 255–82.

19. Testimony of Pvt. John Walker, the lead prosecution witness, transcript, p. 16; testimony of Pvt. Charles Knistrom, transcript, 64; testimony of Pvt. Harry W. Hannon, transcript, 143.

20. Testimony of Sgt. William McGregor, transcript, 106; testimony of Pvt. Michael C. Redican, transcript, 169; testimony of Pvt. Elza Werkmann, transcript, 208; testimony of Pvt. Ross Plummer, transcript, 217.

21. Robert A. Brown, "Report."

22. Testimony of Pvt. Harry W. Hannon, transcript, 22; testimony of Pvt. Leotis Weddle, transcript, 53; testimony of Pvt. Charles Knistrom, transcript, 59.

23. E.g., testimony of Pvt. John Walker, transcript, 3.

24. Testimony of Pvt. Chester Rhoades, transcript, 45.

25. Transcript, 10.

26. Testimony of Pvt. Harry Hannon, transcript, 27.

27. Transcript, 75.

28. Testimony of Pvt. Forest Walker, transcript, 34; testimony of Pvt. Charles Knistrom, transcript, 60 ("Lieutenant Brown made some remark about Private Weidner being worth more than all the niggers in the island"); testimony of Pvt. George A. Garrett, transcript, 70 ("wouldn't give Private Weidner for all the niggers that were round there"); testimony of Pvt. Reuben M. Short, transcript, 269 ("wouldn't have lost Private Weidner for all the gugus in the islands").

29. E.g., testimony of Pvt. Henry Oiler, transcript, 175–76.

30. Testimony of Pvt. Michael C. Redican, transcript, 156.

31. E.g., testimony of Pvt. Henry Oiler, transcript, 172; testimony of Cpl. Michael Maher, transcript, 120; testimony of Pvt. Michael C. Redican, transcript, 145; testimony of Pvt. Elza Werkmann, transcript, 202; testimony of Pvt. Reuben Short, transcript, 259.

32. Robert A. Brown, "Report," Exhibit L'.

33. E.g., testimony of Pvt. David Robinson, transcript, 111; testimony of Pvt. Michael C. Redican, transcript, 146; testimony of Leo C. Norton, transcript, 186; testimony of Pvt. Elza Werkmann, transcript, 204; testimony of Pvt. Ross Plummer, transcript, 211; testimony of Pvt. James D. Bright, transcript, 221; testimony of Pvt. Reuben M. Short, transcript, 259.

34. Testimony of Pvt. Reuben M. Short, transcript, 260.

35. Testimony of Lt. Preston Brown, transcript, 266.

36. Linn, *Philippine War*, 224, describing a March 30, 1900, letter from Brig. Gen. J. Franklin Bell to the effect that threats of violence to obtain information "are necessary and

justifiable," but that he would not be able to protect "any officer whose employment of such methods becomes a matter of complaint or scandal."

37. Testimony of Lt. Paul H. McCook, transcript, 88.

38. Record of examination of Lt. Paul H. McCook, May 19, 1901, Robert A. Brown, "Report," Exhibit A'.

39. Report of Capt. F. P. Fremont, April 30, 1901, Exhibit J, Robert A. Brown, "Report."

40. Robert A. Brown, "Report," 4–5.

41. Mary Mason Brown to Wayne MacVeagh, Oct. 17, 1901, 400729/C, Brown AGO file; Margaret W. Brown to Justice H. R. Brown, Oct. 24, 1901, Brown AGO file.

42. Julius A. P[enn?] to Col. Enoch Crowder, War Department, Nov. 10, 1901, Brown AGO file.

43. Bullard, *Fighting Generals*, 184, 186–87.

44. Synopsis of remarks by Maj. F. A. Smith, inspector general, U.S. Army, commanding Boac and troops on Marinduque Island, May 18, 1901, Exhibit Y, Robert A. Brown, "Report."

45. Record of examination of Lt. Paul H. McCook, May 19, 1901, Exhibit A', Robert A. Brown, "Report"; testimony of Lt. McCook, transcript, 93.

46. Dorman, *Prestons*, 22, 56–57, 223–25.

47. Further remarks of Captain F. P. Fremont, May 21, 1901, Exhibit J', Robert A. Brown, "Report."

48. Statement by Pvt. David Robison, May 8, 1901, Exhibit M, Robert A. Brown, "Report." "Robison" was likely the same private whose name was spelled "Robinson" in the transcript cited in note 32 above.

49. Testimony of Major F. A. Smith, transcript, 15.

50. The findings and sentence are in the transcript, 281–82. Brig. Gen. Wade's suspension of the sentence is a separate document in the Brown court-martial file.

51. See chapter 6 above for more about Col. John Mason Brown.

52. "Trial of Lieutenant Brown," *Army and Navy Journal*, Sept. 21, 1901. See Mary Mason Brown to Wayne MacVeagh, Oct. 17, 1901, Brown AGO file, 400729/C (noting that Roosevelt told Robert Thornton that if the facts were as stated in the *Army and Navy Journal*, Brown would not be reduced in rank); Margaret W. Brown to Justice Henry B. Brown (enclosing the article), Brown court-martial file; Henry B. Brown to Elihu Root (secretary of war), Oct. 28, 1901, Brown court-martial file (enclosing Margaret Brown's letter); Henry C. Corbin to MacVeagh, Oct. 23, 1901, Brown court-martial file (noting that a copy of the letter from Mary Brown would be presented to Secretary Root). See Leech, *Days of McKinley*, 237, for Corbin's importance in Roosevelt's administration.

53. John G. Carlisle to Roosevelt, Sept. 28, 1901; John G. Carlisle to Root, Sept. 28, 1901; R.T. Durrett to Roosevelt, Sept. 28, 1901; William F. Draper to Roosevelt, Sept. 30, 1901; William F. Draper to Root, Sept. 30, 1901; John E. Parsons to Root, Sept. 30, 1901; all in Brown court-martial file. Roosevelt, in his 1899 preface to *The Winning of the West*, began his acknowledgments relating to Kentucky's early history by thanking Durrett for the source material he had provided. Roosevelt, *Winning of the West*, vol. 1, 11–12.

54. Morris, *Rise of Theodore Roosevelt*, 677–79.

55. Mary Mason Brown to Wayne MacVeagh, Oct. 17, 1901, 400729/C, Brown AGO file.

56. W. J. Deboe to Root, Oct. 7, 1901, Brown court-martial files; W.C.P. Breckenridge to Roosevelt, Sept. 26, 1901, Brown court-martial files; Samuel J. Roberts to Roosevelt, Oct. 25, 1901, 400729/F, Brown AGO file.

57. Captain George C. Gatley to AGO, Oct. 18, 2001, 400728/J, Brown AGO file.
58. Taft to Root, Sept. 30, 1901, 400729, Brown AGO file.
59. Cable from Brown to Thornton, Sept. 30, 1901, Brown court-martial file.
60. Bullard, *Fighting Generals*, 185.
61. Harlan to Root, Sept. 27, 1901, Brown AGO file.
62. H. B. Brown to Root, Oct. 28, 1901, Brown court-martial file.
63. MacVeagh to Corbin, Oct. 20, 1901, 400729/C, Brown AGO file; Corbin to MacVeagh, Oct. 23, 1901, Brown AGO file.
64. Chaffee to Corbin, Sept. 28, 1901, Brown AGO file.
65. Roosevelt, *Winning of the West*, vol. 1, 17, 24
66. John Mason Brown to Reuben Durrett, March 29, 1888, Reuben T. Durrett Added Papers, Filson Historical Society, Louisville; Morris, *Rise of Theodore Roosevelt*, 388, 806.
67. Roosevelt, *Winning of the West*, vol. 1, 12.
68. Roosevelt, "At the Banquet," 7–8. The reference to an American sword being carried by Brown's father during the Mexican war seems incorrect, as Brown's father, Mason Brown, was a circuit judge in Kentucky during the Mexican War.
69. Linn, *Philippine War*, 310–21 (quote, 321); see also Boot, *Savage Wars of Peace*, 100–102, 120–123; Jones, *Honor in the Dust*, 221, 225–35, 241–66 (Balangiga and Samar).
70. Memorandum dated Oct. 22, 1901 from George B. Davis, judge advocate general, to Secretary of War Elihu Root, Brown court-martial file.
71. Judge Advocate General Enoch H. Crowder to Secretary of War Newton D. Baker, April 12, 1919, HR No. 23628 (62nd Cong.). Before the 1919 revision, most of the Articles of War dated back to 1806. Crowder knew of Brown's case, having been a lieutenant colonel in the Judge Advocate Corps in the Philippines and having received a letter from a fellow officer in November 1901 asking his help in seeking clemency for Brown. Under Article 92 of the revised Articles of War, manslaughter was to be "punished as a court martial may direct." Among the obsolete provisions deleted were old Articles 52 ("It is earnestly recommended to all officers and soldiers diligently to attend divine service") and 53 ("Any officer who uses any profane oath or execration shall, for each offense, forfeit and pay $1").
72. Corbin's cable to Chaffee is in 407729, and Chaffee's response in 400729/H, Brown AGO file. The final version of Davis's memorandum is in the Brown court-martial files.
73. Linn, *Philippine War*, 3 (first quote); Morris, *Rise of Theodore Roosevelt*, 611 (second and third quotes); Morris, *Theodore Rex*, 79 (fourth quote).
74. First endorsement, Nelson A. Miles, lieutenant general, Dec. 2, 1901, Brown court-martial files.
75. Morris, *Theodore Rex*, 79.
76. Davis Memorandum, endorsement by Secretary of War Elihu Root, Jan. 27, 1902, Brown court-martial files.
77. Commutation of sentence dated Jan. 27, 1902; unsigned typed statement dated Jan. 27, 1902; both in 401849, Brown AGO file.
78. Commutation of sentence, first endorsement, by Maj. Gen. Loyd Wheaton, Manila, P.I., Feb. 11, 1902; second endorsement by Maj. Gen. Adna R. Chaffee, Headquarters, Division of the Philippines, Manila, P.I., Feb. 18, 1902; third endorsement by Judge Advocate General Davis, April 14, 1902; all in 40189, Brown AGO file.
79. Morris, *Theodore Rex*, 98, 104 (first quote), 100 (third quote); Boot, *Savage Wars of Peace*, 120, 122–23 (second quote); Jones, *Honor in the Dust*, 300–42 (uproar over

water cures and wrongful killing of Filipinos, courts-martial of Jacob Smith and Edwin Glenn).

80. Morris, *Theodore Rex*, 127.

81. Morris, *Theodore Rex*, 119, 609.

82. Filipino combat deaths are estimated at around sixteen thousand—more than ten times the number of American combat deaths. Boot, *Savage Wars of Peace*, 125; Bayor, *History of Race and Ethnicity in America*, 335; Smallman-Raynor and Cliff, "The Philippines Insurrection and the 1902–4 Cholera Epidemic," 69–89.

9. An Award from General Pershing

1. G.O. No. 12, War Department, 1919, quoted in Stevens, *Speak for Yourself, John*, 31. The cablegram announcing the award was dated January 8, 1919.

2. Fromkin, *Europe's Last War*, 260, 286–91; McMeekin, "The War of the Ottoman Succession," 2–4.

3. Woodrow Wilson, *Message to Congress*, 63rd Cong., 2nd Sess., S. Doc. No. 566 (Aug. 19, 1914).

4. Stallings, *Doughboys*, 4.

5. Capt. Preston Brown to adjutant general of the Army, April 13, 1914; Lt. Col. W. P. Burnham to adjutant general of the Army, April 14, 1914, both in 2148937, Brown AGO file.

6. Eisenhower, *Yanks*, 12, 303n5 (Regular Army, 127,588; National Guard, 66,594) and n6; Keegan, *The First World War*, 373 (Army, 107,641; National Guard, 132,000); Coffman, *The War to End All Wars*, 38 (number of machine guns); Ambrose, *Eisenhower*, 33–34 (training Tank Corps without tanks).

7. Tuchman, *The Zimmerman Telegram*, 138–41 ("no American will set foot on the Continent!").

8. Keegan, *The First World War*, 375 (fifty divisions); Eisenhower, *Yanks*, 62 (each American division had around 28,000 officers and men, approximately twice the size of a German division).

9. Eisenhower, *Yanks*, 100–103.

10. For a summary of American propaganda efforts and anti-German sentiments and actions (including the stoning of dachshunds), see Farwell, *Over There*, 120–30.

11. Eisenhower, *Yanks*, 25 (draft), 30–31 (appointment as commander of the AEF, role in Punitive Expedition), 40 ("Lafayette, we are here"). Pershing, *My Experiences*, vol. 1, 2–93 ("I am sure that those words were spoken by Colonel Stanton").

12. Eisenhower, *Yanks*, 94; Keegan, *First World War*, 372–73.

13. Eisenhower, *Yanks*, 33–34.

14. Eisenhower, *Yanks*, 82–83 (first American firing and deaths), 94 (AEF size), 106–107 (commencement of Operation Michael).

15. Pershing, *My Experiences*, vol. 1, 352 (Big Bertha), 354 (ground gained by the German offensive); Eisenhower, *Yanks*, 102.

16. Eisenhower, *Yanks*, 125–32, 134–36; Coffman, *The War to End All Wars*, 156–58 (Cantigny).

17. Pershing, *My Experiences*, vol. 2, 62.

18. Eisenhower, *Yanks*, 137.

19. Col. Arthur K. Conger, in the Thirty-Five Year Record of the Yale Class of 1892, quoted in Bullard, *Fighting Generals*, 187; Spaulding and Wright, *The Second Division*, 38–39, 39n2 (on May 31, Brown discussed where to deploy the 2nd Division near

Château-Thierry; "During this conference the discussion became tense, Col. Brown, who spoke French presenting the American point of view").

20. Coffman, *The War to End All Wars*, 216, 260.

21. Report from Major Paul H. Clark, Pershing's representative at General Pétain's head-quarters, "Letters and Messages to John J. Pershing, 1918–1919" (Manuscript Division, Library of Congress), quoted in Asprey, *At Belleau Wood*, 48–49. Colonel Rozet's last statement as to Brown's lack of war experience disregarded Brown's service in the Spanish-American War and the Philippine War. The latter was a guerilla war, to be sure, but according to Benjamin D. Foulois, who had served in the Philippines before taking charge of the American air arm in the First World War, "Anyone who had lived through the fighting in the Philippines could live through anything." Coffman, *The War to End All Wars*, 19.

22. Eisenhower, *Yanks*, 140.

23. Eisenhower, *Yanks*, 144 (casualties of 4th Marine Brigade on June 6), 146 (order of General von Boehm).

24. Farwell, *Over There*, 170; Asprey, *At Belleau Wood*, 173.

25. Coffman, *The War to End All Wars*, 221 (mustard gas casualties), 224 (shell shock cases).

26. Farwell, *Over There*, 172; Eisenhower, *Yanks*, 148–50; Asprey, *At Belleau Wood*, 296; Clark, *The Second Infantry Division*, 6.

27. Lieutenant Tillman, describing the night of June 9–10, Asprey, *At Belleau Wood*, 245.

28. Meyer, *A World Undone*, 674.

29. Eisenhower, *Yanks*, 151–61.

30. Eisenhower, *Yanks*, 141–73; Pershing, *My Experiences*, vol. 2, 211.

31. Coffman, *The War to End All Wars*, 245–46.

32. Pershing, *My Experiences*, vol. 2, 160–65 (advances of the 1st and 2nd Divisions, comments of von Hertling and von Hindenburg).

33. Pershing, *My Experiences*, vol. 2, 167 (congratulation of Harbord and Brown).

34. Marshall, *Memoirs*, 123–24.

35. Bullard, *Fighting Generals*, 189–90.

36. Pershing, *My Experiences*, vol. 2, 172, 175. By the end of the war on Nov. 11, 1918, the U.S. Army numbered 3,685,458, including many who were not in France. Weigley, *History of the U.S. Army*, 358.

37. Eisenhower, *Yanks*, 174–197; Pershing, *My Experiences*, vol. 2, 3–86; Coffman, *The War to End All Wars*, 268–83 (St. Mihiel); Weigley, *History of the U.S. Army*, 385.

38. Eisenhower, *Yanks*, 200–223, 320n13 (Patton: "I hit him over the head with a shovel"), n16 (loss of tanks).

39. Eisenhower, *Yanks*, 224–39 (the lieutenant was Maury Maverick of the 28th Infantry), 232–34, 322n15 (description of high explosives bursting overhead).

40. Coffman, *The War to End All Wars*, 299.

41. Eisenhower, *Yanks*, 240–46, 323n4 ("We cannot win this war any more"); Pershing, *My Experiences*, vol. 2, 342 (German request for an armistice).

42. Bullard, *Fighting Generals*, 190; Pershing, *My Experiences*, vol. 2, 9–40 (3rd Division unable to progress), 352 (Brown given command, Clairs Chênes taken).

43. Eisenhower, *Yanks*, 250–70; Pershing, *My Experiences*, vol. 2, 350–51, 381 ("race for the honor of capturing Sedan"); Coffman, *The War to End All Wars*, 348–53.

44. Eisenhower, *Yanks*, 273–87.

45. Eisenhower, *Yanks*, 288–89. For other estimates, see, e.g., Keegan, *First World War*, 423 (2 million Germans).
46. Verhoeff, "Major General Preston Brown," 246, 249; Bullard, *Fighting Generals*, 184 (Sergeant Haifer), 190–91 (post-war promotions); Stevens, *Speak for Yourself, John*, 31–32; *Who Was Who in America*, vol. 2.
47. In the 2nd Division, 5,155 died in battle or of battle wounds; in the 1st Division, 4,996; in the 3rd Division, 3,401. Stallings, *Doughboys*, 375. Clark, *Second Infantry Division*, 271 (2nd Division most decorated in World War I).
48. John Mason Brown to Edward M. Coffman, April 6, 1964, quoted in Stevens, *Speak for Yourself, John*, 32.
49. R. L. Bullard to General Blanton Winship, Feb. 27, 1933, Brown court-martial file.
50. Bullard, *Fighting Generals*, 185 (greyhound), 186–87 (contemptuous, none indifferent to him), 191 (energy and determination).

10. *The Czar of Halfaday Creek* and Hitler's Toilet Bowl

1. Brown, *To All Hands* (see foreword, page x for Admiral Kirk's description of Brown's duties); Brown, *Many a Watchful Night*.
2. Brown, *Many a Watchful Night*, 24, 32.
3. Brown, *Many a Watchful Night*, 100–108.
4. D'Este, *Eisenhower*, 508; Butcher, *My Three Years with Eisenhower*, 560.
5. Ambrose, *Eisenhower*, 135–36; Eisenhower, *Eisenhower: At War*, 244.
6. Churchill, *The Second World War*, vol. 5,]619–24; Butcher, *My Three Years with Eisenhower*, 559; Dwight D. Eisenhower, *Crusade in Europe*, 251.
7. Butcher, *My Three Years with Eisenhower*, 560 (on morning of June 4, Eisenhower was still resting in his sleeping caravan "surrounded by some new Westerns and Sunday papers").
8. Hendryx, *Czar of Halfaday Creek*, 66, 159.
9. Butcher, *My Three Years with Eisenhower*, 570 (arm-waving); David Eisenhower, *Eisenhower: At War*, 247–48; D'Este, *Eisenhower*, 521–22 (De Gaulle's unhappiness with Eisenhower's proposed remarks).
10. Eisenhower, *Crusade in Europe*, 250 (wind on morning of June 5 "of almost hurricane proportions," rain "in horizontal streaks"); Butcher, *My Three Years with Eisenhower*, photograph after xvi (Eisenhower's draft of release: "Our landings . . . have failed . . . and I have withdrawn the troops"); Eisenhower, *Eisenhower at War*, 251 ("Okay, we'll go"); Ambrose, *D-Day*, 189 ("OK, let's go"); D'Este, *Eisenhower*, 524–26, 782n38 (different versions of Eisenhower's exact words), 783n54 (sources for Eisenhower's decision).
11. Brown, *Many a Watchful Night*, 6–7.
12. Brown, *Many a Watchful Night*, 10–18, 113–28.
13. Brown, *Many a Watchful Night*, 148.
14. Butcher, *My Three Years with Eisenhower*, 567 (early morning, June 6 [D-Day], Butcher finds Eisenhower "silhouetted in bed behind a Western"); McKeough and Lockridge, *Sgt. Mickey and General Ike*, 116.
15. Hendryx, *Czar of Halfaday Creek*, 235.
16. Collier, *D-Day*, 88 (50th birthday of Rommel's wife).
17. Brown, *Many a Watchful Night*, 174–82, 215.
18. Eisenhower, *Crusade in Europe*, 254.

19. Brown, *Many a Watchful Night*, 184–213.
20. Pyle, *Ernie's War*, 282 (wreckage on the Normandy beach), 419 (the dead).
21. Butcher, *My Three Years with Eisenhower*, 834. The book, published in January 1945, is by William Colt Macdonald.
22. Eisenhower, *Eisenhower at War*, *1943–1945*, 555–610; Eisenhower, *Crusade in Europe*, 342–65.
23. Patton, *War As I Knew It*, 175–77.
24. Eisenhower, *Crusade in Europe*, 365.
25. Toland, *The Last Hundred Days*, 176.
26. Ambrose, *The Victors*, 345.
27. Eisenhower, *Crusade in Europe*, 387–94.
28. Shirer, *Rise and Fall of the Third Reich*, 1105–06.
29. Shirer, *Rise and Fall of the Third Reich*, 1038–41.
30. Operation Foxley records are in the British Public Record Office, HS6/624. File Number S.O.E. Germany, No. 8, vol. 1. Some or all of this material was published as *Operation Foxley: The British Plan to Kill Hitler*.
31. Shirer, *Rise and Fall of the Third Reich*, 1116–18; Toland, *Last 100 Days*, 430–32.
32. Toland, *Last 100 Days*, 439–40 (bombing of Berchtesgaden), 529–30 (death of Hitler); Shirer, *Rise and Fall of the Third Reich*, 1132–33; Eisenhower, *Crusade in Europe*, 420 (bombing of Berchtesgaden).
33. Butcher, *My Three Years with Eisenhower*, 831–34.
34. Winters and Kingseed, *Beyond Band of Brothers*, 218–21; Butcher, *My Three Years with Eisenhower*, 860.
35. For a description of Berchtesgaden on June 1, 1945, see Hamburger, "Letter from Berchtesgaden," 51–55. Hamburger noted that the Führer's bedroom had been burned, but the bathroom was in better shape: "It has green tiled walls, in the best *Good Housekeeping* tradition."

Afterword

1. U.S. Census Bureau, *Statistical Abstract of the United States: 2003*, Table HS-1, p. 8 (includes population in 1945); *Rand McNally Cosmopolitan World Atlas*, 146 (settlement of British colonies), 189 (growth in area of the United States). For a comparison of the gross domestic product of the great powers in 1945, see Harrison, *The Economics of World War II*, 10.
2. Does not include actions by U.S. forces to protect American interests during local revolutions; does not include all engagements with American Indians.

BIBLIOGRAPHY

Abbot, W.W., and Dorothy Twohig, eds. *The Papers of George Washington, Colonial Series.* 10 vols. Charlottesville: University Press of Virginia, 1983–1995.

Allan, Elizabeth Preston. *Life and Letters of Margaret Junkin Preston.* Boston, Mass.: Houghton, Mifflin and Company, 1903.

Ambrose, Stephen E. *D-Day, June 6, 1944: The Climactic Battle of World War II.* New York: Simon and Schuster, 1982.

———. *Eisenhower: Soldier and President.* New York: Simon & Schuster, 1990.

———. *The Victors—Eisenhower and His Boys: The Men of World War II.* New York: Simon & Schuster, 1998. Reprint, New York: Touchstone, 1999.

Anderson, Gary Clayton. "Myrick's Insult: A Fresh Look at Myth and Reality." *Minnesota History* 48, no. 5 (1983): 198–206.

Army and Navy Journal. "Trial of Lieutenant Brown." Sept. 21, 1901.

Asprey, Robert B. *At Belleau Wood.* Denton: University of North Texas Press, 1965. Reprint, 1996.

Bailey, Kenneth P. *The Ohio Company of Virginia and the Westward Movement, 1748–1792: A Chapter in the History of the Colonial Frontier.* Spokane, Wash.: Arthur H. Clark, 1939.

Bailyn, Bernard. *To Begin the World Anew: The Genius and Ambiguities of the American Founders.* New York: Alfred A. Knopf, 2003.

Bakeless, John. *Daniel Boone.* Rahway, N.J.: Quinn & Boden Company, 1939. Reprint, Harrisburg, Pa.: Stackpole Books, 1965.

Basler, Roy P., ed. *The Collected Works of Abraham Lincoln.* 9 vols. New Brunswick, N.J.: Rutgers University Press, 1953–1955.

Bayor, Ronald H. *The Columbia Documentary History of Race and Ethnicity in America.* New York: Columbia University Press, 2004.

Birtle, Andrew J. "The U.S. Army's Pacification of Marinduque, Philippine Islands, April 1900–April 1901." *Journal of Military History* 61, no. 2 (1997): 255–82.

Block, Mart R. "'The Stoutest Son': The Mexican-American War Journal of Henry Clay, Jr." *Register of the Kentucky Historical Society* 106 (Winter 2008): 5–42.

Boetzkes, Ottilie G. *The Little Queen: Isabella II of Spain.* New York: Exposition Press, 1966

Boot, Max. *The Savage Wars of Peace: Small Wars and the Rise of American Power.* New York: Basic Books, 2002.

Borneman, Walter R. *Polk: The Man Who Transformed the Presidency and America.* New York: Random House, 2008.

Brown, John Mason (1837–1890). "Traditions of the Blackfeet." *The Galaxy* 3, no. 2 (January 15, 1867), 157–64.

———. "A Trip to the Northwest in 1861: Diary of John Mason Brown, May–November

1861, With an Introduction by His Grandson, John Mason Brown." *Filson Club History Quarterly* 24 (April 1950): 103–36 and (July 1950): 246–75.

Brown, John Mason (1900–1969). *Many a Watchful Night.* New York: Whittlesey House, 1944.

———. *Seeing More Things.* New York: Whittlesey House, 1948.

———. *To All Hands: An Amphibious Adventure.* New York: Whittlesey House, 1943.

Brown, Meredith Mason. *Frontiersman: Daniel Boone and the Making of America.* Baton Rouge: Louisiana State University Press, 2008.

Brown, Preston. "John Mason Brown, 1837–1890, One of the Founders of The Filson Club." *Filson Club History Quarterly* 13 (July 1939): 125–33.

Brown, Robert A. "Report of an Investigation of the Killing of a Native Filipino, by First Lieutenant Preston Brown, 2nd U.S. Infantry, at Binganonan, Infanta Province, P.I., on December 22, 1900," Box 16, June 1, 1901, entry 2330, General Correspondence, Southern Luzon, Records of U.S. Army Overseas Operations and Commands, RG 395, Old Military Records, National Archives, Washington, D.C.

Bullard, R. L. *Fighting Generals: Illustrated Biographical Sketches of Seven Major Generals in World War I.* Ann Arbor, Mich.: J. D. Edwards, 1944.

Bureau of the Census. *Bicentennial Edition: Historical Statistics of the United States: Colonial Times to 1970.* United States Department of Commerce, 1975. http://www2.census .gov/prod2/statcomp/documents/CT1970p1-01.pdf.

Butcher, Harry C. *My Three Years with Eisenhower: The Personal Diary of Captain Harry C. Butcher, USNR, Naval Aide to General Eisenhower, 1942 to 1945.* New York: Simon and Schuster, 1946.

Butterfield, Consul Willshire. *History of the Girtys.* Cincinnati, Ohio: Robert Clarke & Co., 1890.

Calloway, Colin G. *The American Revolution in Indian Country: Crisis and Diversity in Native American Communities.* New York: Cambridge University Press, 1995.

———. *The Scratch of a Pen: 1763 and the Transformation of North America.* New York: Oxford University Press, 2006.

Carley, Kenneth. *The Dakota War of 1862.* St. Paul: Minnesota Historical Society Press, 1976.

Carriker, Robert C. *Father Peter John De Smet: Jesuit in the West.* Norman: University of Oklahoma Press, 1995.

Carton, Evan. *Patriotic Treason: John Brown and the Soul of America.* Lincoln: University of Nebraska Press, 2009.

Catton, Bruce. *This Hallowed Ground: The Union Side of the Civil War.* Garden City, N.Y.: Doubleday, 1956.

Cave, Alfred A. *The Pequot War.* Amherst: University of Massachusetts Press, 1996.

Chernow, Ron. *Alexander Hamilton.* New York: Penguin Press, 2004.

Chernow, Ron. *Washington: A Life.* New York: Penguin Press, 2010.

Church, Albert E. *Personal Reminiscences of the Military Academy from 1824 to 1831: A Paper Read to the U.S. Military Service Institute, West Point, March 28, 1878.* West Point, N.Y.: Military Academy Press, 1879.

Church, Benjamin. *The Entertaining History of King Philip's War, which began in the Month of June, 1675.* Boston, 1676.

Churchill, Winston. *The Second World War.* Vol. 5, *Closing the Ring.* Boston, Mass.: Houghton Mifflin, 1951.

Clark, George B. *The Second Infantry Division in World War I: A History of the American Expeditionary Force Regulars, 1917–1919.* Jefferson, N.C.: MacFarland & Co., 2007.

Coffman, Edward M. *The War to End All Wars: The American Military Experience in World War I.* Oxford University Press, 1968. Reprint, Lexington: University Press of Kentucky, 1998.

Collier, Richard. *D-Day, June 6, 1944: The Normandy Landings.* London: Orion, 2002.

Conway, Moncure D. *The Golden Hour.* Boston, Mass.: Ticknor and Fields, 1862.

Cullen, Charles T., Julian P. Boyd, L. H. Butterfield, and John Catanzariti, eds. *The Papers of Thomas Jefferson.* Princeton, N.J.: Princeton University Press, 1950–2000.

Cullum, George W. *Biographical Register of the Officers and Graduates of the U.S. Military Academy at West Point, N.Y., from Its Establishment, in 1802, to 1890: With the Early History of the United States Military Academy.* Boston, Mass.: Houghton Mifflin, 1891.

Cullum, George Washington, and Francis B. Heitman. *Historical Register and Dictionary of the United States Army from its Organization, September 29, 1789 to March 2, 1803.* Washington: Government Printing Office, 1903.

Davie, Preston. "Personal Reminiscences Concerning Some of the Founders of the Filson Club." *Filson Club History Quarterly* 18, no. 3 (July, 1944): 130–32.

De Forest, John W. *History of the Indians of Connecticut from the Earliest Known Period to 1850.* Hartford, Conn.: Wm. Jas. Hamerley, 1851.

Depew, Chauncey. *My Memories of Eighty Years.* New York: Charles Scribner's Sons, 1922.

de Polnay, Peter. *A Queen of Spain: Isabel II.* London: Hollis & Carter, 1962.

D'Este, Carlo. *Eisenhower: A Soldier's Life.* New York: Henry Holt, 2002.

Dorman, John Frederick. *The Prestons of Smithfield and Greenfield in Virginia.* Louisville, Ky.: Filson Club, 1982.

Douglass, Frederick. *Life and Times of Frederick Douglass, Written by Himself.* Boston: De Wolfe & Fiske Co., 1892.

Draper, Lyman C. *The Life of Daniel Boone.* Edited by Ted Franklin Belue. Mechanicsburg, Pa.: Stackpole Books, 1998.

Drimmer, Frederick, ed. *Captured by the Indians: 15 Firsthand Accounts, 1750–1870.* New York: Dover Publications, 1985.

DuBois, W. E. B. *John Brown.* Armonk, N.Y.: M. E. Sharpe, 1997.

Ehle, John. *Trail of Tears: The Rise and Fall of the Cherokee Nation.* New York: Anchor Books, 1988.

Eisenhower, David. *Eisenhower: At War, 1943–45.* New York: Random House, 1991.

Eisenhower, Dwight D. *Crusade in Europe.* New York: Doubleday, 1948.

Eisenhower, John S. D. *So Far from God: The U.S. War with Mexico, 1846–1848.* New York: Random House, 1989. Reprint, Norman: University of Oklahoma Press, 2000.

———. *Yanks: The Epic Story of the American Army in World War I.* New York: Simon and Schuster Touchstone, 2001.

Ellis, Joseph J. *His Excellency George Washington.* New York: Alfred A. Knopf, 2004.

Ellis, William Arba, ed. *Norwich University, 1819–1911: Her History, Her Graduates, Her Roll of Honor.* 3 vols. Montpelier, Vt.: Capital City Press, 1911.

English, John, and Réal Bélanger, eds. *Dictionary of Canadian Biography Online.* Last modified September 1, 2011. http://www.biographi.ca/009004-119.01-e.php?&id_nbr=7532

Faragher, John Mack. *Daniel Boone: The Life and Legend of an American Pioneer.* New York: Henry Holt, 1992.

Farwell, Bryan. *Over There: The United States in the Great War, 1917–1918.* New York: W.W. Norton, 1999.

Ferling, John C. *The Ascent of George Washington: The Hidden Political Genius of an American Icon*. New York: Bloomsbury Press, 2009.

Ferrell, Robert H., ed. *Monterrey Is Ours! The Mexican War Letters of Lieutenant Dana, 1845–1847*. Lexington: University Press of Kentucky, 1990.

Fitzpatrick, John C., ed. *The Writings of George Washington*. 39 vols. Washington, D.C.: U.S. Government Printing Office, 1931–1944.

Floyd, Letitia, letter to Benjamin Rush Floyd, Feb. 22, 1843. In *The Richmond Standard*, June 5, 1880.

Fowler, William S. "Procurement and Use of Bark." *Bulletin of the Massachusetts Archaeological Society* 37 (1976): 18.

———. "Tomahawks of Central New England." *Bulletin of the Massachusetts Archaeological Society* 12 (1954): 34.

Freehling, William W. *The South vs. the South: How Anti-Confederate Southerners Shaped the Course of the Civil War*. New York: Oxford University Press, 2001.

Fromkin, David. *Europe's Last War: Who Started the Great War in 1914?* New York: Vintage Books, 2005.

Gilder Lehrman Collection. New York Historical Society.

Glanville, Jim, and Ryan Mays. "The Mysterious Origins of James Patton, Part I." *The Smithfield Review*, 15 (2011): 35–64.

Grandjean, Katherine A. "New World Tempests: Environment, Scarcity, and the Coming of the Pequot War." *The William and Mary Quarterly*, 3rd ser., 68, no. 1 (January 2011): 75–100.

Grant, Ulysses S. *Personal Memoirs of U. S. Grant*. 2 vols. New York: Charles L. Webster, 1885–1886. Reprint, *Memoirs and Selected Letters: Personal Memoirs of U. S. Grant; Selected Letters 1839–1865*. 2 vols. New York: The Library of America, 1990. Citations refer to the Library of America edition.

Greever, William S. *The Bonanza West: The Story of Western Mining Rushes, 1848–1900*. Norman: University of Oklahoma Press, 1963.

Hamburger, Philip. "Letter from Berchtesgaden." *New Yorker* (June 9, 1945): 51–55.

Hammon, Neal O. "Captain Harrod's Company, 1774: A Reappraisal." *Register of the Kentucky Historical Society* 72 (July 1974): 224–42.

———, ed. *My Father, Daniel Boone: The Draper Interviews with Nathan Boone*. Lexington: University Press of Kentucky, 1999.

———. "The Fincastle Surveyors at the Falls of the Ohio, 1774." *Filson Club History Quarterly* 47 (Jan. 1973): 268–83.

———. "The Fincastle Surveyors in the Bluegrass, 1774." *Register of the Kentucky Historical Society* (Oct. 1972): 277–94.

———, and James Russell Harris, "'In a dangerous situation': Letters of Col. John Floyd." *Register of the Kentucky Historical Society* 83 (1985): 202–36.

———, and Richard Taylor. *Virginia's Western War: 1775–1786*. Mechanicsburg, Pa.: Stackpole Books, 2002.

Hankla, Mel. "Across the Woods with Kentucky's 'Humble' Gunsmiths." *Kentucky Rifle Association Bulletin* 36, no. 2 (Winter 2009): 1–9.

Hauptman, Laurence M., and James D. Wherry, eds. *The Pequots in Southern New England: The Fall and Rise of an American Indian Nation*. Norman: University of Oklahoma Press, 1990.

Harrison, Lowell H. *The Civil War in Kentucky*. Lexington: University Press of Kentucky, 1975.

Harrison, Mark, ed. *The Economics of World War II: Six Great Powers in International Comparison.* Cambridge: Cambridge University Press, 1998.

Hendryx, James B. *The Czar of Halfaday Creek.* New York: Grosset & Dunlap, 1934. Reprint, New York: Triangle Books, 1942.

Holmberg, James J. "John Mason Brown's 1862 Journal of His Second Trip to the Rocky Mountains." *The Filson* 7 (Fall 2007): 2–5.

Horwitz, Tony. *Confederates in the Attic: Dispatches from the Unfinished Civil War.* New York: Vintage Books, 1999.

———. *Midnight Rising: John Brown and the Raid that Sparked the Civil War.* New York: Henry Holt, 2011.

Howe, Daniel Walker. *What Hath God Wrought.* New York: Oxford University Press, 2007.

Hubbard, Lucius F., and Return I. Holcombe. *Minnesota in Three Centuries.* 4 vols. Mankato, Minn.: Free Press Printing Co., 1908.

Hurd, Duane Hamilton. *History of Essex County, Massachusetts: With Biographical Sketches of Many of Its Pioneers and Prominent Men.* 3 vols. Philadelphia: J. W. Lewis, 1888.

Jackson, Donald, and Dorothy Twohig, eds. *The Papers of George Washington.* Vol. 5, *The Diaries of George Washington.* Charlottesville: University Press of Virginia, 1979. The George Washington Papers at the Library of Congress, 1741–1799. American Memory. The Library of Congress. http://memory.loc.gov/cgi-bin/query/r?ammem/mgw:@field(DOCID+@lit(wd05T000)).

Johnson, Patricia Givens. *James Patton and the Appalachian Colonists.* 3rd ed. Charlotte, N.C.: Jostens, 1983.

———. *William Preston and the Allegheny Patriots.* Blacksburg, Va.: Walpa Publishing, 1976.

Johnston, J. Stoddard. *Memorial History of Louisville from Its First Settlement to the Year 1896.* Chicago: American Biographical Publishing Company, 1896.

Johnston, William Preston. *The Life of General Albert Sidney Johnston.* New York: D. Appleton, 1878.

Jones, Gregg. *Honor in the Dust: Theodore Roosevelt, War in the Philippines, and the Rise and Fall of America's Imperial Dream.* New York: New American Library, 2012.

Karnow, Stanley. *In Our Image: America's Empire in the Philippines.* New York: Random House, 1989.

Keegan, John. *The First World War.* New York: Alfred Knopf, 2001.

Kincaid, Robert L. *The Wilderness Road.* Indianapolis, Ind.: Bobbs-Merrill, 1947.

Knetsch, Joe. *Fear and Anxiety on the Florida Frontier: Articles on the Second Seminole War, 1835–1842.* Dade City, Fl.: Seminole Wars Foundation Press, 2008.

Larsen, Lawrence H., and Barbara J. Cottrell. *Steamboats West: The 1859 American Fur Company Missouri River Expedition.* Norman, Okla.: Arthur H. Clark, 2010.

Lass, William E. *Navigating the Missouri: Steamboating on Nature's Highway, 1819–1935.* Norman, Okla.: Arthur H. Clark, 2008.

Leech, Margaret. *In the Days of McKinley.* New York: Harper, 1959.

Lepore, Jill. *The Name of War: King Philip's War and the Origins of American Identity.* New York: Alfred A. Knopf, 1998.

Linklater, Andro. *Measuring America: How an Untamed Wilderness Shaped the United States and Fulfilled the Promise of Democracy.* New York: Walker, 2002.

Linn, Brian M. *The Philippine War, 1899–1902.* Lawrence: University Press of Kansas, 2000.

Mahon, John K. *History of the Second Seminole War, 1835–1842.* Rev. ed. Gainesville: University Press of Florida, 1985.

Malone, Michael P., Richard B. Roeder, and William L. Lang. *Montana: A History of Two Centuries.* Rev. ed. Seattle: University of Washington Press, 1991.

Mancini, Juli. "Dr. Kevin McBride Lectures on Pequot War Findings." *GrotonPatch,* May 15, 2011. http://Groton.patch.com/articles/dr-kevin-mcbride-lectures-on-pequot-war -findings.

Marshall, George C. *Memoirs of My Services in the World War, 1917–1918.* Boston, Mass.: Houghton Mifflin, 1976.

McBride, Kevin A. "The Historical Archaeology of the Mashantucket Pequots, 1637–1900: A Preliminary Analysis." In *The Pequots in Southern New England: The Fall and Rise of an American Indian Nation,* edited by Laurence M. Hauptman and James D. Wherry, 96–116. Norman: University of Oklahoma Press, 1990.

McConnell, Michael N. *A Country Between: The Upper Ohio Valley and Its Peoples, 1724–1774.* Lincoln: University of Nebraska Press, 1992.

McCullough, David. *John Adams.* New York: Simon & Schuster, 2008.

McDonough, James Lee. *Shiloh—in Hell Before Night.* Knoxville: University of Tennessee Press, 1977.

McKeogh, Michael J., and Richard Lockridge. *Sgt. Mickey and General Ike.* New York: Putnam, 1946.

McKnight, Brian D. *Contested Borderland: The Civil War in Appalachian Kentucky and Virginia.* Lexington: University Press of Kentucky, 2006.

McMeekin, Sean. "The War of the Ottoman Succession," *Historically Speaking* 13, no. 1 (January 2012): 2–4.

Merry, Robert W. *A Country of Vast Designs: James K. Polk, the Mexican War, and the Conquest of the American Continent.* New York: Simon & Schuster, 2009.

Meyer, G. J. *A World Undone: The Story of the Great War, 1914 to 1918.* New York: Delta, 2006.

Miller, Randall M., and William Pencak. *Pennsylvania: A History of the Commonwealth.* University Park, Pa.: Pennsylvania State University Press, 2002.

Mitchell, Robert D. *Commercialism and Frontier: Perspectives on the Early Shenandoah Valley.* Charlottesville: University Press of Virginia, 1977.

Morris, Edmund. *The Rise of Theodore Roosevelt.* New York: Coward, McCann, 1979.

———. *Theodore Rex.* New York: Random House, 2001.

Mosgrove, George Dallas. *Kentucky Cavaliers in Dixie: Reminiscences of a Confederate Cavalryman.* Jackson, Tenn.: McCowat-Mercer Press, 1957.

Musikant, Ivan. *Empire by Default: The Spanish-American War and the Dawn of the American Century.* New York: Henry Holt, 1998.

Mystic River Press. "Tribe celebrates $3 billion milestone." May 20, 2010.

Oates, S. B. *To Purge This Land With Blood: A Biography of John Brown.* 2nd ed. Amherst: University of Massachusetts Press, 1984.

Operation Foxley: The British Plan to Kill Hitler. Darby, Pa.: Diane Publishing, 1998. Reprint, London: Public Record Office, 2001.

Osborn, Richard C. "William Preston of Virginia, 1727–1783: The Making of a Frontier Elite." PhD diss., University of Maryland, 1990. UMI Dissertation Services.

———. "William Preston—Revolutionary (1779–1780)." *The Smithfield Review* 12 (2008): 5–24.

Overholser, Joel *Fort Benton: World's Innermost Port*. Fort Benton, Mont.: Joel Overholser/ Falcon Press Publishing Co, Inc., 1987.

Patton, George S. *War As I Knew It*. New York: Bantam Books, 1980.

Paul, Rodman Wilson. *Mining Frontiers of the Far West, 1848–1880*. New York: Holt, Rinehart and Winston, 1963.

Perdue, Theda, and Michael D. Green. *The Cherokee Nation and the Trail of Tears*. New York: Viking, 2007.

Pershing, John J. *My Experiences in the World War*. 2 vols. New York: Harper, 1931. Reprint, New York: Da Capo Press, 1995. Citations are to the Da Capo edition.

Peter, Frances Dallam. *A Union Woman in Civil War Kentucky: The Diary of Frances Peter*. Edited by John David Smith and William Cooper, Jr. Lexington: University Press of Kentucky, 2000.

Peterson, Norma L. *Freedom and Franchise: The Political Career of B. Gratz Brown*. Columbia: University of Missouri Press, 1968.

Polk, James K. "A Special Message Calling for a Declaration of War Against Mexico." Descendants of Mexican War Veterans. Last modified March 4, 2012. http://www .dmwv.org/mexwar/documents/polk.htm.

Pyle, Ernie. *Ernie's War: The Best of Ernie Pyle's World War II Dispatches*. Edited by David Nichols. New York: Random House, 1986.

Rakove, Jack, ed. *The Annotated U.S. Constitution and Declaration of Independence*. Cambridge, Mass.: Belknap Press, 2009.

Ranck, George W. *Boonesborough: Its Founding, Pioneer Struggles, Indian Experiences, Transylvania Days, and Revolutionary Annals*. Louisville, Ky.: Filson Club, 1901.

Rand McNally Cosmopolitan World Atlas. Chicago: Rand McNally, 1963.

Rasmussen, Barbara. "Anarchy and Enterprise on the Imperial Frontier: Washington, Dunmore, Logan, and Land in the Eighteenth Century Ohio Valley." *Ohio Valley History* 6, no. 4 (Winter 2006), 1–26.

Register of the Officers and Cadets of the U.S. Military Academy, June, 1829. West Point, N.Y.: U.S. Military Academy, 1884.

Remini, Robert V. *Andrew Jackson and His Indian Wars*. New York: Viking, 2001.

Reynolds, David S. *John Brown, Abolitionist: The Man Who Killed Slavery, Sparked the Civil War, and Seeded Civil Rights*. New York: Alfred A. Knopf, 2005.

Rice, Otis K. *Frontier Kentucky*. Lexington: University Press of Kentucky, 1993.

Richardson, H. Edward. *Cassius Marcellus Clay: Firebrand of Freedom*. Lexington: University Press of Kentucky, 1976.

Robbins, James S. *Last in Their Class: Custer, Pickett and the Goats of West Point*. New York: Encounter Books, 2006.

Roland, Charles P. *Albert Sidney Johnston: Soldier of Three Republics*. Lexington: University Press of Kentucky, 2001.

Roosevelt, Theodore. "At the Banquet to Justice Harlan, the New Willard Hotel, Washington, D.C., December 9, 1902." Almanac of Theodore Roosevelt. http://theodore -roosevelt.com/images/research/txtspeeches/35.txt

———. *The Winning of the West*. 4 vols. New York: G. P. Putnam, 1889–1896. Reprint, 1903.

Rothert, Otto. "John Floyd—Pioneer and Hero." *Filson Club History Quarterly* 2 (1927): 168–77.

Russell, Howard S. *Indian New England Before the Mayflower*. Hanover, N.H.: University Press of New England, 1980.

Saltonstall, Nathaniel. *A New and Further Narrative of the State of New England* (London, 1676). In *Narratives of the Indian Wars, 1675–1699,* edited by C. H. Lincoln. New York: Charles Scribner's Sons, 1913: 77–99.

Sanborn, Franklin B. *Life and Letters of John Brown.* Boston, Mass.: Roberts Bros., 1885.

Schutz, James Willard. *Rising Wolf, The White Blackfoot: Hugh Monroe's Story of His First Year on the Plains.* New York: Houghton Mifflin, 1919.

Sehlinger, Peter J. "'At the Moment of Victory . . .' The Battle of Shiloh and General A.S. Johnston's Death as Recounted in William Preston's Diary." *Filson Club History Quarterly* 61 (1987): 315–45.

———. *Kentucky's Last Cavalier: General William Preston, 1816–1887.* Lexington: Kentucky Historical Society, 2004.

Shirer, William L. *The Rise and Fall of the Third Reich: A History of Nazi Germany.* New York: Simon and Schuster, 1960.

Smallman-Raynor, Matthew R., and Andrew D. Cliff. "The Philippines Insurrection and the 1902–4 Cholera Epidemic." *Journal of Historical Geography* 24 (1998): 69–89.

Spaulding, Oliver L., and John W. Wright. *The Second Division, American Expeditionary Force in France, 1917–1919.* New York: Hillman Press, 1938.

Speed, Thomas. *The Union Regiments of Kentucky.* Louisville: Union Soldiers and Sailors Association of Louisville, Kentucky, 1879.

Sprague, John T. *The Origin, Progress, and Conclusion of the Florida War.* New York: D. Appleton, 1848.

Stallings, Laurence. *The Doughboys: The Story of the AEF, 1917–1918.* New York: Harper & Row, 1963.

State Historical Society of Wisconsin. Draper Manuscript Collection. Madison: University of Wisconsin.

Stevens, George. *Speak for Yourself, John: The Life of John Mason Brown, with Some of His Letters and Many of His Opinions.* New York: Viking Press, 1974.

Sunder, John E. *The Fur Trade on the Upper Missouri, 1840–1865.* Norman: University of Oklahoma Press, 1965.

Sutler, Boyd B. "The Hanging of John Brown." In *The American Heritage Reader.* New York: Dell, 1956.

Sword, Wiley. *Shiloh: Bloody April.* Dayton, Ohio: Morningside Bookshop, 1988.

Tapp, Hambleton. "Colonel John Floyd, Kentucky Pioneer." *Filson Club History Quarterly* 15 (1941): 1–24.

Terrell, John Upton. *Black Robe: The Life of Pierre-Jean De Smet, Missionary, Explorer, and Pioneer.* Garden City, N.Y.: Doubleday, 1964.

Thwaites, Reuben Gold, and Louise Phelps Kellogg. *Documentary History of Dunmore's War, 1774.* Madison: State Historical Society of Wisconsin, 1905.

Toland, John. *The Last 100 Days.* New York: Random House, 1965.

Tuchman, Barbara W. *The Zimmermann Telegram.* New York: Ballantine Books, 1985.

Underhill, John. *Newes from America; or, a New and Experimentall Discoverie of New England* (London, 1638). In *History of the Pequot War: The Contemporary Accounts of Mason, Underhill, Vincent and Gardiner.* Edited by C. Orr, 47–92. Cleveland, Ohio: Hellman-Taylor Company, 1897.

United States Census Bureau. *Statistical Abstract of the United States: 2003.* http://www.census.gov/prod/2004pubs/03statab/pop.pdf.

United States War Department. *The War of the Rebellion: A Compilation of the Official Records of the Union and Confederate Armies.* Washington, D.C.: U.S. War Department, 1894–1922.

Veninger, Jacqueline, and Laurie Pasteryak. "Battlefields of the Pequot War, Spring 2011 Update." Friends of the Office of State Archaeology: Selected Reprints. Last modified April 28, 2011. http://www.fosa-ct.org/Reprints/Spring2011_PequotBattlefields.htm.

Verhoeff, Mary. "Major General Preston Brown, U.S.A." *Filson Club History Quarterly* 22 (1948): 246–51.

Villard, Oswald Garrison. *John Brown, 1800–1859: A Biography Fifty Years After.* Gloucester, Mass.: Peter Smith, 1965. First published 1910.

Wallace, Paul A. *Conrad Weiser, 1696–1760: Friend of Colonist and Mohawk.* Lewisburg, Penn.: Wennawoods Publishing, 1996.

Wall Street Journal. "Foxwoods Debt Talks Are Test of Tribal Bets." July 2, 2011.

Wall Street Journal. "Proposed Foxwoods Deal Is Gamble for Creditors." August 15, 2011, C1.

Ward, Matthew C. *Breaking the Backcountry: The Seven Years' War in Virginia and Pennsylvania, 1754–1765.* Pittsburgh, Penn.: University of Pittsburgh Press, 2003.

Watkins, Sam. *Company Aytch, or a Side Show of the Big Show.* Edited by M. Thomas Inge. New York: Penguin Putnam, 1999.

Weigley, Russell F. *History of the United States Army.* New York: Macmillan, 1967.

White, Richard. *The Middle Ground: Indians, Empires, and Republics in the Great Lakes Region, 1650–1815.* Cambridge: Cambridge University Press, 1991.

Wilkins, Thurman. *Cherokee Tragedy: The Ridge Family and the Decimation of a People.* 2nd ed. Norman: University of Oklahoma Press, 1986.

Winders, Richard Bruce. *Mr. Polk's Army: The American Military Experience in the Mexican War.* College Station: Texas A & M University Press, 1997.

Winters, Dick, and Cole C. Kingseed. *Beyond Band of Brothers.* New York: Penguin, 2006. Reprint, New York: Berkley Caliber, 2008.

Woodworth, Steven E., ed. *The Chickamauga Campaign.* Carbondale, Ill.: Southern Illinois University Press, 2010.

———, ed. *The Shiloh Campaign.* Carbondale: Southern Illinois University Press, 2009.

Wyatt-Brown, Bertram. *Southern Honor: Ethics and Behavior in the Old South.* 25th anniversary edition. New York: Oxford University Press, 2007.

Zaslow, Jeffrey. "Mass Production: Ford's Odd Collection Is a Model Museum." *Wall Street Journal,* November 21, 2003.

INDEX

Numbers in *italics* refer to pages with relevant illustrations (including maps).

MEREDITH MASON BROWN is a graduate of Harvard College (where he majored in history) and Harvard Law School. Now a lawyer and historian, Brown is author of *Frontiersman: Daniel Boone and the Making of America.*